THE
WISDOM OF
JOSEPH
MURPHY

All titles in this series

The Wisdom of James Allen
The Wisdom of Joseph Murphy
The Wisdom of Napoleon Hill
The Wisdom of Robert Collier
The Wisdom of Wallace D. Wattles

THE
WISDOM OF
JOSEPH
MURPHY

edited and introduced
by Mitch Horowitz

Published 2020 by Gildan Media LLC
aka G&D Media
www.GandDmedia.com

THE WISDOM OF JOSEPH MURPHY. Introduction, Chapter Notes, Timeline and Afterword, copyright © 2020 by Mitch Horowitz

No part of this book may be used, reproduced or transmitted in any manner whatsoever, by any means (electronic, photocopying, recording, or otherwise), without the prior written permission of the author, except in the case of brief quotations embodied in critical articles and reviews. No liability is assumed with respect to the use of the information contained within. Although every precaution has been taken, the author and publisher assume no liability for errors or omissions. Neither is any liability assumed for damages resulting from the use of the information contained herein.

Front Cover design by David Rheinhardt of Pyrographx

Interior design by Meghan Day Healey of Story Horse, LLC

Library of Congress Cataloging-in-Publication Data is available upon request

ISBN: 978-1-7225-0150-1

10   9   8   7   6   5   4   3   2   1

Contents

You Are As Your Mind Is
Introduction by Mitch Horowitz
9

I
This Is It: The Art of
Metaphysical Demonstration
(1945, revised 1948)
15

II
Fear Not
(1946)
118

III
The Meaning of Reincarnation
(1954)
133

IV
Believe In Yourself
(1955)
197

V
Stay Young Forever
(1958)
251

VI
Nuclear Religion
(1961)
265

VII
Why Did This Happen to Me?
(1962)
311

Afterword
Takeaway Points
325

Joseph Murphy Timeline   329
About the Authors   336

You Are As Your Mind Is

INTRODUCTION BY MITCH HOROWITZ

Many of us grew up with the notion—almost wholly untested—that our moods are, more or the less, the result of our circumstances. That our moods are *symptoms*.

Metaphysical writer and minister Joseph Murphy (1898–1981) upended that point of view. Murphy perceived and documented a different and more powerful way of living—one in which mood, thought, and mental image are *causes* rather than symptoms. Murphy considered this true in the most literal and vital sense. More so, the author reasoned that you, as an individual, are an expression and channel of the Godlike creative powers referenced in Scripture, and that you are, at this very moment, constructing your world through your emotionalized thoughts and mental images.

Beginning with his first book *This Is It* in 1945, the Irish minister combined principles of psychology, self-suggestion, and a cosmological theology, which he had been developing and testing for many years. It is notable that Murphy did not produce his first book until age forty-seven—he first sought to validate his ideas in the laboratory of experience. Once Murphy found his footing as a writer and speaker, his output was prodigious, as you can see from the timeline at the end of this book.

The size of Murphy's readership, which today is growing, is equal to the volume of his output. Part of the reason for Murphy's posterity is that he dramatically and, for many people, convincingly married twentieth-century psychology with the New Metaphysics, specifically New Thought, Science of Mind, Unity, Christian Science, and Divine Science. In so doing, he gave readers a dramatic new sense of their self-potential and their role in creation.

Murphy accepted the traditional premise that we all possess two minds: the outer, rational mind, called the conscious; and the inner, emotional mind, called the subconscious, or what is sometimes called the psyche. The subconscious is generally agreed to be the driving engine of your life—it is the hidden influence that shapes and reinforces your attitudes, affinities, perceptions, self-image, relationships, and experiences. But Murphy went further. He reasoned that the subconscious mind is *programed* by the conscious mind: what we view and accept as valid or perceptively justified—whether or not this is sound or desirable—is acted upon and out-pictured by the subconscious in a complex of ways.

Hence, Murphy reasoned that the mission of the conscious mind must be to protect the subconscious from receiving impressions that misdirect its life-shaping energies. We must consciously filter out or temper suggestions that we do not want the psyche to uncritically accept and act upon. The stakes of this transaction are higher than is commonly understood. The subconscious, Murphy reasoned, mediates between individual experience and the existence of an Infinite Mind, which courses through each of us like the inlets of a vast ocean. Seen another way, the subconscious or psyche is the medium through which Infinite Mind, or what Scripture calls God, creates and actualizes.

This view is largely at home in New Thought. It differs somewhat from Christian Science insofar as Christian Science theology sees the human mind itself not as a mediator between the individual and higher but as an illusion—sometimes called "mortal" or "material" mind, which must be allowed to dissolve like a fog of delusion so that the one Higher Mind can shine through. In effect, however, Murphy's philosophy agrees with Christian Science and the related metaphysical schools: materialism is ultimately a delusion and the one true reality is the fullness and unsurpassed peace of the Higher Mind. In this sense, Murphy endeavored to harmonize the New Metaphysics, biblical revelation, religious symbolism, and modern psychology.

Murphy was a lifelong seeker and traveller, in both inner and outer realms. As such, he was well suited to the task he took on.

Born in 1898 on the southern coast of Ireland, he grew up in a large, devout Catholic family. Murphy's parents urged him to join the priesthood. But the young seminarian found religious doctrine and catechism too limiting. Eager to peer more deeply into the internal mechanics of life, the he left seminary to dedicate his energies to chemistry, which he studied both before and after his religious training.

In the early 1920s, married yet still searching for his place in the world of career and commerce, Murphy relocated to America to seek employment as a chemist and druggist. After running a pharmacy counter at New York's Algonquin Hotel, Murphy renewed his study of mystical and metaphysical ideas. He read the works of Taoism, Confucianism, Transcendentalism, Buddhism, Scripture—and New Thought. The seeker grew fully enamored with the New Metaphysics sweeping the Western world. The causative power of thought, Murphy came to believe, revealed the authentic meaning of the world's religions, the deeper meaning of psychology, and the eternal laws of life.

In arriving at his matured spiritual outlook, Murphy told an interviewer that he studied in the 1930s with the same teacher who tutored his contemporary New Yorker and friend, mystic Neville Goddard (1905–1972). Murphy said they shared the same mentor: a turbaned man of black-Jewish descent named Abdullah. Shortly before his death in 1981, Murphy, in a little-known series of interviews published in French by a Quebec press,* described his encounter with the mysterious Abdullah. Interviewer Bernard Cantin recounted the tale in his 1987 dialogues with the writer:

---

*˜See timeline.

It was in New York that Joseph Murphy also met the professor Abdullah, a Jewish man of black ancestry, a native of Israel, who knew, in every detail, all the symbolism of each of the verses of the Old and the New Testaments. This meeting was one of the most significant in Dr. Murphy's spiritual evolution. In fact, Abdullah, who had never seen nor known the Murphy family, said flatly that Murphy came from a family of six children, and not five, as Murphy himself had believed. Later on, Murphy, intrigued, questioned his mother and learned that, indeed, he had had another brother who had died a few hours after his birth, and was never spoken of again.

After studying with Abdullah, Murphy in the late-1930s began his climb as a minister and writer, soon lecturing on the radio and speaking live on both coasts. He wrote prolifically on the autosuggestive and causative faculties of thought, and reached a worldwide audience in 1963 with *The Power of Your Subconscious Mind*, which went on to sell millions of copies and has remained one of the most enduring books on positive-mind philosophy.

The Wisdom of Joseph Murphy is intended to provide you with the practical essentials of Murphy's outlook and also give you a sense of arc and breadth of his career. Not every idea included here is one that you will necessarily agree with. I do not myself. But I find it useful to evaluate, learn from, and posthumously argue with Murphy as a figure possessed of a range of outlooks, some of which he refined as time passed.

The truly radical and seismic notion at the center of Murphy's work is: *You are as you mind is*. He dedicated a lifetime to studying, proving, harnessing, and supplying seekers with that idea. This book is a testament to the enduring power and effectiveness of his search.

I
This Is It:
The Art of Metaphysical Demonstration

(1945, revised 1948)

This concise book is one of Joseph Murphy's earliest works and it presents his entire system in a nutshell. In This Is It, *Murphy, like his contemporary Neville Goddard, identifies the figures who populate Scripture as symbols for your moods. He also teaches that you are liable to overlook some of the lessons and solutions intrinsic to your nature because you do not trust your intuition or you dismiss something out of hand because you do not recognize it or consider it carefully enough—an important point to remember when watching for the arrival of answers to problems or the actualization of*

cherished projects. Finally, Murphy writes about the malleability of destiny: nothing is foreseen that cannot be changed with the changing of your thoughts and moods.
—MH

1

Divine Guidance

"If thou knewest the gift of God, and who it is that saith to thee, Give me to drink, thou wouldest have asked of him, and he would have given thee living water." —JOHN 4:10.

The living water means inspiration. The word inspiration comes from the Latin "Spiro," meaning I breathe into. We breathe air without effort, likewise we must let the Divine Light or creative essence of God flow through our intellect without tension. The subjective mind in us perceives by intuition. It does not have to reason or inquire as it is all-wise, infinite intelligence. If you say to your subconscious, sometimes referred to as the subjective mind (being subject to the conscious mind), "Wake me up at seven o'clock," you know that you awaken exactly at the time specified. It never fails.

We must realize that herein lies a source of power which is omnipotent. Many good people have erroneous ideas about being inspired. They believe that it is an extraordinary event to be experienced by mystics or highly spiritual people, and they think it applies to prayer and the Bible only. This is not true.

Any business man or woman may be inspired by turning to God, and information or divine guidance may be received for any problem. Your business problem can be solved by turning to God for the answer and your information may be general or specific. For example, if you are an executive of a commercial organization and you want a new idea for your sales program, try the following technique. If you are in business, have a private office where you will not be disturbed; close your eyes; be still; think of the attributes and qualities of God, which are within yourself. This will generate a mood of peace, power and confidence. Then speak in the following, simple manner to the Father within who doeth the works, "Father, thou knoweth all things, give me the idea necessary for a new program." Begin to imagine that you now have the answer and that it is flowing through you. You must not pretend; really believe it; accept it and then drop it. The latter is most important and is the secret of the whole process.

After the silence, get busy; do something; become preoccupied with routine matters. Above all do not sit around waiting for the answer. It comes when you think not and the moment you expect not. The inner voice of intuition speaks like a flash—it is always spontaneous and unannounced. You may get any type of information which will help you along the road to success.

Intuition, which means being taught from within, knows the answer and does not require previous experience. We must realize that God has no problems, if He had, who would solve them? Therefore, when we pray, we know that God has only the answer; He knows no problem, hence we rise to the point of recognition of the answer. The answer flows through the problem and there is no problem. No reasoning power is involved and the amazing suddenness with which the solution comes, sometimes is startling. In our Young Peoples' Forum we now teach intuition and inspiration; they find it fascinating and illuminating.

Intuition is the soft tread of the unseen guest. We must welcome this King of Kings and sing His praises; then He will make frequent visits. The abandonment of the intellectual reason for the wisdom of God is intuition. We abandon our objective reasoning only in the sense of deferring it to a higher guide. After we have received an intuition, we use reason in carrying it out. You may get specific information about anything.

For example, you may be writing a book and require special data, perhaps written 1000 B. C. The information may be in the British Museum or in the New York Public Library. It might take you days or weeks to find it, if you do not know specifically what you want. In such instances, relax; be still and say silently and quietly to your Father (your subconscious), "Thou knowest all things, give me this information." Drop off to sleep with the one word "answer." In that relaxed mood you repeat the word "answer."

Your subjective is all-wise; knows what type of answer you desire and will answer in a dream, as a hunch, or feeling that you are being led on the right track. You may get a sudden flash to go some place—a person may give you the answer. "I have ways that you know not of." Many are led to an old book store, where they pick up the very book that gives them the desired data. We must be ever watchful for impressions as Divine guidance, for when a feeling or idea comes to us, we must be able to recognize it.

There are two reasons why we may not acknowledge our hunches. These reasons are tension and failure to recognize them. If we are in a negative, despondent, bitter mood, Divine guidance is impossible. As a matter of fact only negative guidance will prevail. If we are in a happy, confident, joyous mood, we will recognize the flashes of intuition that come to us; moreover, we will feel under subjective compulsion to carry them out. It is necessary, therefore, to be still and relaxed when you pray for guidance; for nothing can be achieved by tenseness, fear or apprehension.

Who has not had the experience of being unable to remember a name, then dropping the search, have the name come to him later during repose? If you try too hard to hear a telephone ring, you cannot.

Let us consider the failure to recognize the voice of intuition. For example, suppose we are gazing idly into a store window. An eccentric millionaire puts a $500 bill in our hand. We throw it away thinking it is an advertisement for a dance hall or a beauty parlor. We must be on the alert for Divine ideas or feelings that come to us, and be able to recognize them. In emergencies guidance comes immediately, because we lean all our weight on the Christ within; thus we place all our burden on him and are free; then comes salvation. The answer to everything is within. "You would not have sought me, had you not already found me."

For business and professional people the cultivation of the intuitive faculty is of paramount importance. Intuition offers instantaneously that which the intellect or reasoning mind of man could accomplish only after weeks or months of monumental trial and error. When our reasoning faculties fail us in our perplexities, the intuitive faculty sings the silent song of triumph.

The conscious mind of man is reasoning, analytical and inquisitive; the subjective faculty of intuition is always spontaneous. It comes as a beacon to the conscious intellect. Many times it speaks as a warning against a proposed trip or plan of action. We must listen and learn to heed the voice of wisdom. It does not always speak to you when you wish it to do so, but only when you need it.

If we will only believe, and not pretend to believe, that God is guiding us now in all our ways, in all our thoughts, words and deeds, we shall be led along the right road. Artists, poets, writers and inventors listen to this voice of intuition. As a result they are able to astonish the world by the beauties and glories drawn from this storehouse of knowledge within themselves.

Become still, relax, close your eyes and say, "Father, thou knowest all things. I am writing a novel. Give me the characters, names, locations and setting." Rejoice that the answer is flowing through you now; drop off to sleep with the word "novel" on your lips, silently repeating it until you are lost in the deep of sleep. The word "novel" is etched in the subconscious. In the morning or a few days later, you will sit down to write; the words will flow; ideas will come in an unending stream and you will say, "Thank you, Father."

The word "intuition" also means "inner hearing." The oldest definition for "revelation" meant "that which is heard." Jesus said, "As I hear, I judge." Hearing is not the only way to nurture intuition. Sometimes it comes as a thought, but the most common way is to "hear the voice." Many times it is a voice whose texture, color and substance you can hear as plainly as the voice over the radio. The scientist uses his wonderful gift of imagination and in the silence he sees fulfillment. His intuition relates to his particular science.

Intuition goes much farther than reason. You discard reason; then comes intuition. You employ reason to carry out intuition. When you receive intuition, you will often find that it is opposite to what your reasoning would have told you.

This is how one young lady in the advertising business produces her wonderful slogans. She drops off to sleep with the word "slogan" on her lips, knowing that the answer will be forthcoming. It always is—"He never faileth."

2

Power To Choose

Theology has always accounted for the presence of evil in the world by the invention of a devil.

The inner meaning of the Old Testament clearly indicates that its writers did not believe in the devil. You are told—several times openly, and always secretly—that the Lord was responsible for evil as well as for good. The Lord, or law, referred to is the law laid down by man, because of his foolish beliefs in sickness, disease, fear, death, old age and all other ills. This is the law decreed by man, and is different from the laws of the Lord God. The laws of electricity, motion, physics and mathematics are example of these laws. We are learning the nature of these laws and specializing them in numerous ways. These laws are neither good nor bad—they are facts in nature.

In reading the Gospels the word *devil* is not found in the earlier versions. It is mentioned therein "as a spirit of evil." In the teaching of Jesus there is no mention of the theological devil. This was later invented by certain writers. Furthermore, let us realize that the word we have translated as "devil" is "a" spirit of evil, not "the" spirit of evil.

Thus Jesus taught that there were many spirits of evil. Constantly the narrative states that He went around expelling the devil from human beings. The spirits of evil spoken of are the moods of hate, jealousy, revenge, remorse and fear. The many phobias, fixations and other destructive negative thoughts which man is capable of conceiving are also spirits of evil.

Jesus is symbolized in the Scriptures as the great teacher of Truth. He explained the laws of life by recounting parables, allegories and fables to the multitude. "But without a parable spake he not unto them." He healed all men by seeing them as perfect as their Father in heaven. He proved to them that any man can overcome any obstacle—be it what it may—that besets his path. All that was necessary was for man to believe that the God within could do all things. Jesus' whole mission was to teach people how to find the Christ within, or the true self, which does all things in the name of the Father. In those days man thought that it was too good to be true. Today we still find millions believing in powers apart from themselves and living in dread of the unknown. Countless millions are victims of belief in war, crimes, disease and the power of environment and circumstances to hold them down.

This Is It: The Art of Metaphysical Demonstration

It might be said that the devil is God upside down. The devil is God as He is misunderstood by the so-called wicked or ignorant. God is all, and all there is God. He is absolute, the only One, and everything is made inside and out of the Absolute. He has created all things and nothing exists apart from God. He is infinitely good and perfect and the author only of perfect good.

The devil is everything that God is not; therefore, the devil is not. The devil is wrong thinking and feeling; these powers result in wrong action or expression. Man having free will—that is, the freedom to choose happy or despondent moods—creates his own good and his own evil. He is not compelled to love, but he has freedom to love. Love is joyous and spontaneous and we have the freedom to give or retain it. God did create a being out of Himself but did not decree that he must love Him. No, that would not be love, because man would then be an automaton, and all of us would be truth students.

You will realize there would be no joy unless we knew the opposite. How could man know what joy is except he could experience the opposite? Man is conditioned into this world and becomes conscious of opposites—such as north and south, east and west, hot and cold, positive and negative, darkness and light, male and female, night and day, ebb and flow. These constitute man's evil or limitation. He finds that he has to travel from New York to Chicago due to his belief in travel. He will continue to do this until he awakens from his dream of limitation, and finds that all he has to do is to feel that he is in Chicago; really believe it, and he will be there;

for Chicago is within himself. He does not go there—he brings "thereness" here. When we find God or the Oneness, all opposites or sense of duality disappear.

The first thing we must realize is that there is no power to challenge God for His throne. If this were true, God would not be God. He is omnipotent, omnipresent and all-wise. He is infinite intelligence. "Ye shall know the Truth and the Truth shall make you free." Understanding of Truth frees man from want, fear, sickness, all superstitions and false beliefs of the race. The devil has been created by people who were unable to account for the apparent evil in the world. They reasoned in this fashion: God was omnipotent, but was powerless about the devil.

If any man is now dwelling in hate, that is his personal devil and it will hurt him. If any man believes in external forces capable of injury or destruction, this man is really saying, "God is supreme, yet He is not supreme." He creates a devil who becomes His successful rival. God asks you to forgive your enemies; yet He cannot forgive His own; for he has created a place of everlasting punishment for them, even though admittedly He is all powerful; this of course is an absurd position.

From the foregoing analysis it might be said that the only evil is the belief in evil. All things and all activities are from One source—God. It must follow, therefore, that there can be nothing intrinsically evil. The evil comes from our incomplete state of consciousness—from our seeing things incorrectly. Reflect that what we call evil in humans we do not call evil in animals, but it is the conditioned responses to natural instincts. Our incomplete state of consciousness, our misapplication and our misapprehension of Universal laws constitute what the world calls evil. We insist upon doing things that will hurt us, even after we have discovered that they hurt us. We prefer the immediate gain though it blinds us to the consequent pain.

The hell spoken of by some is not the punishment dealt out by an angry God. It is the consequence of man's own acts, brought upon himself. He can free himself from this hell, when he is willing to take the necessary steps and undergo the self-discipline of right thinking, right feeling and right action.

What greater self-discipline is there than the constant application of the Golden Rule? "As you would that men should do unto you, do you also unto them in like manner!" Likewise, as you would that men should feel about you, feel you also about them in like manner. As long as man refuses to believe that God is good, there remains but one way out—the Via Dolorosa—undergoing pain and suffering.

The word that means "devil" in Hebrew is a word meaning "slanderer" or "a liar." The devil is one who tells lies about reality. A slanderer tells lies about man. The eye slanders a fact because it deals only with the outside appearance of fact. People say, "The sun rises and the sun sets," but it neither rises nor sets. We see nothing as it is in reality, because our eyes are geared to see according to our beliefs. If, for example, our eyes were geared in any other way, we would see things differently. We would see circumstances differently, and they could become something else in our sight.

According to the Ancient wisdom the word "mirth" is connected with the letters AYIN, which means the eye. The reason for this is that the surface appearance is different from the reality. AYIN is associated with what seems rather than what is—with illusion rather than reality; this is the most mirthful thing about the "devil." The real meaning of "devil" in the Hebrew language is the "slanderer"—one who tells lies about the Truth.

We might point out that as man awakens, he builds a finer and finer instrument until he no longer needs an instrument—he sees without eyes; then man sees reality, because the illusion of the thing does not stand in his way. With the mind's eye, he sees beyond the form to the reality behind. In other words, he sees divinity beyond the mask. Without eyes the spiritual man sees "Truth" everywhere. He knows that One and not two is the beginning and end of all. However, two—good and evil—are the aspects One presents to mankind, because men are subject to the illusion of duality.

Fools, deluded by outward appearance, create a demon out of the web of their folly. The awakening is that divine understanding which comes to a man who succeeds in meditation, and "the last day" is the time of that achievement. The wise man sees and knows that the demon is the shadow of the Lord. "Happy is the man that findeth wisdom, and the man that getteth understanding. For the merchandise of it is better than the merchandise of silver, and the gain thereof, than fine gold." (Prov. 3:13–14).

The belief that desire is a personal affair is due to a misunderstanding of the Divine urge present in all men. The urge towards growth which everyone feels, is not from the personality; nor can this urge be satisfied by accumulating things of the world. Man's desire for power, authority, possessions and fame are mistaken desires, *the reason being they are all for limited forms*. They set up the law of contraction instead of expansion. Let us have the desire of being rather than of having; then we will unite ourselves with a source of power that no degree of expression can diminish.

It is true, however, that our subjective mind fulfills or grants mistaken desires also, and this is often the cause for our bitter experiences. The desire to get things such as hats, automobiles, fur coats and houses is a disappointing one. When one gets what he desires in the material way, he must then desire something else, but in this way he does not grow spiritually. Eventually he must look for something which will not fade when he gets it. There is only one such desire—that is to give life, love, peace, wisdom and beauty to mankind. "I am come that you might have life and have it more abundantly." As with all other desires the more we get, the more we want.

We must remember, it is more blessed to give than to receive. We do this by seeing the "Untouchable glory of God" in others. The more we see It in others, the more It will shine out in ourselves. By doing this daily, we are preaching the Gospel or good news. The more we give in this manner, the more we have. The true gift is that which we give ourselves in consciousness by feeling the reality of the wonderful state we desire to see manifested in the other. To take our desires from the world of limitation—which is eating of "the fruit of the tree of knowledge of good and evil"—brings us disillusionment and pain. It is by these "stripes" we are healed—made whole in consciousness.

The innermost nature of Being is the tendency to give more life, therefore, all desires may be tested in this manner. Let man ask himself if the realization of his desire will enable him to give out more life, love and beauty to his world. If this is true, it is a desire that is never disappointing. "The more you give the more you have." On the lower scale we find that the more you get, the more you want.

There is an inexhaustible storehouse in man, from which he can draw forth security, peace and happiness—this is the Kingdom of Heaven spoken of in the Bible. Having found peace and happiness within, all other things are added to him. The only time is NOW. All experience is *now*. All Action is *now*. Let us experience the Kingdom of Heaven *now*, for God or our Good is the eternal *now*.

3

Rebirth

It is often asked, "Why do we have dictators, despots and tyrants in the world?" These are extensions in space of the dictator complex present in the hearts and minds of all human beings.

Instead of trying to force our opinions on others, we must learn how to change ourselves and we will change the world.

What is the world? The world is ourselves in aggregation. Napoleon still lives, Ghenghis Khan still lives, as do Caesar and all others. They live in the consciousness of the race. Our boys and girls learn about them at their mother's knees, at school and in college. They burn with resentment and rage at the apparent wrongs committed by these men. They read avidly of the crimes, atrocities, and acts of violence. These states are impressed on their subconscious minds. All of these moods, feelings and thoughts which are entertained become objectified as living realities. Moreover, these boys and girls suffer from nightmares, hysteria and various complexes because these moods of fear, hate, anger and resentment become the ghosts that walk the gloomy galleries of their minds.

Living in these states of mind—dwelling on dictators and tyrants, realizing that whatever is impressed in consciousness must be expressed in the world—man should not be surprised when these tyrants of the past are reborn into our society, because we actually call them forth. It is true in a sense, therefore, that Ghenghis Khan is reborn or reincarnated. He is an embodiment of the state of consciousness of the people, nation, race or world, whatever the case may be. The reader will see, that it is not a man who lived a thousand or two thousand years ago who is being reborn. It is a state of consciousness that is born again.

When a mother places a child on her knee; whispers in his ear that he is God walking the earth and tells him that he can do all that Jesus did, she is seeing her boy as God had planned. If the mother believes her statements, her belief will be automatically transferred to the child's subjective consciousness, and he will become her ideal. "I was young, now I am old, yet never have I seen the righteous forsaken nor their seed beg bread." If parents live the Law, if teachers teach the Law of life—the Truth of Being to the young; then their seed shall never beg bread. This means these children shall never become the beggars, outcasts, thieves and tyrants of the world. No, they shall fulfill the ideals of the parents.

They must fulfill the prayer of the parents because true prayer is always answered.

If parents will impress their subjective minds with wonderful dreams for their boys or girls, then according to their *belief*, "will it be done unto them." By changing our opinions, beliefs, ideas and ideals by teaching the youth of the nation who they really are, by showing them the way, the truth and the light, we can build the Kingdom of Heaven on earth; then we will prevent the rebirth of dictators, despots—former undesirable states of consciousness—which are perpetuated by prejudices, racial hatreds and fear of the unknown.

Let us teach children of the great accomplishments of the poets, artists, engineers, chemists, physicists, astronomers and others. Let them emulate these great men. There is so much for a child to learn about the great writers of the world and the giants of world literature, that the beautiful works of man cannot be exhausted in what is ordinarily called "a lifetime." After he is taught good, the child will emulate good.

In reality we are all dreaming; when man fully awakens he knows that planets are thoughts, suns and moons are thoughts, and his own consciousness is the space which sustains them all. He begins to realize that the whole world is a thought. For example, he becomes aware of the fact that the body is not real, but it is a thought or idea held in consciousness. The body has no life apart from consciousness. He realizes that there is absolutely no reality to matter or the body of man; it is a group of ideas and opinions. Man gives life to ideas and opinions as long as he believes them. When he disbelieves the errors, these ideas have no life in them.

Man was never born and he will never die. There is no death. Death is an idea that exists in the minds of men. As long as man believes in death, he must witness and experience it. Man has no beginning and no end; he always was, just as God always was, is and shall be. "God and man are one." "I and my Father are one."

The man who is always quoting so-called authorities to prove the modern theories of reincarnation is himself without authority. He is still crying in the wilderness and calling other men masters and adepts. Call no man master. "Salute no man on the highway." Salute the God within. The Kingdom of God is within, and if someone tells you it is "Lo here; lo there," believe him not. The Kingdom of Heaven is within man.

Where is the Truth? *It is within yourself.* "Look within—search the Scriptures," said Jesus. This means that all has been written in your subjective mind "from the foundation." All knowledge is within; all wisdom is within; all beings that ever lived are within you *now*. You can project the likeness of any living being, past or present; for all men are states of consciousness—qualities of mind expressed. *All moods, tones, qualities and vibrations are within you, because God is within and He cannot be divided—all is contained in the part.* Christ cannot be divided, and Christ means consciousness. The subjective Self of man—the Christos or Christ-man, the so-called Jesus Christ or God-man knows all men are within himself. He knows that, objectively speaking, all beings are projections in space of himself—the One Man.

Are there not thousands of cases over the world of men who have completely lost their former identity and personality; assumed new lives; entered different professions, and in many cases even remarried? These men were victims of amnesia, or loss of memory concerning their former selves. They could not remember their former wives or children. They had no recollection of their former professions or occupations. They assumed a new role in life. They were changed men entirely, because they had changed their consciousness. There is only consciousness!

Let us stop quoting authorities on spiritual subjects. As long as we quote authorities, we cease to be THE authority. All power is given to us in Heaven and on earth. Let us use it. In the spiritual sense we are all victims of amnesia. We have forgotten who we *really* are, and we tell ourselves that we are worms of the dust.

Take, for example, a man who goes to sleep and when he awakens he has completely forgotten who he is, and gravitates to the slums. His social world becomes the slums. His friends, knowing what has happened, try to coax him back to his former status. Because of amnesia his former way of life is entirely blotted from his memory. He believes his place is in the slums; he only smiles at these old acquaintances whom he no longer knows. He accepts as true the role he now plays.

The day comes when his memory is restored and he awakens to his rightful status. With certainty and promptness he returns to the environment consonant with the dignity of his upbringing. He wonders why he is in the slums. What has transpired is all a dream, a dream of the unreality. "Awake thou that sleepest, and arise from the dead, and Christ shall give thee light." (Eph. 5:14). Let us awake to the Real and return to our Father's house. "Everyone that thirsteth, come ye to the waters, and he that hath no money; come ye, buy, and eat; yea, come, buy wine and milk without money and without price." (Is. 55:1)

Man does not have to become a victim of amnesia in order to change his consciousness. He can read the 10th Chapter of Samuel, book 1, and learn how he can be turned into another man. This is accomplished through prayer. Take the story of the boy born of lowly parents, in a manger, having all the handicaps socially and financially that any child could have at that period in history. It was said, "Can there anything good come out of Nazareth?" (St. John 1:46). The word "Nazareth" symbolizes to sprout or grow, and man should be ever watchful not to despise the day of small beginnings.

This boy Jesus walked the earth and imagined himself to be the perfect man, capable of seeing only perfection in everything. He felt the reality of the wish within him and it became a conviction. Having imagined the state he wished, and having felt the reality of the state imagined, all the necessary qualities for the fulfillment of that state came from within himself. They were always there, but they had to be recognized before they became manifest in the world of man. This boy did as Samuel said man should do, which was, "Go up into the Hill of God—thou shalt meet a company of prophets coming down from the high place playing music, and thou shalt prophesy with them,—and shalt be turned into another man." (Samuel 10:5)

This Is It: The Art of Metaphysical Demonstration

The Hill is a high state of consciousness; the other prophets represent the eternal trinity employed in the creation of all things—consciousness, idea and the joyous feeling or conviction that it is done. *The "feeling" is the conviction that unites consciousness desiring with the thing desired.* The joy of answered prayer is the music of the three prophets. It is the inner silent knowing of the soul. Therefore, any man can turn his back completely on the past—forget all the old beliefs and foolish ideas of the race mind; enter into the joyous thrill of being Jesus (saving consciousness) and do his work. If he remains faithful to this mood and sustains it, he will automatically develop all the qualities necessary to do "even greater work."

The story of Jesus is a portrayal of what all men should be. It is a complete refutation of all age-old beliefs regarding man's handicaps of race, national origin, environment and circumstance. All these things are as naught when man discovers who he really is; so let us keep our eyes on God. It is there, where man sees no obstacle. When he takes his eyes off God, or his good, he sees his limitations and obstacles. NOW is the day of salvation; let us see the light now; for God is the Eternal Now—since time is an illusion of the senses. The awakening takes place now.

We know that everything exists in the Infinite. There is nothing that any man can think of, no matter how fantastic, that does not already subsist in the Infinite. It may be said to exist when we acknowledge it or witness it. *Nothing is made; nothing becomes; all is and all is God.* We are wedded to the belief in time, so we conceive of ourselves conditioned by time. Yet the Bible tells us, "For a thousand years in thy sight are but as yesterday when it is past, and as a watch in the night." (Psalm 90:4).

If time is a belief, which it really is, the common belief of reincarnation cannot be true. The theory tastes good and looks good, but let our prayer be: "lead us not into temptation." God tempts no man, but our conscious mind and five senses are tempted to believe this false doctrine. It becomes a panacea assuaging our wounded pride or feeling of inferiority. Moreover, it causes us to turn back or tempts us to eat of it. "But in the day that thou eatest thereof thou shalt surely die," because we are eating of the fruit of the tree of knowledge of good and evil. This tree means world belief, power in other gods hence the breaking of the first Commandment, "Thou shalt have no other Gods before me."

We must eat of the tree in the midst of the garden, which is man's consciousness—God dwelling within him giving all power to Him. We "eat" of Him by taking part in a psychological feast of being a noble, dignified and Christ-like person. We must see the Christ in all men, sermons in stones and good in everything. When we do this, all other things shall be added unto us. Man's life on this plane is like the several stanzas of a poem or the scenes of a play, because it really is the One Being dramatizing Himself as the many. Common sense is the most uncommon sense, because it is God's or good sense. Wisdom or common sense teaches that illumination or the great awakening to our Godhead can happen here and now. "If it be not now, yet it will come; the readiness is all."

This Is It: The Art of Metaphysical Demonstration

In order to elucidate this point, take a solid, metallic substance and heat it. The temperature rises, but for a while it looks as if no change were taking place. However, the moment that degree of heat is reached, which denotes its melting point, it begins to liquefy, thus changing its shape and seemingly its nature also. Likewise, water can be turned into steam which is invisible—pure steam cannot be seen. Water also becomes snow, ice and hail—all different rates of vibration of the one substance. When a liquid is changed into a gas, these changes are brought about by an increase in the rapidity of vibration of the constituent particles whether they are solid or liquid. The same applies to man. What is true on one plane is true on another, for God changes not. The rebirth comes to that man here and now—not in after life. There is no transforming power in death. Man raises his rate of vibration by lifting himself up to a high state of awareness, by entering into the thrill of being that which he longs to be, and by feeling the joy of accomplishment.

Man is a porous being, plastic and pliable, capable of being moulded into any state he can imagine. He is nothing but "liquid light." In the meditative mood he stills the mind, thereby immobilizing the senses by focusing his attention exclusively on the one ideal—only one. He suggests sleep to himself by feeling sleepy, being careful not to fall asleep, however; the mystic in meditation must always keep control. In this mood he knows, feels and sees himself as being bathed in a sea of liquid light. A flame or lights appear all around him and he knows that in this floating liquid state he can mould, fashion and shape all that he longs to be, to do and to possess.

In this state he contemplates the joy of the answered prayer. The feeling of accomplishment fills him, and he dwells on the reality of his desire for perhaps five minutes, two minutes or ten minutes. By constantly praying in this manner, there is an expansion of consciousness—it is like the heat that melts the solid. The day comes when man melts away all inhibitions, fears and doubts, and becomes the God man here and now. To such a man, physical laws and time disappear. This change may come in the twinkling of an eye like the volatilization of a liquid into a gas.

The reason the modern theory of reincarnation is popular is because man, using his five senses only, is like the five foolish virgins—he has no oil or wisdom in his lamps. He finds that this explanation gives him solace and tells him what he wants to hear. At the same time it seems to unfold many unexplained phenomena. Such acceptance retards spiritual progress, checks the awakening process and is a destructive, superstitious belief. The modern accepted belief in reincarnation is very old; as is the belief in purgatory, hell and the devil.

The Bible mentions reincarnation several times and some of these references are explained in this book. The Scripture informs us that Herod believed in reincarnation. Herod represents the world or the five-sense man, the man ignorant of spiritual laws who subscribes to tradition and family beliefs. A man who believes that John, Elias, or some prophet long since dead, is risen from the dead, is symbolized by Herod. What this type of man fails to see is that it is always God coming forth as a quality, tone, or mood of man himself.

This Is It: The Art of Metaphysical Demonstration 41

Mozart, Bernini, Lincoln, Shakespeare, and Napoleon left their impressions with mankind. We read of their works in history, song and prose. All of them live in the hearts or subjective minds of man. A man's son is his idea or feeling about anything. He can give conception to any state he is capable of conceiving. If a man, therefore, admires and dwells on the qualities and attributes of Napoleon, and would love to give birth to such a son, "as within so without." During the creative act a Napoleon-like character appears resembling the mood of that man. In other words, it is the tone struck during conception or creation that determines the nature of the child.

The worldly-minded man called Herod in the Bible, believes in a physical reincarnation, and he desires to see Jesus, or the Truth as told in the ninth chapter of Luke. However, the Truth student will readily see that such a man cannot see him, "as no man hath seen the Father." The latter is always a subjective perception or feeling within man. Man awakens by degrees, slowly or quickly. On arising from bed in the morning, he rarely awakens all at once. It takes him a minute or so. The thermometer, however, does not skip any degrees. Before man fully awakens from his dream no necessary step in unfoldment will be omitted. All limitations and inhibitions will be dissolved.

The following article about the violinist Zimbalist appeared in "The New Yorker" some years ago: "Nobody told Zimbalist he was supposed to play the piano, too; during the final examinations in his eighteenth year, they handed him a Beethoven Sonata to be read at sight in the presence of the whole faculty. He had never touched a piano except to get his 'A.' He sat down, however, got his breath and played. When he finished he was told to close the book and repeat the whole Sonata from memory. He did so. After a moment of silence the room broke unanimously into applause—an unheard-of demonstration."

The man of the world would not conceive of this as being possible. The power within man is capable of setting at naught all human beliefs and man-made laws. We must begin to take our attention away from the limited, human concept of ourselves; then we shall, like Mozart, compose music at six, statues at seven, and at the age of twelve we will confound the wise men of the world. Many cases are reported where cripples invalided for years leap and run in the presence of fires. In emergencies mothers lift automobiles to extricate their children. Where is this power? It is within themselves. Fires and emergencies are not needed to stir the gift within. Man can do this in the quiet of his own soul. We create in "silence."

4

The Bible and Man

Man cannot interpret the Scriptures in their proper light until he is at a point of spiritual development comparable to the writers of the Bible. Man must get into the meditative mood. He must ask the All-Wise within himself what He, Himself, meant when He (consciousness) wrote that Bible passage thousands of years ago. The reader of this book must realize that he wrote the Bible but he has forgotten it. His subjective mind knows and remembers all. It knows the truth about reincarnation and all other so-called mysteries of life.

Dwelling on the past like Lot's wife, we are turned slowly but surely into a pillar of salt. In other words, we are preserving the past. We are wedded to it and are held in bondage to false beliefs or Karma (evil that has to be expiated here in life), and to many other strange and weird ideas. As long as man believes those things, he must suffer the consequences of his beliefs, ideas and opinions. Disease is ignorance, and the modern, accepted conception of reincarnation is similar to a disease. It is worse than the effects of opiates, alcohol, or hashish, because it paralyzes the mind and destroys the body.

The writer's experience with people who believe in these ideas is that they are nearly all sick. However, they have perfect alibis which act as anesthetics to dull their senses, and to render them both numb and dumb to the truth. The anesthetic they inhale is not ether but much worse, since the effects of the former wear off. Likewise, the opinions, beliefs and foolish race concepts continue in the minds of these well-meaning but misguided people.

One will tell you that the reason she is now a cripple suffering from rheumatoid arthritis which cannot be cured, is that it is a Karmic debt, which she must pay, for a sin or error committed in a former life. Man must see the foolishness of all this. It is a complete contradiction of all the teachings of the Bible, which portray that man is God, individualized—One with the Father. "When you have seen me you have seen the Father." "I and my Father are one." Yes, truly, when you look at any man, you see God.

The Truth is that when man discovers that he is God, and that his unmodified consciousness or awareness is the invisible creator of all things, he will learn to overcome all obstacles, such as disease, suffering and frustration. In overcoming these he will awaken to his true power and his divinity, because he seeks the aid of no man. He then goes forth and proves his Godhood.

Man is both unconditioned and conditioned. The life principle—subjective or subconscious of man—is the awareness of being, or unconditioned consciousness. Man expressed is conditioned consciousness—or God expressing Himself as man. Man becomes that which he believes himself to be. "Whom do men say that I, the son of man, am?" Will you the reader, give the same answer that the world does by saying: "Some say that thou art John the Baptist: some Elias; and others Jeremiah, or one of the prophets?" (St. Matthew 16:14). That is the belief of the world.

Read these words again in the Bible, ponder on their meaning. It will then reveal itself to you and you will not have to ask anyone what it means. "Peter" in the Bible means your inner voice, the Rock of Truth, which cannot be moved or swayed by the opinions of the world. This inner quality of mind is an attribute of God expressed in man. It is the disciplined hearing of the Truth student which reveals that you are Christ, the son of the living God. Now Jesus said, "Flesh and blood hath not revealed it unto thee, but my Father which is in Heaven." (Matthew 16:18). Yes, it is true that flesh and blood will never tell us who we are. It can never reveal the story or truth of re-birth. The flesh and blood spoken of is the world and its opinions, race consciousness, traditional beliefs and the attitude such as, "the old religion is good enough for me." The old religion is not good enough for anyone who seeks the truth on these matters. Blood means life. You give life to your ideas and to the opinions and concepts of the world as long as you believe them. Jesus tells us that Heaven is within ourselves. The Voice speaks and tells man, as it did

Simon Peter, "Thou art Christ, the son of the living God." (Matthew 16:16).

The son is the offspring of the Father and must be like the Father. Is he not the image and likeness of the Father? Man is God conceiving Himself to be man—then man appears. We are here to discover who we are, to awaken from the dream of limitation and ignorance and to prove ourselves to be God. When we discover who we are, we will express the will of God, which is life, beauty, peace and love.

In the seventeenth chapter of Matthew we read: "But I say unto you, Elias has come already and they know him not." Elias means my God Jehovah. It is always God being born. Man does not believe it—neither does he know it. He thinks it is another person being reborn. Man is trying to divide the One, and by so doing he limits the Holy One of Israel.

It is always Elias that is born in the world—the spirit of the one God. Let us awaken here from the dream of limitation and separation. There is no other place or planet for us to go. Man cannot go outside himself. I am you and you are I—for there is but One. The hero and the most degraded criminal are really I also. One Being, God, is incarnated in two and one-half billion persons called the "human race."

People have inverted and distorted the Truth for thousands of years, but that is no reason why man should continue to do so. There are still people living on this globe who believe the earth is flat and that the sun rises in the east. There are millions that subscribe to the belief in disease. Let not man be blinded by his former beliefs. Rather, let him open his mind to the Truth of life.

This Is It: The Art of Metaphysical Demonstration

If he approaches the study of the Bible,—which is purely allegorical, figurative and psychological—he must not approach it with a closed mind. If he does he will color it to meet his former opinions which are fixed within him. Such a man can never find the Truth. You cannot pick up anything if you are holding something in your two hands. If you hold fast to your former beliefs, you are turning back and limiting the Holy One of Israel. A closed mind is unable to grasp the Truth.

When man sheds the garment called the body, he continues to live subjectively in a dream state.

All the moods that he carried over with him into this present state are experienced in the form of a dream. Some of his experiences may be those of nightmares based on the subjective impressions of anger, hate and resentment. In this life man is expressing moods, feelings and ideas which he takes to sleep with him every night. Upon awakening he fulfills the impressions of his subjective mind. He has forgotten many of the moods or feelings that he took into the deep of himself a month ago or a week ago, and he now looks upon any injury as an accidental occurrence. He calls incidents which occur matters of chance or coincidence.

This, of course, is not so. All is Law. "Nothing is lost in my Holy Mountain." Our objective experiences on this plane are the manifestations of subjective impressions. The law is the same on all planes. When we leave the objective plane, we have subjective experiences based on all subjective impressions carried over by us. This is a dream state, just as real as the plane you left.

5

Subjective Mind Impressions

When we speak of mind, we usually refer to two phases of the one mind, objective and subjective. In broad general terms the difference between man's two minds may be stated in the following terms. The objective mind reasons, analyzes, dissects, divides and chooses. It takes cognizance of the objective world through the media of the five, physical senses. It is the outgrowth of man's physical necessities. Furthermore, it may be said to be his guide where his material environment is concerned. Its highest function is that of reasoning. *It is not creative.* "I can of mine own self do nothing." (John 5:30). It is "the Father that dwelleth in me, he doeth the works." (John 14:10).

The subjective mind of man is that which creates and gives form to all impressions made upon it through suggestion or feeling. This phase of man's mind takes cognizance of its environment by means independent of the physical senses. It perceives by intuition. It is the storehouse of memory and the seat of the emotions. It is the Father that doeth the works. It performs its highest functions when the objective senses are in abeyance, as in meditation. It sees without the use of the natural organs of vision. It can leave the body and assume another body and travel to distant lands.

In the absolute sense, man's subjective mind does not have to travel anywhere as the whole world is within it. "Be still and know that I am God." (Ps. 46:10). God does not travel—He is Omnipresent. The subjective mind has the power to read the thoughts of others in the minutest detail. It can read the contents of sealed letters and of books locked in a safe. All wisdom and knowledge are locked within it, because it is the Higher Self of man or God.

For purposes of clarification we will say that the real distinction between the two minds consists in the fact that the "objective mind" is merely the function of the physical brain. On the other hand, the "subjective mind" is a distinct entity, possessing independent powers and functions. It has a mental organization of its own, and is capable of sustaining an existence independent of the body. In other words, it is the Soul. The most important point to remember is that the subjective mind accepts every suggestion given to it, no matter how good, bad or absurd without the slightest hesitation or doubt.

Man must, therefore, learn to entertain only good suggestions, ideas and moods. This is imperative due to the fact that man's subjective mind is amenable to the control of his objective mind, as well as to the suggestions of others. Through discipline he learns to reject all suggestions at variance with that which he wants to hear. The subjective mind expresses the feelings impressed upon it. This is the Law of cause and effect. The cause is the mood, and the effect is the manifestation of the mood.

In the subjective dream state we meet loved ones and we visit places thousands of miles away. This is real, because man is a psychological being and not bounded by space or time. Other people may tell us important things in our dreams. Tigers, lions and other wild animals talk in foreign languages to us, and it seems natural and logical while we are dreaming. However, it is when we awaken to this world of "make-believe," that we think our dream experiences are illogical or unreal. Life on this plane is truly a dream and nothing but a dream.

Is it not foolish to say man is suffering? Can God suffer; can God grow; can God expand; can God contract? It is the illusion of growth, the illusion of travel, the illusion of time and the illusion of suffering or death. If you have a toothache, who is suffering, you or the tooth? If you are hypnotized, for example, and the suggestion is given that "there is no pain," immediately the pain leaves you. On awakening you have no sense of pain. Where did it go? It was only an idea, belief or opinion accepted by your consciousness. A counter-suggestion removed it.

People talk about thousands being killed. Can God die? Can man die? God cannot be slain; neither can man be slain. God as man will come again. When we awaken—and we are

This Is It: The Art of Metaphysical Demonstration

beginning now to remove the scales from our eyes—we will truly become one with God, and shed His light, Love and Beauty to all the world.

We can only conjecture as to the length of time the process of awakening will take. On the other hand if time is not, it must only be the illusion of time. It may appear to be a year or a day, or eight hundred years—for in consciousness a thousand years are as a day. God is the eternal now. He is the God of the living and not of the dead.

Let us reason together. If the world is within you, where can you go? The world you will experience for a time in the after-life will be that of your crystallized beliefs. It will be a dream-world peopled by your prejudices, ideas, opinions and beliefs about peoples and things. Our ideas and beliefs are like individuals—they live and exist as long as we sustain them in our consciousness.

"Why seek ye the living among the dead?" There are no dead. All your loved ones, closest friends, all men, women and children who make their exit from this plane are very much alive and functioning fourth dimensionally. They cannot be seen by the three dimensional mind of man.

This recalling of the lost preserves the beauty of thought without limitation. In other words we must never grieve or mourn for loved ones. On the contrary we must give, "... Beauty for ashes, the oil of joy for mourning, the garment of praise for the spirit of heaviness." (Isaiah 61:3).

By dwelling on the qualities of love, kindness, inner beauty and nobility of thought that was theirs, we resurrect these qualities within ourselves. This is what is meant by praying for the dead. It is a "holy and wholesome thought to pray for the dead." Recognizing the Oneness or Wholeness, we realize that the loved one who has passed on is still alive and dear to us. Meditating occasionally on the fact that the departed are dwelling in a state of peace, beauty and love, we change any nightmares they may be experiencing (due to subjective impressions carried over with them) to lovely experiences.

We make them whole or "holy" by our prayer which is scientific prayer. This is what is meant by giving the oil of joy for mourning. Instead of feeling that they are dead and gone—that their grave is where the body is—let us, by our inner mood, see them dwelling in a state of indescribable beauty; then we truly give the dead "Beauty for Ashes." Under no circumstances must we ever dwell in the mood or feeling of lack, limitation or regret.

6

Hearing and Seeing

Every day of our lives we are only meeting our beliefs. Let us not be fooled, cajoled or tricked by any seemingly miraculous stories or strange phenomena. Many so called strange occurrences, projections and voices are nothing but subjective manifestations. The ghosts we fear are those that walk the gloomy galleries of our mind.

To the intuitive or sensitive person the subconscious is an open book. He reveals the contents of your subconscious to your conscious or waking self. The thoughts and feelings of man can also be read by a deck of cards, sand or other devices. From time immemorial man has given certain values to cards and other symbols. Since man has given authority and power to these things, they must confirm his beliefs symbolically. By getting into a partly subjective or passive state, it is possible to reveal the contents of the subjective mind of a person. The cards, or the marks on the sand serve as an alphabet which, when pieced together intuitively, give a language that will be understood.

We are surprised many times that what is delineated is true, and many of the predictions do occur. To read the character of any individual, it must be done intuitively or in a partially subjective state. If a person is highly intuitive, he tunes in with you and reveals the contents of your subjective mind. Your conscious mind becomes aware of what you formerly were not aware.

As long as man worships at the shrine of graven images and molten idols, so long will he be a slave to his beliefs. Like the surge of the sea, he will be tossed to and fro—"a double-minded man, unstable in all his ways."

What Isaiah or the prophet of God says is only too true, "Thou art wearied in the multitude of thy counsels." (Isaiah 47:13). He is looking for a God outside of himself; he is worshipping constantly at the shrine of the false gods. Whatever man accepts as true becomes a subjective reality. The subconscious mind of man, being absolutely impersonal, no respecter of persons and non-selective, accepts whatever man believes to be true and gives it form. The latter becomes an embodiment, an experience or condition in that man's world.

He is impressed by a suggestion that he will have an accident on the 15th of next month, and that he should avoid auto travel or train travel. This man lives in fear until the 15th; then he decides to lock himself in a room. Having impressed his subconscious with the belief in an accident, and having actuated it by fear, he knows it now must come to pass. He cannot escape. Something happens—he slips in the bathroom and hurts himself or he cuts his hand with a knife—perhaps a fire breaks out; something *must* happen.

Now, if man knows the Law of life and the Truth of Being—that "I and the Father are one" and that "whatsoever ye shall ask in prayer, believing, ye shall receive" (Matthew 21:22)—this man will shape and mould his own destiny. He will laugh at all dire predictions because he knows his consciousness to be God. What he feels as true of himself must come to pass. Not liking what he has heard, he says to himself, "How would I feel were the opposite true?" Then he enters into the spirit of it—gets into the mood that all things are possible to him who believes—enters into the conviction that it is so, and thrills to it. This man has actualized a new state subjectively, and this must come to pass.

If a man believes that he must get hay fever this year, as he always has in the past, let him dispel all such beliefs in powers apart from himself. Let him turn his attention to the God within—yes, turn inward, towards the Real. *This is the internalization of consciousness.* In this state let him dwell in the feeling of perfect health—enter into the spirit or mood of being healed—and he will express health.

God is truly the known God. As Paul says, "If haply they might feel after him and find him . . ." Yes, all that man has to do is enter into the feeling of the answered prayer. His eyes, ears and all his faculties must be turned inward and focused on the One, the Beautiful and the Good. While man is still in this meditative and relaxed mood, he will write on his consciousness the words of Scripture, "It is finished!" We must walk the earth knowing and believing perfect health is ours.

There is absolutely no one who can predict with accuracy for the spiritual man, or the man who "dies daily" through scientific prayer. It cannot be done because this man predicts for himself. The mystic sees the fallacy of fear of the unknown and belief in evil. The mystic, the truth student, who believes in God as taught in the Bible and prays scientifically to the God within himself, is the true prophet. Truly he prophesies for himself all the good that is to come. He is the master of his fate and the captain of his soul. He knows that God shall wipe away all tears and that there shall be no more crying.

When man awakens to the truth, he realizes that Christ is his consciousness. Then he recognizes the great Oneness wherein all men are One. Moreover he knows and understands the meaning of the greatest commandment, "Hear, O Israel; The Lord our God is one Lord." (Mark 12:29). What such a man feels as true of himself, he feels as true of the other. He only sees and feels the good for every living creature.

Such a man is a type of Christ and is capable of seeing or hearing only good for all men. He knows that negative feelings towards another disturb the harmony of the whole or oneness of which he is a part. The whole of God is in the part, for consciousness cannot be divided. "And all mine are thine, and thine are mine; and I am glorified in them." (John 17:10). "And for their sakes I sanctify myself, that they also might be sanctified through the Truth." (John 17:19).

This Is It: The Art of Metaphysical Demonstration

The true prophet or mystic enters into the mood or feeling of the answered prayer. He has the feeling that it is done, and closing his eyes and ears to the world, he comes before His presence with singing. He enters into His gates with thanksgiving and into His courts with praise. Contemplating the reality of the wish fulfilled, he rests. This is the Sabbath or rest of the Lord or Law. By sanctifying himself he makes others whole.

The mystic walks the earth unmoved, unchallenged and unshaken in his conviction that his feeling, "thy will be done," must be manifested. In a little while, perhaps he is still speaking, it appears—the divine image becomes visible on the world's screen. For the first time he becomes consciously aware of it. He has looked "within" and not "without" and found the wisdom, the power and the glory.

Man does not believe that it is possible for him to extend his faculties of sight so that he may actually see, for example, one of his loved ones thousands of miles away, and carry on a conversation as if they had met on the street. Neither does the average so-called wise man of the world believe it possible to carry on a conversation at a distance of thousands of miles without the aid of all the well-known mechanical inventions for this purpose.

In the chapter on "Time and Space" is outlined the remarkable ability of an Indian boy to stop the flow of blood. This same boy, in addition, had the amazing capacity of projecting his voice thousands of miles to Colorado. He did this quietly, and at the same time replies came back through the air in the voice of his brother. It was just as if two persons sat in their living room and conversed.

This is how he did it. He would sit down, close his eyes and begin to talk to his brother named Two Moons. The conversation concerned family ties, health of the mother, death of some friends and some local news. All of his comrades thought he was faking. Some accused him of being a ventriloquist and said they could prove it. They decided to have him ask three questions rapidly which would require a fairly lengthy reply. They stuffed his mouth with a handkerchief, and sealed his lips with adhesive tape. The answers came clearly over the air. These answers were heard by many men present, including the author.

After a lapse of a few minutes his brother in Colorado said, "Why don't you reply?" In answering he had asked him a question regarding a dog named "Sanco." No answer could be given as it was physically impossible for him to open his mouth. To sum it up, this Indian boy believed that he could talk and be heard at a distance only by his brother and father. This was a childhood conditioning based upon belief.

If he could project his voice thousands of miles over mountains, through fog, winds and waves, certainly he should also be able to project his vision and actually see his brother. He could not do that since he had not been informed when he was a boy that he could. His father believed that he, the first born in their family, could talk over distances to male members of the family only, and that their replies would be heard; yet his brother did not have the power, according to him, of initiating a conversation.

This may all seem peculiar and somewhat weird, but it shows in a striking manner what belief can do. If we would believe now that we could walk on the waters, we could do so. Most of us would *like* to believe or want to believe. However we do not really believe we could, simply because our mother and our teacher said, "That is impossible." Now it is a fixed belief in our subjective mind.

The storms at sea, the tempests, cyclones and hurricanes are within man himself. When we are truly at peace others will say, "What manner of man is this, that even the winds and the seas obey him?" (Matthew 8:27).

7

Prayer and Force

Many ask this question, "What shall I do after praying?" "What physical footsteps are necessary?" If you listen to the Voice within, and subjectively hear the answer, which is the feeling, "that it is done," "that it is finished"; then you have literally heard the answer to your prayer. A prayer is a wish to which you have acceded.

When you have fixed the things you want in consciousness (it may be health, peace of mind, love, wisdom or material things), the subjective mind of you will compel you to take all the necessary footsteps to the fulfillment of your dream or wish. You will actually be compelled to do all that is necessary to the fruition of your ideal. You will not ask Tom, Mary or anyone else, as to what you shall do or what you shall wear. No, you will do everything automatically, led by the SELF within. You can call it "being intuitively led," "divinely guided" or whatever term you wish to use. It is a compelling force which, if listened to, is the "divinity that shapes our ends."

After meditation or prayer, if you are still in a quandary, and feel like asking others for advice as to what you should do or where you should go, it means you have not believed. You have not fixed the reality of your desire or prayer in your consciousness. You will know what to do, where to go and what questions to ask. Whatever you do will be exactly according to the "Pattern on the Mount."

When man ascends into the Mount (a high state of consciousness), and enters into the joy that would be his if his ideal or dream were now realized, he has created a Pattern in the Mount. The likeness and image of the pattern appears. Man being both objective and subjective, will do whatever is objectively necessary to the fulfillment of his divine goal. He may seek a teacher. If he does it will be the proper one. He may be led to a library and find the book that will give him the desired information. He may overhear a conversation that will answer his prayer.

These are the objective manifestations of subjective impressions. "I have ways ye know not of." ". . . neither are your ways my ways . . . For as the Heavens are higher than the earth, so are my ways higher than your ways." (Isaiah 55:8–9). "His ways are past finding out!" (Romans 11:33). The disciplined man, the sincere truth student, does not ask how, or when, or in what manner or through what source his good will come. When the gift appears, he instinctively and intuitively recognizes it, accepts it and says, "Thank you Father." "Father, I thank Thee that thou hast heard me and I knew that thou hearest me always." (John 11:41–42). Many pray to God and then ask others to predict the future for them. Had they prayed believing, they would know the future. They would have prophesied for themselves. They would have had the silent inner knowing of the Soul—the awareness that it is—the sensation of having touched "something" within.

Man may not be able to describe his feeling in words as it is a subjective mood, which is the language of the Soul, but he knows that he knows. How can you describe a fourth-dimensional feeling in a three-dimensional language? When he perceives it objectively, he uses the King's English to describe it. This is the experience of everyone who has prayed successfully, whether on the battle field, in the streets or in the privacy of his home.

"Go (tell no man,) and shew John." (Mt. 11:4). John is the world. When your prayer is answered objectively, you show it to the world and your outer senses confirm the conviction that you have entertained within. Such a person does not consult anyone as to the outcome of his wish. He knows himself what the outcome is. He has prophesied and being the true prophet, not the false one, he knows that "HE never faileth."

Those who are consulting strange gods as to their destiny are looking for a sign. You are told in the twelfth chapter of Matthew, ". . . There shall no sign be given to it, but the sign of the prophet Jonas." This refers to the eternal trinity by which all things are created—consciousness, your ideal and the feeling or nail that joins it. The mystic steps to be taken in all metaphysical demonstration include consciousness desiring, uniting with the thing desired and loving it. These steps will fulfill the Law and take you into the Holy of Holies.

8

False Prophets

The false prophets are those people who tell us there is a way out by cheating, lying and by brute force. The way out is through PRAYER; this is the way to overcome all obstacles, impediments and the challenge of the world. "All things, whatsoever ye shall ask in prayer, believing, ye shall receive." (Matt. 21:22).

Inasmuch as prayer accomplishes all things and is the answer to all problems, man's whole life should be prayer. There is nothing but prayer. We do not gain the ear of God by vain repetitions. By entering into the "secret place," which is our consciousness, and communing with our Father Who sees in secret, He will reward us openly. We must touch, through feeling, the reality of the desire for which we pray.

On hearing Truth for the first time, many maintain their old beliefs and still wish to accept the new. As a result, there ensues a quarrel in consciousness and they become neither hot nor cold. This double-minded man, who is unstable in all his ways, cannot hope to receive anything from God.

Man must leave the old with all its works and pomp. He must forget all the idols and false prophets and become the true prophet. The false prophet believes his future depends on circumstances, conditions, environment, influences and forces outside himself over which he has little or no control. The man who believes in powers outside himself is calling God "Baali"—a God of caprice and vengeance, a God of wrath and an inscrutable being whose playthings we are. This type of man conjures a being dwelling in space who must be appeased by sacrifices, fastings, pilgrimages and repetitions of various prayers.

Man must begin now to call God "Ishi," which means "my husband, my lover." Yes, God must be your true lover. You must be close to Him, you must embrace Him. He is a God of love, of justice, of wisdom and power. We must look upon the God within us with love, understanding and absolute trust. We must not regard Him with a sense of fear, doubt and apprehension. He is not the unknown God. "In Him we live, and move, and have our being" (Acts 17:28). Let us look upon Him as the known God.

A question often asked is, "Why is it that predictions regarding future events in my life have come to pass?" Follow the answer to the question carefully and it will be easily understood, and not appear mysterious and strange.

"I am the Alpha and Omega, the beginning and the ending, saith the Lord, which is, and which was and which is to come, the Almighty." It is possible for an intuitive person who is in a psychic, passive or receptive state, to tap the contents of the subconscious of another and reveal these "secrets" to the conscious mind or waking self of man. In other words, in a passive state, a sensitive or highly intuitive person tunes in with the fears, phobias, fixations, desirable states, subjective acceptance of marriage, divorce and various other impressions in the other—be they what they may. The individual who is tuning in with your subjective feelings translates moods and beliefs in his language and foretells accordingly.

We must remember that the subconscious mind is a storehouse of memory, and many suggestions have been accepted of which the conscious mind is wholly unaware. These are brought to the surface by an intuitive individual, and we may become aware of them for the first time. Many times, of course, these things come to pass—for whatever the subconscious has been impregnated with will be objectified in man's world sooner or later unless changed by prayer. Any man, receiving a suggestion or prediction regarding himself of an undesirable nature, can prevent this prediction from coming to pass by prayer. In this way he becomes the true prophet.

The intuitive person who made the prediction saw or felt the beginning and having seen the beginning saw the end; for the beginning and the end are the same. "I am Alpha and

Omega, the beginning and the end." (Rev. 21:22). There is no mystery about it, no trick and no phenomenon. All is according to the laws of mind.

It is possible to predict with a certain degree of accuracy for a person, a group, a race, a nation or the world, because the majority of human beings do not change very much. They live with the same old beliefs, same old traditions, race concepts, the same hates, phobias and fears. They follow more or less a set pattern, which can be easily read by one tuning in psychically or intuitively with the mass consciousness.

What is strange about men such as Nostradamus who tapped the consciousness of the race in the 16th Century and, from the fixed beliefs and moods of the race mind, saw the beginning and the end? Today we are witnessing the drama of the end—at least to some extent. Why should not man be able to peer through the unnumbered centuries and see all?

The prophecies of Nostradamus—or any other man— would mean nothing and could be defied and proved untrue, if men knew how to pray. Through prayer they could change their subconscious and consequently their destiny. Prayer eliminates fear, doubt and hate from the subconscious of man. That is how he weeds his garden so that only beautiful flowers may grow.

The spiritual man refuses to hear something he does not want to come to pass; he changes the beginning by a new concept of himself and, therefore, he changes the end. This is done by the law of substitution or prayer. *Instead of praying something out of existence, he prays the condition he wants into existence.* He becomes a producer.

By illustration, suppose a man is informed that someone dear to him is very ill and may die within a certain time. If he has accepted this as a fact of consciousness and sustains the belief, it must come to pass. Let us further assume the man hears of this principle and applies it, believing in the Law of Reversal. Immediately the false prophecy is nullified and the true prophecy of Life is fulfilled. The prophecy was false because it foreshadowed gloom, doom and disaster. In this way he changes the prediction and defies all the dire prophecies of man concerning things to come.

This is the process to use: first, he must change his conception of the loved one and feel and see him as a radiant being, perfect in health. This is done in a silent meditative mood by calling the subjective image of his loved one before him. He causes the person to smile, to tell him that he never felt better in his life, and that the spirit of God is permeating every atom of his being. He thrills to this annunciation and is happy because "it is so." Dwelling on the joyous answer to his prayer, he goes off to sleep in the arms of the Lord, who receives his gift and objectifies it in a little while. This man has replaced the fear of sickness and death for his loved one with the realization of perfect health. It must be fulfilled.

Whether for good or ill, the Law of the Lord is perfect. It is "a Tree of Life" to those who know how to pray. It is the "Valley of the Shadow of Death" to those who pray amiss.

Let me give you another example: A man heard the false prophecy that his child had only a few hours to live. "The thing I fear most has come upon me." The fear of death causes death. The fear of loss is "Alpha" and death is "Omega"; the beginning and the end are the same. Man changes the beginning and brings about a new end by seeing, feeling and believing his child to be perfect.

In the subjective mood of prayer he lifts the child up— actually sees him running around, playing, enjoying himself and radiating health and happiness. He actualizes this state by feeling and contemplating the psychological reality of it. He rests on this conviction. The new "Alpha" or beginning is that silent inner knowing, the conviction that all is well. It is the joy of the answered prayer. The new "Omega" or ending must be perfect health. The fear is replaced by love. "As within, so without."

By changing our mental attitude, the outer picture must change, too. "Be ye transformed by the renewing of your mind, that ye may prove what is that good, and acceptable, and perfect, will of God." (Ro. 12:2). "Thou shalt love thy neighbor as thyself." (Matt. 19:19). *This is the law that will change your world*. No one can prognosticate for a spiritual man. He shapes his own ends, because "he dies daily" to the untrue. He prays unceasingly. The mystic, or spiritual man, through prayer and meditation, changes the subconscious part of his mind. Prayer wipes out fear and purges the subjective Self of all false ideas and superstitions which have been causing all the trouble. Let us face the facts and realize that every condition, circumstance, or experience in our lives is the outpicturing of a belief in the subconscious.

We must also realize that all sickness, accidents and disease of every nature are the embodiments of negative ideas or fears in our subconscious. Always remember, ". . . Though your sins be as scarlet, they shall be white as snow; though they be red like crimson, they shall be as wool." (Isa. 1:18).

9

Far-Seeing

The following is an experience of the author, which may answer many questions in the minds of the inquiring reader. He wanted to go to a certain city in the Orient in the capacity of a chemist for a large, international, chemical organization with which he was at that time associated. This is the procedure that he used: he relaxed in an armchair in the back of an old church which still stands; closed his eyes and became still. The writer imagined himself in the Orient by an inner perception of a typical Oriental setting. He felt the tropical breeze on his face and actually felt his toes being cooled off by the salt water on the sands of the seashore. He dwelled on this realization for two or three minutes, and felt the joy of being where he wanted to be. At the end of five minutes contemplation, the words of the prophet Isaiah came to his mind: "So shall my word be that goeth forth out of my mouth: it shall not return unto me void, but it shall accomplish that which I please, and it shall prosper in the thing whereto I sent it." (Isa. 5:11).

The sequel to this prayer is very interesting. A short time afterwards, the opportunity came to the author to visit the Orient. All arrangements were made to proceed by plane. However, the morning preceding his departure for the Orient, in a dream, came the vivid realization of things to come in two or three years hence. A friend appeared in the dream and said, "Read these headlines—do not go!" The headlines related to war. The writer "dreams literally."

The subjective mind of man always projects a person whom you will immediately obey, because you trust and love that person. To some people a warning may come in the form of a mother who appears in a dream. She tells them not to go here or there, and gives the reason for the warning. Your subjective is all-wise. It knows all things. It will speak to you only in a voice that your conscious mind will immediately accept as true. It would not be someone whom you distrusted or disliked. Oftentimes the voice of a mother or loved one may cause you to stop on the street, and you find if you had gone another foot, a falling object from a window might have struck you on the head. This is not the voice of your mother, or teacher or loved one. It is the voice of your subjective and it speaks in a tone or sound that you instantly obey.

As proof of this, I questioned my mystic friend. He assured me that he knew absolutely nothing about the warning "he" had given me subjectively. No, it is man's subjective that is ever portraying the drama of its contents in the form of a dream or a vision of the night. If man suggests to himself that he will remember and understand the symbolism portrayed therein, he will know the outcome of many things. He will also learn to change the dreams; for by changing his consciousness he changes the dream, and as he dreams, so shall he become.

Joseph was warned in a dream. God spoke to Solomon in a dream and offered him his choice of gifts. Solomon chose wisdom, and God added long life and riches. With all our getting, let us get understanding of this principle; then our pillars of strength will be the two great pillars—"Boas and Jachin"—Wisdom and Understanding.

Possessing the wisdom which the Bible teaches, and the understanding to apply the psychological principles therein, man's inner righteousness will show itself in his world. He will need no man-made rules of conduct to guide him; for he will be led by the wise Power within him. If the thing that you now want will bless yourself and others, it is the Divine Will. "I am come that they might have life, and that they might have it more abundantly." (John 10:10). "Heretofore have ye asked nothing, . . . ask and ye shall receive, that your joy might be full." (John 16:24).

In prayer realize the great oneness and feel the end of the answered prayer. The Being within you sees the beginning and also sees the end. It shows you the end in a feeling, "In a dream, in a vision" or by a voice. Listen to It. It will talk to you. Obey It, because It is Wisdom speaking to you. "In a dream, in a vision of the night, when deep sleep falleth upon men, in slumberings upon the bed; then He openeth the ears of men, and sealeth their instructions." (Job 33:15–16). ". . . He giveth to his beloved in sleep." (Ps. 127:2).

The writer, in consequence of his dream, immediately cancelled the trip, cashed the tickets and sought no reason. He was under subjective compulsion to do so. A subsequent event—the tragedy of Pearl Harbor—proved the truth of the Inner Voice. "Trust in the Lord with all thine heart." (Prov. 3:5). Thus shall ye walk in the land, verily ye shall be fed. Let him be a "lamp unto my feet." (Ps. 119:105).

10

Missing The Mark

Our sin is in missing the target of perfection. Though in the beginning the archer misses his target a thousand times, he gains skill through the practice of aiming again and again at his mark. So does the fruit of sin, which men call punishment, perfect the skill of His chosen one. An ancient meditation points out, "Sin and punishment are one and the fire of punishment is the fire which refineth My works." "Even in the sinner I AM the actor and I, too, am the sufferer, in the experience of punishment. Thy pain is My pain, thy suffering My suffering. Thy sorrows pierce My heart, thine anguish is My anguish. I stand not aloof, unmoved, watching my handiwork as a potter watcheth the clay upon its wheel. Nay, not so, for I am clay, and the wheel, and the potter too. I am the work and the worker, and the means of working."

"The delusion of separateness passeth with the completion of the work for which I enter into manifestation and because nothing can prevail against Me even the worst of sinners shall come in their appointed time to liberation."

Yes, all men shall see the Light. When man awakens to his true Self, he will experience the radiance of the Light Limitless, and from the field of sin and punishment he shall pass into the boundless freedom of the divine perfection. Let us realize the Truth of the following verse from Arnold:

> *"Never the spirit shall die.*
> *The spirit shall cease to be never.*
> *Never the spirit was not.*
> *End and beginning are dreams.*
> *Birthless and deathless and changeless—*
> *Remaineth the spirit forever.*
> *Death hath not changed it at all.*
> *Dead though the house of it seems."*

11

Oneness with God

"I am the Lord, and there is none else, there is no God beside Me." (Isaiah 45:5). You, the reader, are the one and only being there is. When you say "I AM," that means the sum-total of all the personalities in the world. All other conceptions are projections in space of the one being, yourself. In the Bible, which is a text book on psychology—metaphysics and man's moods and feelings—the "I AM" is constantly referred to as, "I am the way, the truth, and the life." (John 14:6). "I am the Resurrection and the Life." (John 11:25). "I am that I am." (Ex. 3:14). These and similar sayings shine forth in all their true brilliance when once we see that Jesus, the Christ, was not speaking of Himself personally, but of the principle of Being inherent in all mankind.

What Truth students fail to see is that there is only one man, for the same reason that there is only one God. God and man are one—"I am in the Father, and the Father in me." (John 14:11). You cannot divide the One; infinity cannot be divided or multiplied. The seeming divisions are the illusions of separation. We must give recognition to that innermost Self which is pure Spirit, and which is not subject to any condition whatsoever. We feel that we are conditioned by time and space, but these conditions have no place in essential Being. The true recognition of the "I AM" is the acknowledgment of the Self within you. God, the Father, eternally subsisting in His own Being, sends forth all forms of His will. Likewise, all forms return to the formless One, according to an immutable law.

You, the one man, can comprehend the infinite Self within you by a limitless expansion of your conception of God. You thus return to the Universal Being as a son coming home to his father. The more we study the Bible the more we realize that, by the art of meditation—i.e., by going inward—we become greater in our knowledge and comprehension of the mysteries contained therein. The road inward is the road to greatness, the Royal Road of the Ancients, and for all men who desire to become united with the Supreme Cause, the root and substance of all.

Rebirth means to ascend inwardly from the lesser to the greater by an inner realization, or by the lifting up of consciousness from one step to another. The consciousness, being lifted up by contemplation, dwells on the fact that I am now the being I long to be, and to make it real I must feel it. This realization is an inner awareness of the new state of consciousness or rebirth.

There is not a single note that was ever played that any man cannot play. Anything that has ever been felt by any holy man, any man can feel. There are no facts or secrets hidden in the dim past that any man cannot bring to light. You are the only Being there is. You have a memory of all that has passed, consequently all tones, moods, vibrations, knowledge and wisdom are within you. There is no language that ever was spoken that you cannot speak. There is no voice that you cannot reproduce, because all is within you.

YOU have always lived! "Before Abraham was, I AM." (John 8:58). "When all things cease to be I AM." You, man, wrote the Bible! You may have forgotten it, but if you meditate on its passages, the subjective self within you will reveal to your conscious mind what you meant, when YOU wrote it thousands of years ago.

Time is an illusion; God is the eternal NOW. Thousands of years are as an instant. Aeons are as a day. Therefore, shed now the belief in time and the idea that we have to come back again and again to this earth plane—one time as John, another visit as Mary—in order to gain more experience, to perfect ourselves and become as Jesus, the Christ.

We are sometimes told that it is almost impossible for us to become as Jesus, or Moses, or Elijah in one lifetime; it takes several lifetimes; moreover, many say that we have some "karma" to work out in this life. In other words, we must expiate for the sins and crimes committed in past lives before we can be purified. Some state that it is almost impossible to change certain physical conditions in this life, particularly, if one happened to be born with a congenital disease or deformity.

This teaching is false and a contradiction of everything the Bible teaches, namely, "Behold, I am the Lord, the God of all flesh: is there anything too hard for Me?" (Jer. 32:27). "I will restore health unto thee, and I will heal thee of thy wounds, saith the Lord." (Jer. 30:17). ". . . Who healeth all thy diseases; Who satisfieth thy mouth with good things, so that thy youth is renewed like the eagle's." (Ps. 103:3, 5). "I will ransom them from the power of the grave, I will redeem them from death." (Hosea 13.14).

A cripple is not instantly healed because of his or your belief. Likewise, if a man's leg is amputated, the reason he does not grow another leg is because his father and mother, the authorities of certain text books, plus tradition and race belief, all contributed to the false belief and teaching he received as a baby. He holds a firm conviction within himself now that God cannot grow another leg for him. He firmly believes that nothing can be done for him except to wear an artificial leg. "Thy faith hath made thee whole." (Luke 8:48).

Regarding the belief of some people that we must suffer for errors of the past or for sins committed centuries ago, there is no basis for this false concept. If a person believes that he must suffer for something he has done, he will suffer. It is all based on belief.

The only loss, limitation, restriction or evil in the world is our belief in loss, our belief in limitation, our belief in

This Is It: The Art of Metaphysical Demonstration

restriction and our belief in evil or disease. This is known as "the son of perdition" or sense of loss spoken of in the Bible. "Come now, let us reason together, saith the Lord: though your sins be as scarlet, they shall be white as snow; though they be red like crimson, they shall be as wool." (Isaiah 1:18). "And their sins and iniquities will I remember no more." (Hebrews 10:17). "For thou, Lord, art good, and ready to forgive; and plenteous in mercy unto all them that call upon thee." (Ps. 86:5).

The reader should stop, think and realize for a moment that a God who says, "Love your enemies, do good to them that hate you," by necessity of His greater Love, blots out all of the past. He wipes away all tears, and forgives you immediately. Can you imagine a God asking you to forgive those who trespass against you, and in another breath refusing to forgive Himself? "He shall call upon me, and I will answer him." (Ps. 91:15). "I, even I, am he that blotteth out all transgressions for mine own sake, and will not remember thy sins." (Isaiah 43:25).

Man completely detaches himself from the past by partaking of a great psychological and mystical feast of peace and happiness. Realizing the presence of God within him, he rises in consciousness to the joyous conviction that he is NOW the being he longs to be. Having fixed this state within him, a silent inner knowing possesses him; all former doubts and fears pass away and shall be remembered no more. By sustaining this silent inner feeling, that which he felt inwardly becomes expressed outwardly.

12

Forgiveness

Your consciousness is God and there is no other God. If a seeming wrong or injury has been committed against you, therefore, you must forgive. Now, there is no other—so there is no other to forgive. You give something for the feeling of resentment or hate that you now hold in your consciousness. You give way to a feeling of love, peace, harmony and joy.

In other words, it is the age old law of substitution in consciousness. To "forgive" means to give something for. If you have a headache, and you take a pill for the condition you are giving yourself something for the headache. Likewise a person who happens to be in a mood of resentment must replace this mood he is entertaining by forgiveness. The only way he can forgive himself for entertaining such a negative mood is by the indwelling gift of love and peace within his own consciousness.

You must radiate this feeling to all around you. When you think of John or Mary, who formerly was what you thought the "cause" of resentment, you will see the Christ in him or her and rejoice. You become exceedingly glad that they are expressing all they long to be. You are seeing the Truth behind the form, the Divinity behind the mask. "Love thy neighbor as thyself," says Jesus. Your neighbor is yourself. All love is to oneself. All treatment is to oneself, consequently all hate, jealousy and bitterness is to oneself. If you decide to hate someone, or injure someone, whom are you injuring? Yourself only! "I am The Lord that is my name: and my glory will I not give to another." (Isaiah 42:8). As is well known, many people are healed by absent treatment, and the teacher or healer does not know anything about the details of the case in question. The blending of the patient with the healer is not essential. The Scriptures point this matter out clearly. Jesus raised Lazarus who was dead four days. A dead man cannot ask you to pray for him or blend with him; neither can the insane ask you to heal them; yet the Scriptures reveal that they were healed.

The only reason the disciples could not heal an insane child was because of their unbelief. If you wish to treat a person at a distance, even though he has not requested you to do it, you must feel the reality of the healing within yourself. You actualize this state within your subjective mind. Since there is only one subjective mind, what you have felt as true of the others, must be manifested in the other's world. There is no other, for there is only the One.

This question comes up occasionally wherein someone says, "Oh, I had a remarkable spiritual healing, but some weeks or months later there was a relapse to the former state." No teacher or healer can guarantee the continuance of the healed state, due to the simple fact that man is not an automaton, but has freedom to choose. He has freedom to be sick or well as he chooses. The day following the healing, he may re-infect himself by accepting a suggestion of fear or by entering into an emotional outburst of anger or hate.

Man must change his habits of thought and adopt for his rule and guide: *right thinking, right feeling and right action*. Teaching is healing; consequently a very important function of the healer or teacher is to point out to the sick person the cause of his trouble and how to eliminate it. The sick person, realizing that all his troubles of whatsoever nature were effects of causes set up within himself, must decide to discontinue the wrong thinking which produced the ill effects in his world. He learns that the Christ within can accomplish all things. Having learned the causes for the misfortunes and chaos in his world, he will then maintain the consciousness of health, peace and harmony. He will, thereby, prevent a relapse or re-infection of former destructive moods.

In the eleventh chapter of St. Mark, we read these wonderful words: "What things soever ye desire, when ye pray, believe that ye receive them, and ye shall have them." (Mark 11:24). There are no conditions laid down. It is not necessary that one be a holy man or a great mystic to manifest the innermost desires of his heart.

The man we call the murderer, thief, or the person of ill repute could, if he desired, become Jesus, the Christ, instantly. Shocking as this may sound, all that such a being would have to do—according to the law of spiritual consciousness—is to forget completely the past by turning within; feeling with all his heart and soul that he is the Christ and is doing the works of Christ Jesus on earth. As a man thinketh in his heart, so shall it be done to him. In the twinkling of an eye he could be changed.

Paul, according to the New Testament, persecuted his fellowmen, testified against them, and had them put to death. He is a shining example of the state of consciousness that can be attained instantly if desired. Paul was illuminated on the road to Damascus by turning within, changing his conception of himself, and finding that he really was the Christ. We can do this! If this is not true, the whole teaching of the Bible collapses and is false. *But it is true*, "the same yesterday, today and forever."

The truth is we are all that we ever will be now, but we fail to recognize it. The mass murderer or the violent assassin can in one moment become the Christos, the illumined one. This person need merely rise in consciousness to the conviction or feeling that he is the Christ, and doing the works of Him that sent him.

We are told the story of the boy born in the stable, of lowly parents. We are informed that He was a carpenter. It was said, "Can there any good thing come out of Nazareth?"

(John 1:46). Yet this boy, born with all the social and worldly handicaps, became one with the Father. He walked the earth the God man, seeing only perfection, beauty, order, symmetry and proportion in everybody and everything. Why? *Because by uplifting his consciousness these qualities were established and made manifest within himself.* "What thou seest, that thou beest." The meaning of the story of Jesus is that any man, woman, boy or girl can become the Christ. The command is, "Go thou and do likewise." The Jesus Christ state of consciousness is not born of woman, but comes *out* of the imagination of man. We must refuse to believe the idle, foolish statement that it takes man one hundred or one thousand years to become a Jesus. There is no time in God. "That which is to be hath already been." In other words, you are all that you will ever be NOW—yes, this very instant. Even fifty million years hence will not make any difference to the Reality within you.

Do you not realize the everlasting Truth of the ages that you are God, individualized in a fleshy body? All conceptions that you ever conceived or will conceive, all growth, learning, wisdom, expansion and contraction are the illusion of growth and expansion. God cannot learn or become wise. He is All-wise. He knows all. Hence it must be the illusion of evolution. It is simply the grand masquerade of the One.

Yes, there are deep, heavy scales on our eyes. If we will let the scales fall, we will see the light within. Our prayer should be, "God give me eyes to see the Light." "Awake thou that sleepest, and arise from the dead, and Christ shall give thee light." (Eph. 5:14). If you think for one moment that you are unworthy to see the Light and become the perfect man, then dwell on these words: "But if the wicked will turn from all his sins that he has committed, and keep all my statutes, and do that which is lawful and right, he shall surely live, he shall not die, all his transgressions that he hath committed, they shall not be mentioned unto him: in his righteousness that he hath done he shall live." (Ezekiel 18:21, 22).

13

Outpicturing Man

All outer manifestations of man's life are projections of an inner state or image contained within his consciousness. Man must learn that the only way to create a better world is to build the constructive images within his consciousness that he wishes to see expressed in the world. The world is an outpicturing of our mental beliefs and attitudes.

We look at a man and we say that he is lame, deaf, blind, ragged or poor. We have clothed him in rags, in garments of blindness, deafness and poverty, but in absolute Truth he is God and can never be any less than He is. Let us awaken from the dream, and clothe every man in the garment of Christ, the Anointed One. "Who is blind as he that is perfect and blind as the Lord's servant?" (Isaiah 42:19).

This Is It: The Art of Metaphysical Demonstration

The perfect man cannot see a blind man or a deaf man; neither can he see any man in rags. He sees only divine perfection, the divine idea behind all form. He sees the ever-flowing reality, justice and beauty in all things. In other words, he sees God in all things. He does not see another. His command is that of a King: "Take ye away the stone." (John 11:39).

The perfect man, giving complete, recognition to God and realizing that all things are possible to Him, cannot see any lack anywhere. Hence his request for abundance is automatically granted. He is blind to all evidence of the five senses and worldly beliefs or powers outside of himself. His eyes are forever turned inward towards the Real.

If you have a lesion on your face, and a friend prays for you, the latter does not inwardly see the lesion on your face. On the contrary he hears you telling him that you are overjoyed that God has granted you a perfectly beautiful, smooth face. If he succeeds and the scar disappears, "he saw the perfect face." This manifestation may have occurred the same moment you were telling him the foolish details of the difficulty you experienced so far in treating it, and all the resultant failure. Where did the lesion go? Where did it disappear to? The truth is that it existed only in your imagination and belief.

When you have learned these great truths, you have "reincarnated" indeed. To learn these truths is to know them, and to know them is to live them and witness them. Man is playing a role in the great drama of life. When the curtain comes down, he puts off his garment, hangs it up and disappears from sight. He ultimately returns to the Source. From Him we all come forth—to Him we all at last return. There is no other place to go. "They shall not hurt nor destroy in all my holy mountain." (Isaiah 11:9).

When John or Mary "dies"—as we usually employ the term—it means that John or Mary, as the case may be, lives on in each one of us. A person never dies. The quality, tone, or mood of the Infinite, which was his always existed and always will. The subjective afterlife may be a nightmare or a lovely dream—depending entirely on what man has impressed on his subjective mind before passing over. Let us play the melody of God here, and listen to the overtones of life. In this way we will be better equipped to play the game of life in the next dimension.

All things subsist in the Infinite and when we call forth the expressions by our feelings, then it may be said to exist. "I am Alpha and Omega, the beginning and the ending, saith the Lord, which is, and which was, and which is to come, the Almighty." (Rev. 1:8). ". . . I girded thee, though thou hast not known Me." (Isaiah 45:5). We fail to see that it is always God coming into the world when a child is born. That child is its own father and mother. There is only the One Father and He is "Our Father." "It is He that hath made us." (Ps. 100:3).

14

Inequality of Man

It does not make any difference whether man was born deaf, dumb or blind, the "works of God" can now be made manifest. The Divine Love of God in action is omnipotent in healing. It is invincible; therefore, Jesus or the illumined consciousness can enter into the realization, "It is done." Many ask this question: "Why is an innocent child born blind, deaf or crippled?" Obviously, they have not read the Scriptures, for the same question is asked in the ninth Chapter of John: "Master, who did sin, this man, or his parents, that he was born blind?" Jesus answered, "Neither hath this man sinned, nor his parents: but that the works of God should be made manifest in him." (John 9:2–3).

The work of God is the nature of God, which is goodness, truth and beauty. Man's conscious mind is "father" and his subconscious "the mother." Man creates by his feelings or moods. In the creative act, the mood at the moment of conception determines the nature of the child. "I form the Light, and create darkness, I make peace and create evil: I, the Lord do all these things." (Isaiah 45:7). This means the Lord (law) can be used two ways, but through our ignorance we misuse it. Our moods create! What is the nature of our mood? What tone do we strike during the creative act? If there is someone in the parent's world whom they hate the sight of, or if there is a voice that they wish they would not hear again, a corresponding expression must be brought forth. A blind or deaf child will be born—as within so without—as above so below—as in Heaven (consciousness) so on Earth.

The law is impersonal and no respecter of persons. It gives to all men that which they ask according to their mood or belief. The nature is the feeling or conviction within man. If man feels he is healthy, realizing his state of consciousness as the determining factor, he cannot express illness. The child be it deaf, dumb or blind is judged good and very good, because it is the perfect image and likeness of the consciousness which produced it. ". . . Every creature of God is good." (I Tim. 4:4). "His work is perfect." (Deut. 32:4). "And God saw everything that He had made, and, behold, it was very good." (Gen. 1:31).

You will see that whatever "tone" is struck by the parents, a corresponding voice or mood comes forth by the law of reciprocal relationship. No child is subject to so-called laws of heredity. "What mean ye, that ye use this proverb concerning the land of Israel, saying: The fathers have eaten sour grapes, and the children's teeth are set on edge? As I live, saith the Lord God, ye shall not have occasion any more to use this proverb in Israel." (Eze. 18:2–3).

Yes, the father may be insane, tubercular or criminal, but the only thing passed on to children is the spirit or mood of the father and mother. It is possible for a so-called criminal to have a son who becomes a Beethoven, a Shakespeare, a Lincoln or a Jesus. It depends on the moods of the parents or the states of consciousness at conception. "I, if I be lifted up from the earth, will draw all men unto Me." (John 12:32). If you are lifted up in consciousness to the point of acceptance or belief that your son will be the noble, dignified, Christ-like being you dream of, according to the law of reciprocal relationship a corresponding mood or quality of the Infinite comes forth.

If man realized that God walked and talked in him, he would change the whole course of his life. God is indivisible. There are not two Infinites, but only One. It is impossible to divide infinity. The whole of God, therefore, is in the seeming part of man. All beings in the world live and have their existence only in the consciousness of man.

Let us get away from any idea of separateness. Some wish an eternal continuance of themselves as John, Mary or Joe, coming back again and again for more experience. They do not realize they have experienced everything—have seen all things and have always lived.

". . . The works were finished from the Foundation of the world." (Heb. 4:3). It is not the personality known as John, Mary or Joe coming back. It is always the spirit of the one God. "Elias is come already." (Matt. 17:12).

The personality, John or Mary, is simply the mask of God—it is the sum of the appetites, moods, feeling and beliefs of each of us. In other words, we tincture or color the one Spirit by our beliefs and impressions. God does not repeat himself; therefore, objectively, we look different. Subjectively we are all one. The subjective is the Real—the objective—the mask. John, for example, might have lived in New Orleans. We will say he died; then the quality which was John lives on in all beings throughout the world.

Now, during the creative act, in some part of the globe the tone or quality that was John is struck.

This could be in China or Japan or elsewhere and that quality or mood of the One God comes forth. It is not the personality we knew as John; it is ever the spirit of God. The same instant that John died, instantaneously, the same vibration could come forth in a member of another race and country.

Cycles of 500, 800 or 1,000 years have nothing to do with this law. God is timeless; all tones are in the one. When we are playing on the grand piano, it will respond according to the notes we strike. Man is the one who measures, and "the measure he metes shall be measured unto him." "Whatsoever he sows, that shall he also reap." You sow the seed in consciousness and you reap the fruit of the seed; it will be the exact likeness of the seed sown. *Let us sow beautiful thoughts; let our hands play divine melodies; let our eyes see the beauties of God; let our voices be those of praise and thanksgiving. Then surely we will reap what we sow.*

15

Time and Space

A question frequently propounded is this: "Why do I say I have been here before; I have seen this place before?" Is there any place in which you have not been? The world is within you.

You do not have to travel to any point in order to describe any place, country or area in the minutest detail. God is omnipresent; He does not travel. You are both God and man. You are both unconditioned and conditioned—the unconditioned or formless awareness is God Almighty. This is the Real Self of you.

You have forgotten who you are, and you believe that you must travel to India in order to see it. You can sit still and see all of India. "Be still, and know that I am God." (Ps. 46:10). Your "I AM-NESS" is God. God is everywhere and in all things. There is nothing outside yourself. You are the center of all creation and all revolves around you. As long as we believe in travel, time and disease, we must experience them. In other words, we must have proof of our convictions.

Consider this explanation: John wishes to take a trip to Killarney. He dreams about the trip and plans for it. He buys a ticket; arranges for passage and passport. He knows that he is going to take the trip. John goes to his Father every night and takes all his moods, feelings and beliefs with him as gifts. The Father always acknowledges whatever his son etches on consciousness.

While asleep, John's subjective has taken the psychological trip to Killarney, visited his friends and heard their voices and comments. John awakens and takes the trip physically. Eventually he motors to Killarney from Cove and does not need to ask directions from anyone. WHY? He was there before; he visited it a few weeks ago, psychologically, while asleep on his couch. Now he knows the way. He hears a voice and stops suddenly, saying loudly and excitedly, "I've heard that voice before, even that same expression." "Why I know this cottage, I've lived here before!" A dozen different expressions pour forth from him. Consciously, he has forgotten, but the subconscious is the storehouse of all memories and experiences—the seat of all knowledge.

His experience has nothing to do with previous incarnations. John has been visualizing a wonderful trip, impressed his subconscious and "went to sleep on it." His subjective, knowing all, accepted the suggestion and dwelt there psychologically. When the conscious mind arrived there, it experienced all the subjective states. "I go to prepare a place for you, and if I go, I will come again and take you unto Myself, that where I Am there ye may be also."

When he hears the voice and feels the loving caress of a dear one, it is the objectification of his own desire and then it registers. "I come to make the blind see and those that see blind." This means that all things exist now but we refuse to believe it and accept it.

For example, the writer some years ago met a boy who was considered ignorant and stupid by his comrades. This boy could not read or write, neither did he know the classics. Yet he could stop the flow of arterial blood, which flows freely, by closing his eyes and saying, "Stop it." When he opened his eyes, the bleeding had ceased. He believed that his prayer would always be answered and even though others mocked, he never failed. "Charity (love) never faileth." (Cor. 1: 13–8).

That is why belief is not necessary on the part of the sick person. Yes, truly the woman can have an issue of blood for twelve years, and by touching the hem of His garment, she shall be made whole. To touch the hem of His garment means to feel the thrill of accomplishment on the inside of the subjective self.

It is the inner silent knowing. It is the feeling within that "It is done." We must always seek the end. Having felt the end, we have already determined the means to that end.

How did the so-called ignorant boy mentioned in a previous chapter have this ability? His explanation was as follows: As long ago as he could remember, his father told him that the power to staunch blood was a tradition in the family, and was handed down from father to son. The first born in the family had the gift, but the other members, such as sisters and other members, such as sisters and other brothers did not possess this power.

The boy grew up in this belief and fully accepted the fact that he could stop the flow of blood. If he saw it, he closed his eyes to it, and issued the command which was always obeyed. He really did not know how or why it should stop. He knew practically nothing about God. The reason the blood stopped flowing was because of his *belief.* (He stated that at home in Colorado he frequently was called upon to stop cases of hemorrhage.)

A very peculiar thing about this healing capacity was that he believed that he had to be present and see the blood flow, and so he could not heal anyone out of sight. Not aware of the laws of mind or the working of the conscious and subconscious faculties of man, this shows what could be accomplished with a youth if conditioned properly by someone who knows and understands the laws of life and the Truth of Being. For example, no amount of words or explanation would convince this Indian boy of the fact that he could stop the flow of blood at the request of a third person—even though he did not see the patient. This was a belief implanted in his subjective mind at an early age and he accepted it as a part of the tradition of his tribe or family.

Children, particularly under seven, are living mostly in the subjective state and very amenable to suggestion, especially from parents whom they trust and love. This boy was unconscious of the "fact" that it could not be done, just as many of us believe that the technique of stopping the bloodflow is only possible through the use of blood coagulants and a tourniquet. It is all a question of how "free consciousness" has been bound and conditioned by belief, opinion and custom.

16

The Journey Beyond

Frequently is the author asked: "Will we meet our former parents, brothers and sisters in the after-life?" In the 22nd chapter of Matthew, the question reads like this: "Therefore in the resurrection whose wife shall she be of the seven? for they all had her?" (Matt. 22:28). Jesus answered them, "In the resurrection they neither marry, nor are given in marriage, but are as the angels of God in Heaven." (Matt. 22:30).

We must not think that our former wives or husbands will be lined up to greet us. Family relationship is for this three dimensional plane. Believing in the old concept of reincarnation, just imagine what it would mean! Maybe two million wives would be waiting for us. Where there is a deep, unselfish love of a mutual nature, there will be a meeting and a joyous reunion.

When you learn to love, and are prepared to serve others, your solo will cease, as Dunne says in "New Immortality," and become part of a duet. Thus you join through love other players and produce orchestral effects. Finally one day we will discover we are playing in the symphony of all creation. There is no lost Soul and even the child that dies in the womb, still lives. Yes, it grows; expands and through love it goes from "glory to glory."

When we awaken, all are one in consciousness. In the absolute state, all tones are one. There is nothing but a great Oneness. "There is neither Jew nor Greek, there is neither bond nor free, there is neither male nor female." In God the sinner and the holy man are one. Black, white, yellow and brown races are all one. He ". . . hath made of one blood all nations of men for to dwell on the face of the earth." (Acts 17:26).

"I am the resurrection, and the life." (John 11:25). Your I AMNESS is the only living Reality. "In Him we live and move and have our being." (Acts 17:28). An angel is an attitude of mind, a voice, a tonal quality or mood. God, being infinite, consists of an infinite number of angels or "angles." Man is God in infinite expression. There is no end to his expansion of consciousness, because God is without beginning or end.

All our friends, relations and all those people who are past and gone, are within ourselves. They are angels of heaven—and where is heaven? Jesus says, "The Kingdom of Heaven is within you." There is, therefore, no place for them to go except within our consciousness, which is God, the Absolute. "Do not I fill heaven and earth? saith the Lord." (Jer. 23:24).

"There is but one God, the Father, of whom are all things, and we in Him." (I Cor. 8:6). Our Father is in heaven and heaven is within us. All your loved ones, when they finally awaken, subsist in the eternal stream of consciousness as angels of God, in perfect peace, and they are one with their Father. All men, women and children in the world are notes in a vast musical composition. Let us become lost in the unity of the whole, and all sense of separateness leaves us. The sum total of all creatures does not comprise unity,—no more so than the fractions contained within the number, one, bring about the fundamental unity of that number, by being added together. We may regard multiplicity as a way of experiencing that unity. When we enter the world of Reality by a process of withdrawal into the enduring self ("I die daily"), we no longer persist as individuals, surrounded by a world which is not ourselves. *We are all that is*, and our individuality has merged in the *all*. We are the life of all creation.

The eternal continuance of John or Mary Smith as a personality is the nemesis of the uninformed. This is the point where foolishness and wisdom hopelessly divide. As long as John desires to be separate, he desires to be separate from that Universal One, who is the root and substance of all things. The universe of the foolish man is one containing spheres, planets and planes through which he passes forever—a universe becoming greater all the time.

The Truth student looks at things somewhat differently. He knows that this Spirit within him, which he is trying to individualize, is not an individual at all. He knows that the life within him has never been separate from God and never

This Is It: The Art of Metaphysical Demonstration 103

can be. What the illumined one calls "being alive" is eternal Life living in him. Man is playing against fate when he wishes to be John Smith forever. He might be referred to as an egoist, who thinks that as personal self, he is sufficiently important to subsist for aeons of time.

Let us be real Truth students. Let us realize that that which lives and abides in us, is eternal Life. If it were true that the personal John Smith was the Thinker—if it were true that he was the Life—it would be different. These are appearances due to the illusion of the material state.

In contemplation and in deep meditation, we realize these profound truths about man. It is Thought thinking him. He is not thinking thoughts. Is it not LIFE living in him? He is not living LIFE. Is it not eternity concealed or hidden within non-eternal natures? All of us are an inevitable part of the unity of God and inevitably destined to be reabsorbed into His unity. We need not fight on forever. We can "stand still, and see the salvation of the Lord." (Ex. 14:13). The absorption of the particular by the universal is the end of individual existence, as we know it on this plane of consciousness. We could liken it, as the return of the spark to the flame, the return of the water to the sea.

Man is forever asking, "What shall I be in the afterlife? What will Mary be? What will all individuals be?" We are victims of centuries of false beliefs. Over thousands of years we have begun to believe in a strange complex of separation or apartness from our Father. Yes, man is always asking, "Will we lose this individuality of ours." The word "individual" means that which is indivisible. The answer must be,

"What is individuality?" Is it not the One Life looking out through the countless windows and eyes? This Life is ever at one with Itself and It shall not be anything less. Man is not an individual; he never was. His emotions, beliefs and intellect tried to make him something apart. All things in this relative world of ours are expressions of the absolute. The one life is expressed in countless modes. It is all One Reality. The one in the many, and the many in the one. The apparent separate manifestations are notes in a grand symphony. There is a difference in the notes, and they are grouped differently into chords and harmonies; yet, we must remember the symphony is One. Grace notes, somber notes and notes used to form part of a magnificent opening chord are not separate; they all are the symphony and the symphony is one and indivisible. The composition is one Reality. Every note shares the joy and beauty of every other note, and shares the Life of every other note. The life of the whole is in each note. The part is in the whole, and the whole is in the part. You are the Grand Symphony. You are the Creator and the Hymn of Creation. We are the Supreme Reality sharing the life of all things.

"Everywhere in heaven is Paradise. Even though the grace of the Chief Good does not reign there after one only fashion!" Does not this mean that the mystery of the ultimate Reality is multiplicity in Unity?

The reason for all the chaos and misery in the world today is given to us in Chapter 2 of Jeremiah: "For my people have committed two evils; they have forsaken me the fountain of living waters, and hewed them out cisterns, broken cisterns, that can hold no water." (Jer. 2:13). Millions of men today pray to a God in space whom they look toward as some being living in the skies, consequently, their prayers are not answered, because they do not know how to pray. They have forsaken the God within, and have created a God outside of themselves. They also have given power and authority to conditions and circumstances.

Instead they must realize that rather than permit the world to control, influence and frighten them, they should control what now controls them. We have the choice to control our outer manifestations or be controlled. The world with all its pomp and ceremony is the cistern that holds no water and if man drinks of this, he will thirst again. He must go back to the fountain of living water and drink of it in order to become free of the limitations of matter and circumstance. Man must leave the world of sound; go back to the "Silence," and dwell in His peace, strength, wisdom and power.

17

Finding Oneself

Let us once and for all awaken from the dream of being separate. Actually, we never have been separate and never have been individuals. When we completely die to all of our false beliefs, we are back again in the Garden of Eden. "Thou hast been in Eden the Garden of God; every precious stone was thy covering." (Ezekiel 28:13). This is the illusion removed and the Fact made known. The ancients called it the awakening from a dream. It is an awakening from the recurrent dream of self to find the "Selfless One."

"... Awake thou that sleepest, and arise from the dead, and Christ shall give thee light." (Eph. 5:14). This means that when you awaken, you learn all has been a dream—all wars, crimes, one's mistakes and misfortunes. All the chaos of the world is a nightmare—unreal, to be forgotten and remembered no more. The reality of this awakening is to find oneself in a kingdom of love, peace and happiness with the Light of Truth always shining. Beholding the Truth, dwelling upon it, accepting and rejoicing in it, we realize that the streams of "manyness" all lead to the Oneness.

The Gospel of Good Tidings is the realization that the One alone lives, and that the One alone is the end all men are seeking, the one Self that stands supreme midst the illusions of the not-selves. Then man knows for the first time what the ancients meant in their meditations, when they said: "Neither is there anywhere injustice, and the semblance of it is the delusions of separateness. The strife, the quarrels, the contentions that thou witnesseth day by day are the plays of light and darkness which I am. All sense of effort, all semblance of exertion—know these as illusions and with thy mind's eye see Me entering into all."

One man, a friend of the writer, who has read twenty or thirty books on reincarnation, is no longer worried about which wife he will meet in after life. He said, "You know I must have had millions of wives, also fathers and mothers." He is now at peace, having read the 22nd Chapter of Matthew. He is no longer worrying about which one to claim. He was under the impression that there might be strife in heaven over him.

Man is told what the true reincarnation or rebirth means in Chapter 3 of John, "Except a man be born again (of water and the spirit), he cannot see the Kingdom of God." (John 3:3). Millions have read this chapter, however like Nicodemus, they fail to see the light or true meaning. They say, "How can these things be?" (John 3:9).

Obviously pouring water on the head of a person does not bring about a spiritual awakening or change of consciousness. There must be another meaning. The simplicity of Truth is its greatest stumbling block. Children who believe in Santa Claus operate this law very successfully, because they believe in "make-believe." That, after all, is what the whole world is and all things contained therein—a vast "make-believe"—nothing more and nothing less.

At one time a little Spanish girl lived a few doors away from the author. He knew the family well, and often visited at the home of the little girl's parents. She was about eight years of age and attended the local parochial school. For months she had been asking her parents for a bicycle to ride in Central Park. The mother's constant answer was: "Stop bothering me. You know there is a war on and no bicycles are available." She continued to ask, however, much to the annoyance of her parents.

This little girl was a typical tom-boy, fought with the boys in the neighborhood and "got a black eye" occasionally. One night the writer of this book said to the little girl: "Mary, you can get a bicycle, and I know where." Immediately her eyes expanded and she was all ears and exclaimed, "Where?" The following dialogue took place between us:

TEACHER: "Go to bed immediately and close your eyes. Now imagine clearly that your boy and girl playmates are riding your bicycle in Central Park, and just see their smiles."

MARY: "I won't give my bicycle to anyone if I get it."

This Is It: The Art of Metaphysical Demonstration 109

TEACHER: "Then, Mary, I am afraid you can't get the bicycle. The person who is willing to give you the bicycle wants you to share it with your playmates who have no bicycle, so that you can make them happy. He insists that you make your friends joyful and merry."

MARY: "Oh, all right, if that's the kind of person he is. I suppose I must agree."

TEACHER: "Fine, Mary, that is the proper feeling. Now, Mary, Christmas is coming shortly and there is a big boss over all the Santa Clauses, who tells them what they can give to little girls and boys who are good."

MARY: "Mother said Santa Claus could not or would not bring a bicycle."

TEACHER: "Now, Mary, your mother is very busy; you annoy her too much and she does not always realize what she says. This is the way you can get the bicycle before nightfall tomorrow."

MARY: "Really, promise?"

TEACHER: "Mary, you know I always keep my promises. I take you to the movies when I promised, and buy you ice cream when I promise."

MARY: "I believe you. Tell me how."

TEACHER: "Mary, close your eyes and imagine yourself riding a bicycle in Central Park."

MARY: "I can see the bicycle I want!"

TEACHER: "See your playmates riding the same bicycle, one at a time. See them smiling and laughing and full of fun. Now the Big Santa Clause is listening to you and is pleased, because you believe he has the power to give it to you. He is glad, also, because you are going to share it. He will give it to you tomorrow, before nightfall. Go off to sleep, sound asleep, deep, deep sleep."

About six o'clock the next evening Mary was at Woolworth's—78th Street and Broadway, New York City—when she suddenly began to cry. A lady nearby noticed this and speaking gently said to her, "Little girl, what is the matter? Did someone hurt you?" Mary replied, "No, but there was a man at our house last night and he told me the boss over Santa Claus would give me a bicycle before nightfall. It's getting dark now and there is no bicycle." The lady was moved and said: "That man had no right to promise such a thing." She took the little girl to her apartment nearby, and gave her a bicycle, which her daughter, who had died two years previously, had used. She told Mary that she always wanted to give it to a child who loved God.

This is all that prayer is—simply "make-believe." That is all "reincarnation" is. If you do not like what you are, make-believe you are that which you long to be. Accept it, sustain the mood or belief and you will embody that state. The water spoken of in the Third Chapter of John is "consciousness," and the spirit is the spirit of joy in possessing that which you long to be or to do. The Kingdom of Heaven is the peace and stillness that follows the answer to your prayer.

We are here to experience the joy of living and for no other purpose. Out of the great silence comes God, appearing as man. Man has dreamed a dream away from reality and found that which he calls evil and sin—to be an illusion of the senses. Man must return to the Silence, and in the presence of Truth all these so-called evils fade away, since they never really existed.

18

Renewal of the Mind

You may transform your mind, body and affairs through the water and the spirit (3rd John) by re-educating the subconscious (water). One way of getting at the subconscious is by affirmation; that is, saying a thing over and over again. This is the way with some; but all these affirmations are only abstractions. What is needed is something concrete—an inner perception, a firm conviction within yourself. You must actually feel yourself as the Doer and the Seer. This is the "Spirit."

If your desire is to be a great teacher of the Law, the following suggestions could be used. Close your eyes, which shuts out the evidence of your senses; still the mind by dwelling on God; ask yourself, "What does God mean to me?" The answer automatically comes—God is Love, Beauty,

This Is It: The Art of Metaphysical Demonstration

Infinite Intelligence, Omniscience, Omnipotence, Omnipresence and All Wisdom. Then feel yourself to be the great teacher. You must feel the reality of it; the joy and thrill must course through your veins with the mood of actual accomplishment.

It is as if you went to the theatre, came home, sat down on the couch, closed your eyes and began to review all the scenes in a contemplative mood. You hear the voices, and you see the beautiful scenery, lights and costumes. You are witnessing that which has already taken place. Prayer is contemplating the reality of the wish fulfilled and reacting to the joy that, "It is finished." (John 19:30). "Enter into his gates with thanksgiving, and into his courts with praise: be thankful unto him—and bless his name." (Ps. 100:4). NOW YOU ARE BORN OF WATER AND THE SPIRIT.

When we pray, it is essential that we realize nothing is achieved by desperate effort. We grow, not by trying to grow, but rather by permitting the fact of growth to assert itself or be manifest in ourselves. Man cannot become the Great Teacher or Healer by any direct effort. "The father that dwelleth in me, he doeth the works." (John 14:10). The result is due to an attitude or mood of the mind that the Wisdom, which is ever present, is made manifest in us. We do not create wisdom, virtue and knowledge. We reform and reverberate these attributes by a renewal of the mind, thereby releasing ever-existing principles and qualities into manifestation.

19

Meditation

The discipline of looking inwardly is Meditation. What we understand we do naturally. What we do not understand we force ourselves to do. Students so often tell the teacher how hard they tried. The very effort meant failure, for meditation is always effortless. Tension, exertion or force result in failure.

An excellent way to still the mind is as follows: imagine yourself on a mountain top, looking into a lake. In the placid surface you see the sky, the stars, the moon and those things above the earth. If the surface of the lake is disturbed, the things seen are blurred and indistinct; thus it is with you. You are not "still"—not at peace—and the answer to prayer comes only to the man who dwells with all tranquility on the joy of already having received that for which he prayed.

Meditation is the internalizing of consciousness. It is the pilgrimage within. If an eight year old child can operate the Law successfully, we can. We first must become as the little child. Half an hour a day spent in meditation upon your ideals, goals and ambitions will make you a different person. In a few month's time the gentle, silent acknowledgment comes that God is within you, that the spirit of Almighty God is now moving in your behalf and that which you long to be, to possess or do is already a fact of consciousness. Man actualizes this state by feeling the thrill of accomplishment; when he has succeeded, he will no longer be worried, anxious or apprehensive.

Moreover, he will not ask anyone for advice, because he will be under compulsion to do that which is right. His subjective mind compels him to take all the necessary steps to the completion of his goal or objective. After prayer, if a man is still doubtful and begins to argue with himself as to which course to pursue, it means that he has not fixed the desired state in consciousness; then let him go back again and dwell in the reality of it.

"Verily I say unto you, Among them that are born of woman there hath not risen a greater than John the Baptist: notwithstanding he that is least in the kingdom of heaven is greater than he." (Matt. 11:11). This means that any man who prays successfully and touches Reality by getting into the proper mood or feeling is greater than the wisest man. Most of us live life looking outwardly. The wise learn to look inwardly. The disciplines of looking "inwardly" are termed together, "Meditation."

Detachment is the key to meditation. That is, we must sever ourselves completely from all worldly beliefs and opinions, and focus silently upon our ideal state. It is the effortless-effort which causes us to flow towards that which we realize without conflict. Detachment does not mean that we give up what few earthly possessions we may have. It means that we must give up possessiveness in ourselves, or release the attachments that peculiarly limit us to a human viewpoint in all matters.

"Be still and KNOW." Stillness is not only keeping quiet; it means that the causes within the Self, by which the inward life is rendered discordant, have been removed. It indicates that there must be no inner dissonance, but rather when man goes within himself, he must find perfect and abiding peace. Knowing that God is within himself makes man live in a world that is ever peaceful. The lack of it makes him live in a series of conditions which grieve him to the end. He fusses about things which, if he saw them differently, would not cause one moment of unhappiness.

Every day of our life we should meditate on beauty, love and peace. We should feel that these qualities are being resurrected in us. As we meditate daily on this inner beauty, let us feel that we are Jesus the Christ, the illumined man. Let us actually conjure the mood that would be ours were we actually doing his works and healing the blind, the halt and the lame. As we walk the earth, we must sustain this mood or conviction that we are Jesus and those qualities, which he portrayed, will be resurrected within us. They were always within us! This state of consciousness is not born of woman.

This Is It: The Art of Metaphysical Demonstration

Jesus is born out of the imagination of man and nowhere else. It is the second birth or spiritual awakening of man.

The birth of Jesus the Christ truly takes place in man as he practices the disciplines and meditates on the ideal state.

By moving inward, the mystic finally finds the Real. As he goes inward he realizes first that this thing called the body is very unreal, and this earth upon which we are seated becomes unreal. The external life becomes the dream; the internal life awakens and moves further and further inward. Finally it seems to merge, and suddenly the meditating Self perceives that, by going inward, it has found the Universe. The suns, moon, stars and planets are within. For the first time he knows that planets are thoughts; that suns and moons are thoughts; and also he apprehends that his own consciousness is the realization which sustains them all. Temporarily in space are moving the dreams of the Dreamer; worlds, suns, moons and stars are the thoughts of the Thinker. His eyes are closed; He is meditating, and we are His meditation. It is CONSCIOUSNESS meditating on the mysteries of Itself!

This inward journey ultimately leads man to the Real. It leads man away from the sense of the small "I" to the realization of the eternal Self. The mystic's mind, through meditation, finds the peace, the strength and fortitude for further steps. The practice of the discipline of meditation bestows beauty, love, peace, grace and dignity upon every impulse, every attitude and every act.

In conclusion, let us meditate on these lines, written by the finger of God, the Ancient of Days, which have come to us, down through the ages—ever the Ageless Wisdom:

"Of all existence I am the source, the continuation and the end. I am the germ, I am the growth, I am the decay. All things and creatures I send forth. I suppose them while they yet stand without, and when the dream of separation ends, I cause their return unto myself. I am the Life, the Wheel of the Law, and the Way that leadeth to the Beyond. THERE IS NONE ELSE."

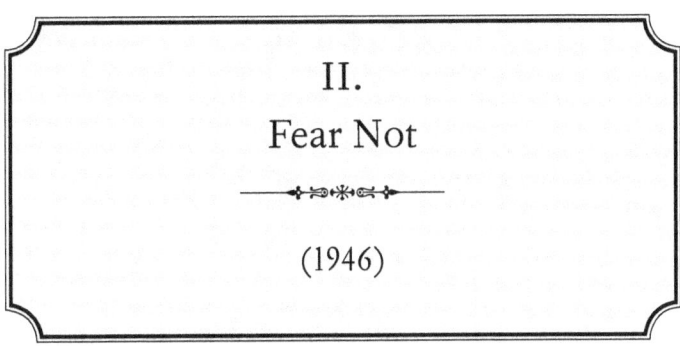

II.
Fear Not

(1946)

Fear, anxiety, and unnamed dread are the maladies of modern life. This is probably truer today than in Murphy's time. In this pamphlet, Murphy diagnoses fear as the *inability to recognize the omnipotence of your own Mind. When you come into the realization of your true nature, you realize that all circumstances are subject to self. Murphy writes that even the prisoner can be free if he follows the formula: "Learn to imagine the thing desired, and then feel the reality of the state sought." The worldly path to freedom may be impossible to foresee. "My ways are past finding out." (Romans 11:33) But with the thought arrives the means—and the incarcerate will go free. This promise holds true for you if you recognize the power that you are.* —MH

Fear Not

"The Lord is my Light and my Salvation; whom shall I fear? the Lord is the strength of my life; of whom shall I be afraid?"   Psalm 27:1.

"For in the time of trouble he shall hide me in his pavilion: in the secret of this tabernacle shall he hide me: he shall set me up upon a rock."   Psalm 27:5.

Who is your Lord and master this very moment? Your Lord is your predominant, mental attitude; it is your conviction or belief about yourself, people, and things; this Lord can be a tyrant. For example, if your mood is now one of resentment, that is your Lord or tyrant that governs all of your actions and all phases of your life. If you want to invest some money, buy a new home, or some property, while in this attitude, you will do the wrong thing and say the wrong thing, because your predominant mood is negative. The law is: "As within, so without." You are fearing your good, and you would react negatively. Fear is a lack of faith or trust in God, which is a denial of His Omnipotence.

"The Lord is my light and my salvation." "The Lord" referred to is the Lord God, or the law of God or good. To put the law of good into operation—thereby banishing fear once and for all—enthrone in your mind the thoughts of power, courage, and confidence. These thoughts will generate a corresponding mood or feeling, which will banish the arch enemy of your success and health.

Fear, this self-made enemy of yours, must be completely destroyed before the Lord God can shine through you. Your fear is the cloud that hides the sunshine of God. Men have made personal devils out of fear of the past, the present, and the future. They fear friends, gremlins, elementals, banshees, and other strange things. There are no ghosts, werewolves, gremlins, or banshees; they exist only in the gloomy galleries of man's mind.

It is our attitude toward life that determines the experiences we are to meet. If we expect misfortune, we shall have it. Knowing the law of God or good, the truth student expects only good fortune. The world is not harsh; it may seem to be, because we fail to affirm or claim the Presence of God. Men fear criticism so much, that many of their most beautiful thoughts never see the light of day. To the man who believes that God is the only Presence and the only Power, there is no past; he knows that if he believes in the power of the past, he is disbelieving in God. God is the Eternal Now; there is no future and no past.

This is the Gospel—the good tidings. There is no such thing as past karma; there is only man's foolish, stupid, false belief in it. *"Now is the day of salvation!"* The Kingdom of Heaven is at hand. Your good, your health, and your success are here now; feel the reality of them; thrill to them. Enter into the conviction that you are now the being you long to be.

The only guilt there is, is the consciousness of guilt. "If your sins are as scarlet, they shall be white as snow, though red like crimson, they shall be as wool." This is the Christ message. The only moment that matters is the present. You can live only in the now, experience in the now, plan in the now, and think in the now. Whatever you are planning or dreading, you are planning it now. When you realize that every form of lack and limitation is the result of your wrong thinking and feeling, you shall know the Truth that sets you free. The mountains will be removed.

Aboriginal tribes and primitive man feared nature. Modern man fears his fellow man. To a great extent we have dispelled the ghosts of ancient days. We have combatted the plagues, and we will soon control the elements. Man is doped by modern propaganda. Some men are afraid to live, and afraid to speak. Mothers fear for their children. All this is due to a superstitious belief that there is another power to challenge God.

The only evil there is, is due to a lack of knowledge of the laws of life. If we put our hand on an open wire, we get a shock, but if it is insulated properly, we do not. The evil or shock was due to our ignorance; yet any man will admit that electricity is not evil; it blesses humanity in countless ways. Electricity is used to play music, drive trains, fry eggs, vacuum the floors, and light the world. Evil or fear is our misapplication and incomplete comprehension of the Omnipresence of God or good. Where fear is, love cannot be; for error cannot dwell with understanding.

The wealthy fear they are going to lose; the poor fear they shall not gain. The only wealth and the only security are found in the consciousness in which we abide. If we are conscious of being wealthy, nothing in all the world can stop us from being prosperous in our bodies and affairs. The things men fear are unreal. Only the One alone is real; only the One alone is Law; only the One alone is Truth.

The jungle doctor of old has passed on many of his superstitions; consequently, countless cults today instill fear into the minds of many individuals. The various creeds have, like humanity, ignored the one fundamental truth and stressed differences, so that today so called religion is a ghastly travesty of the name religion. They say, "Our Father" and have forgotten the brotherhood of man. I and my Father are One—One Man, One God, One Truth, and One Law. Let us face the facts. The cause of most fear is man's fear of his fellow man. Many men pray together on Sunday, and prey on each other on Monday.

The answer to the fear problem is understanding. All fear is due to ignorance. In order to express harmony, we must think and feel harmonious thoughts. When we enter into the mood of success, confidence, and happiness, we will express similar results in all phases of our life. When man knows that every form of discord, sickness, and lack is due to wrong thinking, he will know the Truth which sets him free.

Learn to imagine the thing desired, and then feel the reality of the state sought. This is the easiest and quickest way to get results. Some get results by convincing themselves of the Truth—that God is the only Presence and the only Power; this is one of the most wonderful things in all the world to know.

Regardless of the cause of the fear, you have no one to treat or heal but yourself. You have to convince yourself that you are now expressing Life, Love, and Truth. Let us not fear anything or anybody; let us be busy radiating courage, confidence, and power. In this way we will crush all obstacles in our path, and the mountains will be cast into the sea.

We are one with Infinite Strength. If we say we are weak or infirm, we are telling a falsehood about God. Fear turns the love of God or good away from us in the same way that a poverty consciousness attracts poverty in health, money, business, and love relationships. Man must stop preaching fear to his fellow man, and unite in teaching all of the Truth.

The Truth is that there is no hell, devil, purgatory, limbo, or damnation of any kind; moreover, there is no past karma for which we must expiate here; there is no future evil. God is the Eternal Now! This is one of the most dramatic and significant statements in the whole Bible: "Now is the day of Salvation." This very moment all that you do is turn to God and claim for yourself that which you long to be; accept it; believe it, and go thy way rejoicing. "Though your sins be as scarlet, they shall be white as snow, though red like crimson they shall be as wool." "Forgive till seventy times seven." "This day thou shalt be with me in paradise."

Let us stop instilling fear into the minds of the youth; let us teach them the real facts. We must not preach religious tolerance except we live it. We must teach the Truth. We must not distort the Truth, so that we may hold a position, or because we are afraid that the people will not come back; this type of fear results in spiritual stagnation and frustration. Shall we give a lasting message on Truth or condition it on crowds of people? We must keep our eye on the Kingdom of Heaven, not upon the kingdom of earth. We must teach man to know the Truth, and the Truth shall make him free. The Truth is: Man is belief expressed!

There is no fear where faith in God rules. There is no fear of man where integrity rules in one's consciousness. There is no fear of criticism where the consciousness of kindliness enters into the mind of man. Religion is integrity in action or the application of Truth. We have seen, therefore, that fear is man's basic weakness, and it is based solely on ignorance.

"In time of trouble he shall hide me in his pavilion; in the secret of his tabernacle shall he hide me: he shall set me up upon a rock." "The pavilion" is a canopy or covering; this means the covering shall be the garment of God (mood of good). Think about God. Begin to ask yourself, "What does God mean to me?" Realize that God, or I Am, is the Life in you, your own consciousness, and It is Omnipotent.

For example, if a man is in prison, he automatically desires freedom. God and good are synonymous. He begins to think of this Infinite Power and Wisdom within him; he knows that It has ways of freeing him which he knows not of. He imagines, therefore, the opposite which is freedom. Though he is behind bars, in meditation he imagines that he is at home talking to his loved ones. He hears familiar voices, and feels the welcoming kisses of his children on his cheek. This is hiding in the *pavilion*. The prisoner actualizes this state by feeling the joys of being home. It is possible to rise high enough in consciousness in five or ten minutes to bring about a subjective conviction. This is the meaning of, *"In the secret of his tabernacle shall he hide me."* The law is: Whatever is impressed is expressed; consequently, the prison doors are open for him in ways that he knows not of. "My ways are past finding out."

We read in the Scriptures: "Fear not, little flock, it is your Father's good pleasure to give you the kingdom." Jesus tells us this Kingdom is within us—this Kingdom of Heaven or harmony is within every one of us. Infinite Wisdom, Divine Intelligence, and Infinite Power are available to all men, because God is within them, and He is the very Life of them. Any one can prove to himself that the Kingdom of Heaven is at hand. It is right here now; Jesus saw it, and lived in it; we are color blind; that is why we do not see it; the blindness is due to ignorance and fear. We are blinded by centuries of false beliefs, superstition, creeds, and dogmas. The Truth is so shrouded by false dogmas, that we have created God and a heaven of our making. God is to us what we believe Him to be. Man has created a horrendous creature in the skies; he visualizes a God of caprice and vengeance, or an inscrutable being who sends wars, plagues, etc. We create our own hell and our own heaven, based upon our concept of God. Anyone can prove that the Kingdom of Heaven is at hand.

Let me tell you the story of a young girl who proved it. She was living with a father who came home drunk every night, and sometimes treated her brutally. She lived in constant fear of her father. She kept house for him. Due to frustration, her face was covered with acne.

We are not living with people; we are living with our concept of them. Realizing this truth, the girl in meditation closed her eyes and dwelt on the God Power within her. She no longer clothed her father in the garment or mood of a drunkard. Instead, she saw a loving, kind father, who had perfect balance, poise, and equilibrium. She clothed him in righteousness, and her judgment was "a robe and a diadem"; which means that she saw her father as he ought to be. The fact that her father was drinking heavily, meant that he was seeking escape to conceal an inferiority complex or a subjective sense of loss. In other words he was trying to run away from himself.

This girl spoke the word which healed him. She relaxed her whole body, closed her eyes, and began to say to herself, "How would I feel if my father was loving, kind, and peaceful?" She dwelt on the solution, which generated a mood of peace, confidence, and joy within her; this was clothing him in righteousness. Her judgment was a "robe and diadem."

When you pass judgment, you come to a decision. It is the final verdict, and you are the judge passing judgment; "As I hear, I judge." Her verdict was an inner hearing or feeling, wherein she saw her father smiling, happy, and joyous; she imagined he was telling her how wonderful he felt, and that he had found peace, balance, and poise. She also heard him telling her how wonderful she was; she thrilled to the fact that her father was healed and made whole. "He wore a seamless robe"—no holes, no patches, and no seams; this means she meditated on the mood of love, peace, and oneness with her ideal. All doubts and fears were absent (judgment as the robe). "Judgment as the diadem" means she gave "beauty for ashes," which signifies she saw beauty in her father and felt it. Beauty was expressed on the screen of space.

After one week's treatment her father was completely healed; moreover, he was a changed man. His attitude was completely transformed, and they are devoted to each other. She proved the Kingdom of Heaven (harmony and peace) is at hand NOW. What are we afraid of? "If God be for us, who can be against us?" The thing you fear does not exist.

For example, a man lives in fear that his business will fail. His business is not failing; neither is he in bankruptcy. Business is as usual, and it may be booming; the failure does not exist save in his imagination. Job said, "What I fear most, has come upon me." Job is every man that walks the earth. Therefore, as the successful business man continues to sustain the mood of failure, sooner or later his mood crystallizes into a subjective conviction or impression.

Any feeling impressed on the subconscious mind is made manifest by an immutable law of life. The subconscious, being impersonal and no respecter of persons, says, "John wants to fail in business." So it proceeds in ways that he (John) knows not of to bring this failure to pass. Everyone realizes that he brought this failure on himself through imagination and feeling.

I know a lady who read of an aeroplane wreck. She was contemplating a trip by air to Los Angeles, but she lived in fear of an accident. A negative thought cannot do you any harm, except it is energized by a charge of fear. It must be emotionalized before it becomes subjective. This lady did not know what she was doing; she was ignorant of the laws of life. This ignorance is the cause of all of our accidents and misfortunes. Having imagined herself in an aeroplane accident and having emotionalized this negative thought with fear, it became a subjective state. When she took the trip two months later, she had the accident that she *knew* she would have.

If a woman fears her husband is going to leave her, this is how she conquers her moods. The fear is a negative feeling which is communicated to him. If he does not know the laws of life, her conviction of him will be made manifest. In other words, he will do the thing she feared he would do, because this was her conviction of him. Instead of this fear, she supplants it by seeing her husband radiating peace, health, and happiness. In meditation morning and night, she radiates the mood of love and peace, and feels that her husband is the most wonderful man in all the world. She feels that he is loving, kind, and devoted. She imagines he is telling her how wonderful she is, and how happy, free, and balanced he is. Her mood of fear is now changed to a mood of love and peace. This is the Spirit of God moving in her behalf. As she continues to do this, this mood jells within her. She now knows, "He never faileth," and that "Perfect love casteth out fear."

Our daily prayer or daily mood must be one of joyous expectancy or a confident expectancy of all good things; this is our greatest prayer. If we expect the best, the best will come to us. It is our mood that is vital.

The modern metaphysician of today teaches that God is *pure feeling*. If you feel full of confidence and trust, this is the movement of the Spirit of God within you, and It is all powerful. "None shall stay its hand and say unto it, What doest thou?" Man's own consciousness is God; there is no other God. By consciousness is meant existence, life, and awareness.

You, the reader, know that you exist. This knowing that you exist is God. What you are aware of is your concept of God. Each man must ask himself, "What am I aware of?" The answer to this question is his belief about God. It is what he knows about God. When he says, "I am aware of want. I am fearful. I am sick," these are lies and have no truth in them. When man says, "I am fearful," he is saying God is full of fear which is nonsensical. When he says, "I am in want," he is relating a lie and a denial of God's abundance and infinite supply. His faith is in failure, and he succeeds in being a failure. He believes in a lie, but he cannot prove the lie. The false condition seems real as long as he dwells upon it. When he ceases to believe it, he is free and healed.

III
The Meaning of Reincarnation

(1954)

This is one of Murphy's most original and little-known books. I think it possesses peaks and valleys in terms of insight. But it is worth reading to experience the best of his arguments and to question the lesser. Let me state up front that I do not agree with, nor am I sure a more seasoned Murphy would agree with, his conclusions here about the thought patterns of parents resulting in illness or disability of a child. Murphy himself later moved away from that perspective to suggest that the pool of thoughts of all humanity, extending to antiquity, could be the responsible factor. I do not share that view either, since it borders on randomness which con-

flicts with the rest of his philosophy. Rather, I think that in this sphere we experience many laws and forces; the law of mind is ever operative but it is impacted by other experiences in our physical framework, just as gravity is impacted by mass. I explore this in greater detail in One Simple Idea *and* The Miracle Club. *To Murphy's credit, I believe that certain of his insights coalesce with primeval Vedic ideas about reincarnation, especially when he writes about all of humanity emerging from and returning to original thought substance. In this regard, Murphy's ideas about reincarnation run closely to the outlook of Madame H.P. Blavatsky. I include this rare book not to instill belief but to provoke question and search.* —MH

1

The Meaning of Reincarnation

The time has come in the field of New Thought thinking, living, and practice to make a clear-cut decision as to *what to do* with the mill-stone labelled, "Reincarnation," which is discovered hanging from both oriental and occidental necks.

The highest light in the theory of reincarnation is melioristic; that is, man is becoming better by the slow, *exoteric* process of putting on and off different habiliments of flesh and emotions. Nothing is done in this unconscious process, rooted in mere habit transmission about the ringing challenge: "Be ye perfect even as your Father in Heaven is perfect."

New Thought Philosophy and application must not capitulate to a racial error perpetuated by the pronouncements of unillumined men. We should get started in the "business" about which Jesus so earnestly labored. Let us begin the program with tenacity of purpose and perseverance by putting on the Garment of Christ which is Wisdom, Truth, and Beauty instead of the garment of "poor man, rich man, beggar man, and thief," through the weary cycles of time-space-frames of reference.

Einstein has with great labor brought us to the gate of the Temple Beautiful. The false Gods of time and space have been toppled over, and become mere relativities before that "Which is, and Which was, and Which *is* to come, the Almighty."

We now stand naked before the gates stripped of all disguises and "but little lower than the angels," ready to take our just place at the right hand of Cause—The Father. This means essentially the willful cessation of the automatic, weary round of rebirths, refleshing ourselves in the menial garments of the slave to carnal, materialistic thinking and living.

The scientific, mental thinker looks at the theory of reincarnation from a new standpoint altogether. The scientific thinker starts with, "the pattern on the Mount," wherein man is one with God, and starts from there.

We must cease building an edifice based on a slow-paced dream wherein millions of human beings—east and west—have been laid in the Procrustean bed of karma and reincarnation to arise retailored in garments ill befitting an invited guest to God's Wedding Feast. If you do not wear the proper garment which is the royal, seamless robe, you will be cast out again into the outer darkness of spiritual ignorance.

By believing in the theory of reincarnation, or countless cycles of carnal rebirths, I believe you drift from safe mooring, and fall from spiritual grace.

What is your concept of God? The Bible gives you the answer: "The high and lofty One that inhabiteth eternity, whose name is Holy."

Atomic, H-bombs, and other thermo-nuclear weapons are knocking at your doors calling upon you for a new Declaration of Emancipation from all traditions and false beliefs of man—no matter how time-honored on oriental altars. Let us begin to put out all karmic, purgatorial fires by true faith and conviction in God's Love and Beauty here and now, and press on to the virgin fields of consciousness. You must not be deterred by a mirage of mere meliorism. Refuse to be satisfied by anything but the promised land of Spiritual Reality.

In materia-medica circles it is customary to discard the textbooks of yesterday's pathologies and nostrums. Likewise, you must discard the old garment of "sick man, poor man," and arrive at the hour of decision in your own mind where *"none but the best wine"* of spiritual wisdom shall be put forth for the guests who hunger for a more wholesome fare.

The new, nuclear physics with great courage and faith has also without hesitation discarded the gross atomistic concepts of yesterday. Their courage and faith have demonstrated their own miracles, such as nuclear transubstantiation, time-space fusion, television, radio, inter-atomic energy, etc. Science is also beginning to kneel and pray before the Altar of Being.

By laboring in the vineyard of your own mind, you, too, can bring forth better fruit. The Bible explains the course of action which the student of truth must take in these times when the Holy Spirit is being "poured upon all flesh." All unworthy concepts must go into the limbo of spiritual ignorance; foremost among these stands this well-regarded theory of reincarnation, whereby mole-like progress is decreed by age-old, earth-bound thinking.

When Jesus said, "My kingdom cometh not with observation of, lo here! lo there!" was he not anticipating the relativity of time-space concepts? When he declared: "Behold now *is* the accepted time!" "Believe that ye receive them, and ye shall have them!" "Before Abraham was, I am!" was he not collapsing time and space in this "business" of soul-saving and man redeeming from the thraldom of erroneous oriental and occidental beliefs?

Jesus demonstrated instant resurrection, thereby short circuiting all reincarnation lagging on the way to the promised land of spiritual realization.

Become *now* a true, mental scientist, and agree with the bold declaration: "Behold, I make all things new." "I have overcome the world." "Believe me that I *am* in the Father, and the Father in me." *The me* means the conscious, inner realization of God's Presence in you and in all men.

Free yourself mentally from the belief in self-imposed fleshy, psychologically imprisoning embodiments. The "sons of God" must "leap for joy" beneath "the morning stars" of Light, Love, and Truth which light up the heavens of your own mind.

Once I prayed for a friend who believed he was the victim of karma, that he had to suffer, and that God was punishing

The Meaning of Reincarnation

him. A healing of his mind and body followed; this was God reincarnated or made manifest in a body ill at ease or in disease. The malignant growth was stopped, and the glory of God was made manifest. This *glory* waits "neither for time nor tide," but is instant with the One Presence which always comes with healing on Its wings.

Leave all lesser altars and idols, and come before God with a pure heart and noble purpose. True reincarnation is the birth of God in the mind of man, where man becomes seized with a Divine frenzy and becomes God-intoxicated. The Spiritual rebirth comes to the man here and now who goes on a great psychological, spiritual feast in peace, happiness, and joy; then he begins the task of Divine regeneration, resurrection of God's ideas, and ascension into the bosom of God's Eternal Love.

Emma Curtis Hopkins tells of a wonderful event recorded in the archives of a state penal institution; this is the essence of it: A man was sentenced over half a century ago to be hanged. In the interim between his sentence and its time of fulfillment, he sought the Face of God, which means the Truth about God. If I look at your face, I recognize you. Look to God and His Love; there is no condemnation there. God does not condemn or judge any man. "All judgment is given to the son." You are the son, and you are always judging yourself by the concept and beliefs you entertain. You are always choosing thoughts; thereby passing judgment on yourself. God sees you perfect. The Perfect One cannot see imperfection. When man rises in consciousness to the point where he forgives himself and cleanses his mind and heart, the past is forgotten and remembered no more.

Karma, or reaping what you have sown, turns out to be inexorable only as long as you do not pray or meditate on the Truths of God. As soon as you pray, you rise above karma, and the unpleasant consequences of past mistakes begin to be wiped out. No matter how awful the crime,—be it murder, or any other heinous offense,—it can be expunged from the mind together with all the punishment that would ordinarily follow. Mere reading of affirmations and perfunctory prayer will not change matters. A deep hunger and thirst for God's Love and Grace, plus an intense desire to transform, is essential to wipe out the punishment that must otherwise follow negative and destructive thinking.

I have known murderers to become completely transformed by an inner realization of God's Presence; they were completely reborn; they were so changed that it would be impossible for them to repeat the mistakes of the past.

The murderer of whom Emma Hopkins speaks sought the Face of the All-Good. He had read that God was "the bad man's deliverer," and this man had committed the murder for which he was sentenced. To the great confusion and perplexity of the officers of the law, when the man was led to the gallows, the platform of which would tip ordinarily at the slightest weight, became firm the moment the condemned man stepped upon it. They tried again and again to no avail, until finally he was given his freedom.

Did not the efficacy of the High Watch halt the so-called karma of the ordinarily mandated treadmill of cause and effect, and enable this murderer to step off into a new order of emancipated consciousness and experience?

The Love of God indeed passes all understanding, and It does illumine the path we tread. The wonders and blessings of God know no ending.

Modern science is beginning also to penetrate the wonders of the world; it says that we live in an ever-changing, fluidic universe of dancing forces, and that the universe is a mental phenomenon. The ultimates of science are on precisely the same footing as our intuitions of Goodness, Truth, and Beauty of God. Our reason must listen to the subtler voices of intuition and revelation. With a new vision religion and science may both understand the mystic overtones of this ancient meditation.

> *"Of all existences I am the source*
> *The continuation, and the end.*
> *I am the germ;*
> *I am the growth;*
> *I am the decay.*
> *All things and creatures I send forth;*
> *I support them while yet they stand without;*
> *And when the dream of separation ends,*
> *I cause their return unto myself.*
> *I am the Life,*
> *And the wheel of the Law,*
> *And the way that leadeth to the Beyond—*
> *There is none else."*

2

Does The Bible Teach Reincarnation?

Reincarnation is God incarnating again and again. It is the One Being coming back repeatedly.

Troward says, "If a thing is true, there is a way in which it is true." Let us see the way in which Reincarnation is true. In reading the ninth chapter of Luke, we find these words, "Now Herod the tetrarch heard of all that was done by him: and he was perplexed, because that it was said of some, that John was risen from the dead; And of some, that Elias had appeared; and to others, that one of the old prophets was risen again. And Herod said, John have I beheaded: but who is this, of whom I hear such things? And he desired to see him."

Herod means the world-mind, race belief, and acceptance of the traditions of the past. Such a mind believes it is John the Baptist risen from the dead or Elias come again, but what it fails to see is that it is always God coming forth as a quality or mood of man.

The people in the days of Jesus believed in reincarnation, but everywhere in the Bible, as we shall point out, Jesus rejects the belief completely. If you read this book with a fixed belief in your old ideas, you will not really grasp what is being written. You only hear what you are ready to receive. Many hear what they want to believe. Where will you find the authority for the Truths of the Bible? They are within yourself! Your subjective or Invisible Self is the authority; It knows all, and It will illumine your conscious mind.

Herod is the tetrarch; the latter means the fourth part of the province, or the ruler of the fourth part of a country. You have four parts: You are spiritual, mental, emotional, and physical. *The physical*, or the body, is the tetrarch referred to. The body, or the worldly belief, is that a man dies and comes back in another body in cycles of 500, 800, etc. The man with the worldly belief desires to see Jesus, but he cannot. Jesus symbolizes the Truth.

Truth is an inner perception; It is subjectively perceived and understood. You say, "I see," when you comprehend, or understand the solution to a knotty problem. Many people believe that we come back again and again, in order to expiate for our sins committed in former lives. They believe they have to work out their karma until they are free from bondage. It is a solace and a comfort to many people to realize that their misfortunes and troubles are due to errors in their past lives. This belief is indeed a panacea; it answers their problems; puts them at ease, and it acts as an opiate to these poor people.

Again I wish to emphasize that Jesus does not teach reincarnation, as commonly understood. He teaches a spiritual rebirth. Let us examine the third chapter of John: Jesus said to Nicodemus, "Verily, verily, Except a man be born again, he cannot see the Kingdom of God. Nicodemus saith unto him, How can a man be born when he is old? Can he enter the second time into his mother's womb, and be born? Jesus answered, Verily, Verily, I say unto thee, Except a man be born of water and the spirit, he cannot enter the Kingdom of God."

Nicodemus means a ruling state of consciousness within man; he is still wedded to the old thought of a physical or carnal rebirth; yet he is dissatisfied, and is seeking light. He is a man of the Pharisees, meaning that he is one who adheres to the letter of the Law, but lacks the spirit which giveth life. He represents the average man of today who does not know that his own Awareness, Beingness, or Consciousness is God, his Creator, Redeemer, and Saviour. Let us see this drama or dialogue as taking place within man.

When Jesus says, "I am the Truth," he is not referring to himself as a man, but to the Principle which he teaches.

"*I AM*" means Pure Being, Life, Awareness, Consciousness, or The Unconditioned One. Our "I AMNESS" is God. "I am all things to all men." This Formless Awareness becomes that which man conceives It to be; this is the law of believing—the corner stone of life which the world rejects. When we read the word, "Verily, Verily," it means stop, look, and listen! *To be born again* means a spiritual rebirth—the birth of God in man.

Nicodemus, or man seeking, questions the Truth, asking, "How can a man be born when he is old?" The average man thinks of God as far off; he considers heaven as a place to which he goes when he leaves this plane. He fails to see that anyone can enter the second time into the mother's womb, psychologically, and be reborn spiritually. Man can enter the womb of God again and again, and be reborn mystically. *The womb of God* is man's own inner feeling.

Here is how you may enter the womb of God and be reborn: Get still and quiet by relaxing the mind and body. Detach yourself from the old way of thinking and form a new concept of yourself, a new estimate. Meditate on the reality of this new concept to the point of conviction. Imagine and feel the reality of the new ideal; live with it; envelop it in love; woo it; then the ideal will be resurrected in you, and you will become a changed man.

I knew a murderer one time who confessed to me that he had killed a man. He had an intense desire to transform himself, and be reborn mentally and spiritually. I wrote down the qualities and attributes of God for him. He began to still the wheels of his mind. For fifteen or twenty minutes several times daily, he would quietly, silently, and lovingly claim and feel that God's Love, Peace, Beauty, Glory, and Light were flowing through his mind and heart, purifying, cleansing, healing, and restoring his soul. As he did this regularly, these qualities and attributes of God were gradually resurrected within him. In other words these qualities came out of his mother's womb, which was his own feeling or mood as he prayed.

One night this man's whole mind and body, as well as the room he was in, became a blaze of Light. He was actually blinded like Paul by the Light for awhile. He said to me that all he could remember was that he knew the whole world was within him, and that he felt the ecstasy and rapture of God's Love. His feeling was indescribable. It was in other words the moment which lasts forever. He was a changed man; truly he expressed the real Incarnation of God in his mind and heart. He began to teach others how to live, and I am sure he is still doing it somewhere.

He was born of water and the spirit. *Water* will take the shape of any vessel into which it is poured, so will your mental attitudes and beliefs assume form and shape in your world.

Spirit is a feeling, a mood, or animated state of consciousness. *To be born of water and the spirit* is, therefore, to begin to think in a new way; to get a new mental attitude, and to begin to feel the joy of the answered prayer within you.

Let us take a simple illustration. Suppose you wish to be a great teacher of God's Truths: Close your eyes tonight. Still your body. Imagine you are expounding hidden mysteries or the Truths of the Bible to others, and that they are being illumined and inspired. In your imagination, you see the multitude; feel the reality of it; realize the wonder of it all. Dramatize it within yourself! You are the actor in the drama. ("Act as thou I am, and I will be." This is an old philosophical quotation containing a great Truth). Feeling yourself as being the great teacher, living, and acting the role in your imagination, you are focused on your ideal, and you become one with it as you remain persistent. As you regularly enter this meditative state, you will touch Reality, and you will objectively express what you subjectively saw and felt.

Your true rebirth is when you leave the kingdom of man and his false beliefs, and enter the Kingdom of God and His Glory within you.

3

Are We Victims Of Karma?

We must not be wedded to a belief in karma (evil that has to be expiated here in life). As long as man believes that he is going to be punished, he suffers the consequences of his false beliefs, ideas, and opinions.

To believe that God is punishing you for the mistakes of the past is to have a false concept of the One True God. Whatever concept you hold of God, has its effect on your life. If you have a false, superstitious concept of God, there will be confusion and chaos in your life.

Ask yourself, "What do I really believe as true about God?" Your answer is the most important thing in your life; it must come from your heart. It is not adequate to say, "I believe in God."

For example, begin to believe that God is Omnipotent, All Wise, Boundless Love, Infinite Intelligence, and Infinite Perfection, and that what is true of God must, therefore, be true of you; for God and man are one. God is man made manifest; the Formless and the formed are one, the Unconditioned and the conditioned are one. Spirit and form are one. Life and its manifestation are one.

If you really believe in your heart that God is All Love, Light, Truth, and Beauty in the same way as you believe you are alive; then everything in your life will begin to change. All the departments of your life will begin to improve, such as, your health, wealth, love, and expression; you will go from glory to glory, and your good will multiply exceedingly until "the day breaks and the shadows flee away."

To believe that we must come back again and again to work out our karma or suffer for past misdeeds is a sort of an opiate; it dulls the mind and destroys the body.

I have heard people say, "This is my karma; I cannot overcome this; you know, I must have done something bad in a former life."

This is a form of alibi which acts as an anaesthetic to dull the senses. We must really see the foolishness of such a belief. It is a complete contradiction of the teachings of the Bible and the Ageless Wisdom. Jesus healed the blind man immediately; thereby rejecting all such beliefs.

The only loss, limitation, restriction, or evil in the world is our belief in loss, our belief in limitation, our belief in restriction, and our belief in evil or disease; this is known as the "son of perdition," or sense of loss spoken of in the Bible. "Come now, and let us reason together, saith the LORD: though your sins be as scarlet, they shall be as white as snow; though they be red like crimson, they shall be as wool." "And their sins and iniquities will I remember no more."

Can you imagine a God asking you to forgive those who trespass against you, and in another breath refusing to forgive Himself? You are already forgiven in the eyes of God. Forgive yourself now. "He shall call upon me, and I will answer him." "I, *even* I, *am* he that blotteth out thy transgressions for mine own sake, and will not remember thy sins."

Some people state that it is almost impossible to change certain physical conditions in this life, particularly, if one were born with a congenital disease or deformity. This is a contradiction of everything the Bible teaches, namely, "Behold, I *am* the LORD, the God of all flesh: is there anything too hard for me?" "I will restore health unto thee, and I will heal thee of thy wounds, saith the LORD." "Who healeth all thy diseases; Who satisfieth thy mouth with good *things; so that* thy youth is renewed like the eagle's." "I will ransom them from the power of the grave; I will redeem them from death."

A cripple is not healed instantly because of his belief. A man whose finger is amputated, for example, believes he cannot grow another finger; he has been told that by his parents; the textbook he studied says it cannot be done, plus the tradition, and race belief. He now holds a firm conviction that the Living Intelligence which created his finger cannot grow another.

Elsie Salmon in her book, *He Heals Today*, tells about a child whose three fingers were missing, and how through prayer the three fingers began to grow normally. Jesus said, "Thy faith hath made thee whole."

In the eleventh chapter of Mark we read these wonderful words, "What things soever ye desire, when ye pray, believe that ye receive *them*, and ye shall have *them*." There are no conditions laid down.

It is not necessary that one be a holy man or a great mystic to manifest the innermost desires of his heart. The man we call the murderer, thief, or the person of ill repute could, if he desired, become transformed in the twinkling of an eye; this could be accomplished through a great rise in consciousness, accompanied by an intense desire and hunger for God's Love and Peace. It is possible for a criminal to completely forget the past; turn within to the God-Presence with all his heart and soul, feeling that he is immersed in the Holy Omnipresence, to be bathed by the Light from Above, and have an inner experience of God's Glory and Beauty. In the twinkling of an eye he could be changed.

Paul, according to the New Testament, persecuted his fellowmen, testified against them, and had them put to death. He is a shining example of the state of consciousness that can be attained instantly. Paul was illumined on the road to Damascus by turning within, changing his conception of himself, and finding that he really was the son of the Living God. We can do this. If this were not true, the whole teaching of the Bible collapses, and it is false—but it is true, "the same yesterday, today, and forever!" The truth is: We are all that we ever will be now, but we fail to recognize it. The mass-murderer through an interior, God-like change of the heart could in one moment become illumined and transformed.

Begin now to rise in consciousness by contemplating you are the Christed, Illumined One, and that you are doing the works of Him that sent you. We must refuse to believe the statements and theories that it takes a hundred or a thousand years to become healed or illumined. There is no time in God. "That which is to be hath already been." In other words, you are all that you will ever be Now. Yes, this very instant! Even fifty million years hence will not make any difference to the Reality within you. God cannot learn or become wise. He is All-Wise. All growth, learning, expansion, and contraction are illusions of growth and expansion. How could God suffer? It must be the illusion of suffering.

Dwell on these wonderful words: "But if the wicked will turn from all his sins that he hath committed, and keep all my statutes, and do that which is lawful and right, he shall surely live, he shall not die. All his transgressions that he hath committed, they shall not be mentioned unto him: in his righteousness that he hath done he shall live." You are told in these verses that if a man will forsake the ways of the past, and begin to practice right thinking, right feeling, and right action, he will transform himself. A new beginning is a new end. Get a new concept of yourself; walk forward in the light.

The Bible tells you, "Behold, now *is* the accepted time." And another passage: "There are yet four months, and then cometh harvest? behold, I say unto you, Lift up your eyes,

The Meaning of Reincarnation

and look on the fields; for they are white already to harvest." Jesus said to the people in his day that the truths which he expounded were available now. "This day is this scripture fulfilled in your ears."

Do not postpone your good. Why say, "Next year I will be happier," or "Six months from now, I will be healed." The Healing Presence is available now. The Divine answer is awaiting you. God knows only the answer. The fulfillment of your desire is now. "Before they call, I will answer; and while they are yet speaking, I will hear." The inner meaning of this biblical passage means that before you ask, the answer is already knocking at the door of your mind. Infinite Intelligence has no problems; it knows the solution instantaneously. It is timeless and spaceless. No matter what you are seeking exists Now. "Now is the day of salvation." "In thy Presence is fulness of joy."

The joy of God is available now. Do not say, "Some day I will be joyous and free." Enter into God's joy now by claiming the joy of God and His Love are flowing through you like a gentle river. It is God's river of peace and His waters of joy. God's Love, Beauty, and Power are available now. These Qualitites of God always were, are now, and always will be. Time is psychological; it is a state of consciousness.

If you begin to think that because the earth is moving on its axis every twenty-four hours bringing in day and night, and things are going to be better, you will remain confused. God is here now; the very Presence and Life of you. When you say, "I AM" that is God. We do not speak of God to come. God is here already—your own I Amness—the Eternal Now. Accept your good now; unite with your desire in consciousness. Enter into the finished state of accomplishment. Let your psychological time-clock be, "It is done!" "It is finished!"

Never say, "Oh, next year business will be better." *The time* the average man speaks of means his relationship to earth in its diurnal motion, and the position of the sun; it means his relationship to the events of today and tomorrow.

Prolonged desire and failure to realize your heart's desires give rise to frustration, illness, and neurosis. The ideal, the desire of your heart exists now. It is the concrete living reality in the next dimension of mind. Remember that thoughts are things. Recognize the power of your thought; it is supreme in your life. Go within now, and enter into the mental atmosphere that your prayers are answered—your dreams are fulfilled. Accept your good now. Say from your heart, the thing I am seeking already exists, otherwise, I could not even desire it. I accept the fulfillment of my desire completely now, and I rest in the conviction that "It is done."

If you are sick, claim health now; feel it; give thanks for your perfect health. The Healing Principle exists now; do not delay your healing or postulate it in the future. As you identify yourself with the Healing Principle there will take place a rearrangement of the atomic structure of your body, and health will be revealed. You will realize the Truth of the statement that, "Now *is* the accepted time." I accept my prosperity now—not in some future day. I give thanks for it now—this moment—and enter into the joy of the answered prayer.

4

Inequality of Birth

Many ask the question, "Why is an innocent child born, deaf, lame, or crippled?" We find the same question asked in the ninth chapter of John: "Master, who did sin, this man, or his parents, that he was born blind? Jesus answered, Neither hath this man sinned, nor his parents: but that the works of God should be made manifest in him."

The law of cause and effect is a changeless principle. You may consciously use the law. If you have been nursing or misdirecting the law, you can reverse your mental attitude; then you change the sequence of events. "I form the Light, and create darkness; I make peace and create evil: I the LORD do all these *things*." This means the LORD (law) can be used two ways.

Our feelings and moods create. What is the nature of your mood? What tone do you strike during the creative act?

For example, if there is someone in the parents' world whom they hate the sight of, or if there is a voice that they wish they would not hear again, a corresponding expression is brought forth. These are blind and deaf states of consciousness from which blind and deaf children come forth. Whatever "tone" is struck by the parents, a corresponding expression comes forth by the law of reciprocal relationship. The child is not a victim of heredity. In Ezekiel is written: "What mean ye, that ye use this proverb concerning the land of Israel, saying, The fathers have eaten sour grapes, and children's teeth are set on edge? As I live, saith the Lord God, ye shall not have occasion any more to use this proverb in Israel."

The only things passed on to children are the moods, mental states, or beliefs of the parents. It is possible, for instance, for anyone to have a son who may become a Shakespeare, Beethoven, Lincoln, or a Jesus, depending on the moods of the parents, or this state of consciousness at the moment of conception.

I knew a tubercular father and mother to give birth to a wonderful boy; he is an illumined soul, and doing remarkable work in the world today.

If you are lifted up in consciousness to the point of acceptance or belief that your son will be a noble, dignified, God-like being you dream of; then according to the law of reciprocal relationship, a corresponding mood or quality of the Infinite comes forth. "The fathers have eaten sour grapes, and the children's teeth are set on edge," in this manner. The sins of the fathers are the fears, superstitions, false beliefs, and anxieties which disturb their mind. These moods and mental states are transmitted to the children, and disturb them mentally and physically. *Sins* are mistakes of the mind or misuse of the law. We *sin* when we miss the mark of harmony, health, and peace. The bad or evil acts of parents or grandparents can only be transmitted through the mind. In this way the superstitions, fears, and the errors of the past generation are given to the present.

By illustration, a father instills the fear of God into the son by painting a false picture of the Deity; the son grows up believing in a God of wrath, or vengeance, a sort of a despot living in the skies, ruling the world according to his whims and caprice. The son grows up believing these false ideas, and passes them to his own son, and so on for generations.

The Bible says, "to the third and fourth generation." The numeral *three* means the conviction of God's Presence, and man awakening to the real truth about himself. *Four* means the Love of God made manifest in the mind and heart. All of us have been brought up under the hypnotic spell of the world, its terrors, and false beliefs. We have been expressing illness, confusion, and lack.

Now you begin to realize that your own thought and feeling are your destiny; this is the *third* and *fourth* generation spoken of in the Bible. It represents a state of mind wherein you know that you fashion, mould, and direct your own destiny by transforming your mind. You begin to reject all the thoughts and beliefs of the past. As you begin to realize the Omnipotence of the Spirit within and the power of your own thought, you cease giving power to anything else. You enthrone the concepts of freedom, peace, and health in your mind, and you live with these ideas, entering into the reality of them. In other words you sense and feel you are a son of God, and heir to all the qualities, powers, and attributes of God. You declare your freedom, and write your declaration of independence and freedom in your heart. You begin to love all things good; the law responds accordingly by opening for you the windows of heaven, and pouring out a blessing that there is not room enough to receive.

The following quotation is from Ezekiel, "As I live, saith the Lord God, ye shall not have occasion any more to use this proverb in Israel." The word *Israel* means the man of God, or the mind awakened to the Spiritual Truth. When you are awakened to the Presence of God within you, plus the realization of its response to your thought, you stop looking back on the past; moreover you realize you can overcome the past, and you cease blaming your father or mother, conditions, and circumstances, and you move, onward, upward, and Godward.

When a child is born, it is always the spirit of the One God. "Elias is come already." *Elias* means Jehovah or God. The personality, John or Mary, is the sum of the thoughts, feelings, and beliefs of each one of us. We tincture and color the One Spirit by our beliefs and impressions.

Let us say John, who lived in New York, died; then the quality which was John lives in all beings throughout the world. Now, during the creative act in some part of the globe

The Meaning of Reincarnation

the tone or quality that was John is struck; this could be in China or Japan, or elsewhere, and that quality or mood of the Infinite comes forth. It is not the personality we knew as John coming back, it is the tone of the Infinite coming forth. The same instant that John died, instantaneously the same vibration could come forth in a member of another race and country. Cycles of 500, 600, and 1,000 years have nothing to do with this law. God is Timeless; all tones are in the One. When you play on the grand piano, it will respond according to the notes you strike. Man is the measurer, and the "measure he metes shall be measured unto him." "Whatsoever he sows, that shall he also reap." You sow the seed in consciousness, and you reap the fruit of the seed; it will be the exact likeness of the seed sown. Let us sow beautiful thoughts; let our hands play Divine melodies; let our eyes see the beauties of God; let our voices be those of praise and thanksgiving; then we will reap what we sow. It is definitely wrong to believe that you or anybody else are suffering because of errors made in past incarnations, or because of hereditary influences.

They asked Jesus, as we pointed out at the beginning of this chapter, if the blind man sinned or his parents that he was born blind? In those days they believed that the sins of the parents were visited on the children to the third and fourth generation. In other words if a father was tubercular, his children would be also; if the father or mother were lame, the children would be, too. We have learned it is only the mental influence or state of consciousness that is passed on. Others believed the blind man of the Bible was a victim of karma.

Jesus rejected completely both theories or beliefs, and turned to the spiritual Power; He healed the man instantaneously.

Those of you who have read Troward know that he teaches that we are all born into the race mind or law of averages, and are bound by the race consciousness until we pray ourselves out of it. Jesus did not say to the man, "You must work out your karma." No, he healed him instantaneously, for God condemns no one, and though a man is a cripple, he can be healed; if he is deaf, he can hear; he does not have to work out some karma.

No one in the world is condemned to live in a prison of fear, sickness, and pain which he in his ignorance created. He can rise above any circumstance by feeling the joy of the answered prayer within him, and according to his belief is it done unto him.

Mozart, Lincoln, Shakespeare, and Napoleon left their impressions with mankind. We read of their works in history, song, and prose. All of them live in the hearts or the subjective mind of man. A man's *son* is his idea or feeling about anything. He can give conception to any state he is capable of conceiving. If a man, therefore, admires or dwells on the qualities and attributes of Napoleon, and would love to give birth to such a son—"as within so without." During the creative act a Napoleon-like character appears resembling the mood of that man. The dominant mood prevails. In other words, it is the tone struck during conception or creation that determines the nature of the child.

A man eighty or ninety years of age who becomes crippled, blind, or deaf is under the same law as the child in the womb or the cradle. Jesus says, "Except ye repent, ye shall likewise perish." This means all are immersed in the race or world mind; suggestions of the world are continually impinging upon our consciousness. Our mind receives according to our degree of receptivity.

If we do not think for ourselves, and if we do not cleanse our minds, we will suffer, because we allowed fear, false beliefs, and erroneous concepts of the world to impinge themselves upon us; then the world-mind does our thinking for us, and acts upon us bringing accidents, disease, suffering, etc., into our lives. The world-mind is the mind which believes in disease, failure, misfortune, terror, and superstition. If we do not pray and cleanse our mind regularly, we may also get into trouble. There is no chance or accident; for all is Law. There is a mind, a state of consciousness, which is the cause of all.

When they asked Jesus why the tower of Siloam fell on the eighteen men, he said, "Suppose ye that these Galilaeans were sinners above all the Galilaeans, because they suffered such things? I tell you, Nay: but, except ye repent, ye shall all likewise perish."

To repent means to think in a new way, to transform the mind, to think in one direction, i.e., to think of God and His Qualities, and realize what is true of God is true of you; then you will find that all your ways will be ways of pleasantness; all your paths will be paths of peace.

Suppose you put your hand on a naked wire; you would get burned. Why blame the law of electricity? You must learn the law, and use it to bless yourself and others. It was your misuse or ignorance of the law that caused the burn. It is not God punishing you; neither is it karma that you are working out.

Suppose you jumped into the ocean, and you did not know how to swim, you would drown. It is not your karma; neither is it a vindictive, cruel God punishing you; rather it is your lack of knowledge as to how to swim and keep afloat. The waters will hold up a boat or any man who learns how to swim or navigate.

You can fall off a cliff, because of carelessness in climbing, or paying no attention to the instructor who is teaching you how to climb the Alps. The Law of gravitation is impersonal; in falling you hurt yourself. We hurt and punish ourselves.

Children are at the mercy of the moods, feelings, and atmosphere of the home. Quimby said of children that they are like an old fiddle; anyone can come along and strike a tune on them. Children are like a white tablet on which all members of the family write something. Psychosomatic physicians and psychiatrists are all familiar with the fact that children, until they begin to reason for themselves and pray scientifically, grow in the image and likeness of the mental atmosphere of the home.

A man of ninety is still a child, though he may be a good man in the eyes of the world, i.e., he gives to charity, is kind to neighbors, goes to church, and pays his taxes; yet he has heart trouble, perhaps, cancer, or is crippled by arthritis. You say, "Is it fair? Is it just?" There is only one Law.

If I hold up a horrible painting in front of a mirror, it will reflect exactly the picture held before it. The mind is the mirror; that is why the Law of the Lord is always perfect. Our world is always a perfect reflection of our inner state of consciousness. The above man may have lived in fear; he may be a victim of the various propaganda scares, or it may be the race mind which moved in upon him, and precipitated as certain diseases. If he had prayed scientifically; turned to God, and cast out all fear of any other power; if he had worshiped the One Power only, and loved His Qualities; then he would be one with God. All good would follow him all the days of his life. He would dwell in the house of God forever.

There is not one law for a man ninety, and another for the child in the mother's womb. No matter what the problem is, we can solve it through prayer; we can forgive ourselves instantaneously, and be healed; this is the glorious Truth.

"Come now, and let us reason together, saith the LORD: though your sins be as scarlet, they shall be as white as snow; though they be red like crimson, they shall be as wool." (ISAIAH 1:18).

"And their sins and iniquities will I remember no more." (HEB. 10:17).

"For thou, LORD, *art* good, and ready to forgive; and plenteous in mercy unto all them that call upon thee." (PSALM 86:5).

"He shall call upon me, and I will answer him." (PSALM 91:15).

"I, even I, am he that blotteth out thy transgressions for mine own sake, and will not remember thy sins." (ISAIAH 43:25).

You can now detach yourself completely from the past by partaking of a great psychological and mystical feast of peace and happiness. Realize the Presence of God within you, and rise in consciousness to the joyous conviction that you are Now the being you long to be. Continue at regular intervals to do this, until the state is fixed within you which you recognize by a silent, innerknowing. Sustain this silent conviction, and you shall wear the garment of God. It is wonderful!

5

Preventing Birth of Dictators, Despots, Tyrants, Etc.

It is often asked, "Why do we have dictators, despots, and tyrants in the world?" They are extensions in space of the dictator complex present in the hearts and minds of all human beings. By changing ourselves we change our world. The world is ourselves in aggregation.

Napoleon still lives. Ghenghis Khan still lives, as do Caesar, and others. Boys and girls learn about these men at their mother's knees, at school, and in college. They learn about the wars in which their country was involved, and in some instances they are taught to hate the neighboring nations. These children are born with resentment and rage at the wrongs committed by these men. They read avidly of the crimes, atrocities, and act of violence. These states are impressed on their subconscious minds. All of these moods, feelings, and thoughts which are entertained become objectified as conditions, experiences, and events. Whatever is impressed in consciousness must be expressed in the world. Man should not, therefore, be surprised when these tyrants of the past are reborn into our society, because we actually call them forth. It is true in a sense, therefore, that Ghenghis Kahn is reborn or reincarnated. He is the embodiment of the state of consciousness of the people, nation, race, or world; whatever the case may be. It is never a man who lived a thousand or two thousand years ago who is being reborn. It is a state of consciousness that is born again.

We can prevent the birth of tyrants and despots this way: Let each mother place her child on her knee, whisper in his ear that his Father is God, and that he can do the works of God—his Father. As the mother inculcates this great truth into the mind and heart of her boy, he will believe it, and he will become her ideal. "I have been young, and *now* am old; yet I have not seen the righteous forsaken, nor his seed begging bread."

"I was young" meaning I did not understand the laws of Life; *"now am old."* Age is not the flight of years, it is the dawn of wisdom. I am now spiritually wise and understand the way the mind works; then the righteous are never forsaken. *The righteous* are those who use the Law rightly by right thought, right feeling, and right action.

If parents or teachers teach the Laws of Life—the Truth of Being—to the young, their seed shall never beg bread; this means these children shall never become the beggars, outcasts, thieves, and tyrants of the world. On the contrary, they shall fulfill the ideals of the parents. In other words, the children must fulfill the conviction held by their parents. If parents will impress their deeper mind with wonderful dreams for their boys and girls, then according to their belief, "will it be done unto them."

By teaching the youth of the nation who they really are, by showing them the Way, the Truth, and the Light, we can build the Kingdom of Heaven on Earth; as a result we will prevent the rebirth of dictators, despots, and former undesirable states of consciousness which are perpetuated by prejudices, racial hatreds, and fear of the unknown. Teach children to dwell on the great Truths of God. Teach them of the great accomplishments of the poets, artists, engineers, chemists, physicists, astronomers, and others. Let boys and girls emulate these great men.

Man gives life to ideas and opinions as long as he believes them. When he disbelieves the errors, these ideas have no power.

Where is the Truth? It is within yourself. "Look within—Search the scriptures," said Jesus. This means that all has been written in your subjective mind from the foundation. All knowledge is within; all beings that ever lived are within you now. You can project the likeness of any living being, past, or present; for all men are states of consciousness—qualities of mind expressed.

All moods, tones, qualities, and vibrations are within you, because Infinity is within, and Infinity cannot be divided; all is contained in the part. All beings are projections of yourself—the one man.

We must awaken from the dream of limitation, and declare our freedom as sons of God here and now. There are thousands of cases of men who have completely lost their former identity and personality; assumed new lives, entered different professions, and in many cases even remarried. These men were victims of amnesia, or loss of memory concerning their former selves. They could not remember their former wives and children. They had no recollection of their former professions or occupations. They assumed a new role in life; they were changed men entirely, because they had changed their consciousness.

In the spiritual sense we are all victims of amnesia. We have forgotten who we really are, and we tell ourselves that we are worms of the dust. Take, for example, a man who awakens from sleep, and he has completely forgotten who he is; he gravitates to the slums. His friends, knowing what has happened, try to coax him back to his former state. Because of amnesia his former way of life is completely blotted from his memory. He believes his place is in the slums; he only smiles at these old acquaintances whom he no longer knows. He accepts as true the role he now plays. The day comes when his memory is restored, and he awakens to his rightful status. With certainty and promptness he returns to his environment consonant with the dignity of his upbringing. He wonders why he is in the slums. What has transpired is like a dream to him, a dream of the unreality of it all.

We will prevent the birth of the dictator complex and the undesirable state of consciousness when we awaken to the

Divine Presence within us. "Awake thou that sleepest, and arise from the dead, and Christ shall give thee light." Let us awaken to the Real Presence and Power, recognizing the supremacy of the Omnipotence of the Spirit within, plus the power of our own thought. "Everyone that thirsteth, come ye to the waters, and he that hath no money; come ye, buy, and eat; yea, come, buy wine and milk without money and without price."

Every boy and girl as well as adults should be taught how to go up the hill of God. "Go up into the hill of God; thou shalt meet a company of prophets coming down from the high place playing music, and thou shalt prophesy with them, and shalt be turned into another man."

You go up the hill when you turn in recognition to the God-Presence within, realizing God is Boundless Love, All Bliss, All Joy, Indescribable Beauty, Infinite Wisdom, Infinite Perfection, All Glory, and Peace. Dwelling on these Truths of God, you are lifted up.

The Prophets you meet represent the eternal trinity employed in the creation of all things. First is the awareness of the I AM or God-Presence within and its Omnipotence. Second is your idea or desire. Third is the feeling or conviction that your prayer is answered.

The *feeling* is the conviction that united you with your desire; it is like the nail that joins two pieces of wood together.

The *joy of the answered prayer* is the music of the three prophets. It is the inner, silent knowing of the soul.

Any man can turn his back completely on the past; forget all the old beliefs and foolish ideas of the race mind; enter into the joyous thrill of being what he longs to be. If you remain faithful in this mood and sustain it, you will automatically become what you long to be.

Begin now—today—by going on a great psychological feast of being a noble, dignified Christ-like person. Begin to see God in all men, sermons in stones, and good in everything. When we do this, all other things shall be added to us. What we need is the spirit of Goodness, Truth, and Beauty in our minds and hearts.

Man's Life on this plane is like the several stanzas of a poem or scenes of a play; because it really is the One Being dramatizing Himself as the many. Wisdom teaches that illumination or the Great Awakening to our God-hood can happen here and now. "If it be not now, yet it will come; the readiness is all."

In order to elucidate this point, take a solid, metallic substance, and heat it. The temperature rises, but for awhile it looks as if no change were taking place; however, the moment the degree of heat is reached, which denotes its melting point, it begins to liquefy, thus changing its shape, and seemingly its nature also. Likewise, water can be turned into steam which is invisible, since pure steam cannot be seen. Water, also, becomes snow, ice, and hail; all are different rates of vibration of the One Substance.

When a liquid is changed into a gas, these changes are brought about by an increase in the rapidity of vibration of the constituent particles whether they are solid or liquid. The same law applies to man. What is true on one plane is true on all planes; for God changes not.

The Meaning of Reincarnation

Raise your rate of vibration, and transform yourself by lifting yourself up to a high state of awareness through the contemplation of God. In this meditative, quiet, lovely state, enter into the mood or feeling of being what you long to be, and feel the joy of accomplishment. You still the mind, and enter into this meditative mood, by asking yourself, "What does God mean to me?" In this quiet state, your senses are immobilized by focusing your attention on the one ideal—only one. In this sleepy, meditative state your conscious attention is in control. In this wonderful mental, spiritual atmosphere you mold, fashion, and shape all that you long to be, to do, and possess. By constantly praying in this manner, there is an expansion of consciousness; it is like the heat that melts the solid. The day comes when man melts away all inhibition, fears, and doubts, and becomes the God-man here and now. To such a man physical laws and time disappear. This change may come in the twinkling of an eye, like the volatilization of a liquid into a gas.

The man full of worldly thoughts, race beliefs, and third dimensional concepts of things would not conceive of the possibility of awakening to the God-man here and now. But the Power within man is capable of nullifying all human beliefs and man-made laws. We must begin to take our attention away from the limited, human concepts of ourselves; then we shall, like Mozart, compose music at six; statues at seven, and at the age of twelve we will confound the wise men of the world.

Cases are reported where cripples invalided for years leap and run in the presence of fires. In emergencies mothers lift automobiles to extricate their children. Where is this Power? It is within themselves. Fires and emergencies are not needed to stir the God-Presence within. Man can do this in the quiet of his own soul. We create in the "silence." Truth is lived in the silence; Truth is heard in the silence; Truth is transmitted in the silence; for God abides in the silence.

When you unite with God, you are in union with that which is above and beyond time; surely then you can be free of that which has taken place in Time. If you have a problem, you turn from time and space to the Eternal One within; in other words you go from Time to Eternity. You find rest unto your soul.

6

Have I Lived Before?

One of the interesting factors discussed by many people is that they remember their previous incarnations; furthermore in remarkable detail some say that they were priests in ancient temples giving the period, location, and other interesting highlights. There is no doubt that some people seem to remember previous existences. They relate that the only ways such memories can be explained is that they actually have lived before.

We are all immersed in a great pool of mind, or to point out simply like Quimby did: "Our minds mingle like atmospheres." Your mind is a great reservoir containing the mental experiences and reactions of the ages. Some clairvoyants are capable of seeing what took place thousands of years ago.

The Mind-Principle is neither past nor future. All things co-exist in the Mind-Principle as an Eternal Now.

Have you considered the fact that the sensory impressions of all men who ever lived are within you? You can easily tune in to the vibration of some previous experience which someone else had, and think it is your own. The truth of the matter is that the Infinite One is within you. "Be still, and know that I *am* God." Your "I AMNESS" is God. God is everywhere and in all things. All that you ever were or ever will be exists now. The "I AM" within you, the Reality or Life of you, has played all roles, has been everywhere, has seen everything, and experienced all things. When you awaken to the truth of your own Being, you will discover you do not have to travel to any part of the world to describe it in detail. Clairvoyants can do this; yet the faculties of clairvoyance and clairaudience are within all men.

You are both God and man. You are both Unconditioned and conditioned. The Unconditioned or Formless, Invisible Life is God within you; This is the Real Self of you.

When you say that you remember having lived in a certain city before, and everything seems familiar to you, it means you are awakening to that which was always known, and which always existed within you.

You may meet a man whom you are convinced you have always known. The reason is he is an intimate of your mood. All tones are within you. You have now becomes aware of that which always existed. All notes and tones are in the piano; the tone you strike always was.

Once I took a trip to Killarney; on arrival I knew my way around. All the streets and the lakes were very familiar to me. When I heard voices, I said to myself, "I have heard these voices before."

Let us look at this above experience psychologically for a moment. Knowing I was to visit Killarney, the Subjective Self traveled there while I was sound asleep. The Subjective Self really doesn't have to travel; It is Omnipresent, but we will use the term psychological travel. I travelled there psychologically; conversed mentally with many people; heard their response and voices; furthermore, in that psychological, mental journey, I saw all the beauties of the countryside.

I had been visualizing a wonderful trip; impressed my subconscious mind, and "went to sleep on it." The subjective knowing all, accepted the suggestion, and dwelt there psychologically.

When I consciously and objectively arrived there, I experienced all the subjective states. What I saw and heard objectively, I had seen and heard subjectively. Of course, I had heard that voice before, and had seen that place before! The real truth is that no one, no matter who he is, can go any place, hear anything, or experience anything that does not already exist. Why is this? Because Infinity is within. God does not have to travel, to learn anything, to experience anything, grow, expand, or contract. All is, and the All is God. All things exist now.

Emerson refers to this Truth when he says, "There is one mind common to all individual men." Every man is an inlet to the same, and to all of the same. He that is once admitted to the right of reason is made a free man of the whole estate. What Plato has thought, he may think; what a saint has felt, he may feel; what at anytime has befallen any man, he can understand. Who hath access to this Universal Mind is a party to all that is, or can be done; for This is the only Sovereign Agent.

Of one thing we may be certain; it is possible to remember anything that has ever transpired on this planet. It is also possible to see what might happen in the future, except it is changed through prayer. The real truth about you is this: I am referring to the Eternal You—the I AMNESS within you, your own Consciousness, or Awareness. You have been all men who ever lived, who live now, or whoever will live. You have been Jesus, Moses, Beethoven, Lincoln, and Shakespeare. Your Consciousness or awareness has played all roles; It has been everywhere; It has seen everything—all is within It—even the whole universe is within your own I AM-NESS.

Your Consciousness or Awareness wrote all Bibles, and spoke all languages; therefore you—the Invisible Self of you—knows the meaning of every part of the Bible. Ask yourself what did I mean when I wrote the Bible two thousand or five thousand years ago? The Deep Self of you has the answer.

There is only God, and God appears as man—The One Being—forever dramatizing Himself. All men are extensions of yourself. Every man is yourself. Remember there is only One Being. Why think of another? The Life of you is One and Indivisible. It wears many garments. The word

The Meaning of Reincarnation

humanity means the One Being limiting Himself by his belief in being man.

God cannot die; God cannot be slain. Never, therefore, think of John or Mary as dead; they live forever, as they live on in each one of us, also. A person never dies, The quality, tone, or mood of the Infinite, which was his, always existed, and always will exist. "I am Alpha and Omega, the beginning and the ending saith the Lord, which is, and which was, and which is to come, the Almighty." "I *am* the Lord, and *there* is none else, there is no God before me; I girded thee, though thou hast not known me."

Always remember it is God coming into the world when a child is born. That child is its own father and mother. There is only one Father, and He is "Our Father." "It is He that hath made us." The Bible tells you where you came from. "Thou hast been in Eden the garden of God; every precious stone was thy covering." *Eden* is the place of Boundless Bliss, Joy, Beauty, and Peace. In other words you came forth from God, the Boundless One, where you lived as God in Indescribable Beauty, Absolute Bliss, Fullness of Joy, Boundless Love, Absolute Peace, All Perfection, and All Harmony. These qualities of God are the precious stones which covered you. You were in the Absolute State before being born. When you came forth, it was God being born, and assuming the form of a child. "Before Abraham was, I am." This means the same thing; i.e., before any manifestation or form appears, it first comes out of the Invisible—the Formless Awareness of Life called I AM, The Living Spirit Almighty. Where do you go from here when you leave this plane? You go from glory to glory, ever onward, until you awaken from the dream of limitation, and return to the Glory which was yours before the world was.

Job asked the question, "Where wast thou when I laid the foundations of the earth? declare, if thou hast understanding." Where upon are the foundations thereof fastened? or who laid the corner stone thereof? when the morning stars sang together, and all the sons of God shouted for joy? This is a question asked by man of his Inner Self. We have forgotten that we were one with God when the foundation was laid. There is but One God and One Man, and we have made many out of the One. It is God appearing as many—the One in Infinite Differentiation. We are here to discover the joy of living, and return to the Source from whence we came. We are here to awaken. "Awake thou that sleepest, and arise from the dead, and Christ shall give thee light." This means that when you awaken, you learn all has been a dream. Yes, all wars, crimes, one's mistakes, and misfortunes are dreams. All the chaos of the world was simply a night-mare—unreal, to be forgotten and remembered no more. The reality of this awakening is to find oneself in a Kingdom of Love, Peace, and Happiness with the Light of God always shining. Beholding this Truth, dwelling upon It, accepting, and rejoicing in It, we realize that the streams of "manyness" all lead to the Oneness. "For the LORD shall be thine everlasting light, and the days of thy mourning shall be ended." "The sun shall no more go down; neither for brightness shall the moon give light unto thee; but the Lord shall be unto thee an everlasting light, and thy God thy glory."

7

The Mystery of Prodigies

There is an account of the early career of Zerah Colburn, published when he was under eight years of age taken from the *Annual Register* of 1812. This young boy in Vermont struck everyone with astonishment by his extraordinary mathematical powers. He was asked by an investigator how many minutes there were in 48 years; before the question could be written down he replied 25,228,800; also he instantly added the number of seconds in the same period. This child was entirely ignorant of the common rules of arithmetic. He could not perform upon paper a simple sum in multiplication and division. This singular faculty extended not only to the raising of numerical powers, but to the extraction of the square and cube roots of the number proposed, as these and many more complex, mathematical calculations were answered instantaneously by the boy.

Hudson points out in "The Law of Psychic Phenomena" that this child was placed in school, and trained on objective methods of mathematical calculations. It was believed that when he was more mature and grown up, that he would be able to impart to others the powers by which his calculations were made; however his powers did not improve by objective training. Hudson adds this interesting statement: "On the contrary, they deteriorated in proportion to his efforts in that direction, and his pupils derived no benefit from the extraordinary faculties with which he was endowed." This has been the invariable rule in such cases.

The subjective mind of you, or of anybody, knows the answer to any mathematical problem. As pointed out previously, any note that was ever played, or any song ever sung, is recorded on the Universal Mind within you—your subjective self; furthermore all languages are within. The Subjective Intelligence knows only the answer; It does not have to reason, investigate, calculate, or analyze. The mathematical, artistic, or musical genius is one who is en-rapport with his subconscious mind, enabling him to tap the answers which are there.

Very young children are living in a partly subjective state. There are numerous instances of early, remarkable, musical, mathematical ability which have subsequently diminished as their objective faculties were cultivated.

Quoting from Hudson's Law of Psychic Phenomena: "Musical prodigies furnish further illustrations of the principle involved; of these the most remarkable is the negro idiot, known as Blind Tom. This person was not only blind from birth, but was little above the brute creation in point of objective intelligence or capacity to receive objective instruction; yet his musical capacity was prodigious. Almost in his infancy it was discovered that he could reproduce on the piano any piece of music that he had ever heard. A piece of music, however long or difficult, once heard seemed to be fixed indelibly on his memory; usually he could reproduce it with a surprising degree of accuracy. This capacity for improvisation was equally great; a discordant note rarely, if ever, marred the harmony of his music. These well-known facts of Blind Tom's history furnish complete illustration—first of the perfection of subjective memory; secondly, of the inherent powers of the subjective mind to grasp the laws of harmony of sounds, and that, too, independent of objective education. Music belongs to the realm of the subjective."

From the facts in the above quotation it is obvious to perceive that certain powers are inherent in the subjective mind. The Subjective Intelligence comprehends all the laws of nature, as well as the harmony of sounds, laws of mathematics, or harmony of colors. It would seem absurd to think that Infinite Intelligence had to reason inductively. To *reason* presupposes an inquiry—a search for the answer. How could Infinite Intelligence ask a question? It knows only the answer! To say that God or Infinite Intelligence had to reason, investigate, calculate, or arrive at a conclusion would be to negate and deny the Omniscience of God. The objective, reasoning mind of man is necessary on this objective plane—or this third dimensional world.

While all music is within man, a musician should certainly learn everything he can objectively about it, so that he can better express himself. If, like the great philosophers of old, he heard inner melodies or the music of the spheres, he should have the objective knowledge and education enabling him to write it down as a composition; be able to play it, and give it to the world. The ideal situation is the harmonious accord or rapport of the objective and subjective mind.

I believe that many people now are teaching their children that all Wisdom is within. The intellect of man can be anointed by the Wisdom of God; then his inventive genius will be used to bless humanity.

Intellect must be married to the deep Wisdom and Love of God. The objective mind learns by education, observation, and experience. Supposing you had a dream, and you heard and saw the words of a beautiful poem; if you did not know, for example, the English language, or any language, you could not give it to the world. You express God through your objective senses in your speech, vision, hearing, etc. You are to use your conscious mind to carry out the promptings of the Divine.

In the third chapter of Mathew it relates how Jesus came to John to be baptized. "But John forbade him, saying, I have need to be baptized of thee, and comest thou to me? And Jesus answering said unto him, Suffer *it* to *be so* now: for thus it becometh us to fulfill all righteousness." One of the meanings of the word *John* is intellect or conscious, reasoning mind; one of the meanings of *Jesus* is Wisdom of God, or illumined reason. We must not deny the intellect; we must use it wisely.

You may not type, but if you practice, you can type; the same is true with swimming, walking, dancing, etc. If you have a wonderful idea to do something, you must use your intellect to express it; e.g., Jesus is baptized by John, and John says, "Why comest thou to me?" Jesus says, "Suffer it to be done." *Suffer* means to allow, or to permit. In other words Jesus is the voice of Wisdom within you coming forth; you are aware of it; therefore you must baptize or use this Inner Wisdom or Voice of Intuition by recognizing It, and seeing It take place in your world. Our intellect or conscious mind does not know the secret of the subjective, or how it works.

Do you know how a seed grows? or how or why a sperm divides? There is a Divine Voice within you which knows the way. It has the secret of all things, for It created all things. Many people think they can write poetry, and all kinds of wonderful music. However it is necessary to go to school and learn to read and write, so that the poetic phrases and the inner, harmonies heard by the inner ear can be suitably expressed. A musician should, therefore, learn the scales, geometry, and mathematics.

When the subjective mind revealed the idea of Insulin for diabetes to the Canadian doctor some years ago, he used his intellect and knowledge of glands, physiology, and chemistry to bring it to pass objectively; thereby millions have been helped, and their suffering alleviated.

Let Jesus baptize John, meaning let the Wisdom of God anoint your intellect. When you do not know the answer or solution, defer to a Higher Guide; This Higher Guide is God's Eternal Wisdom within you.

Learn everything you can objectively; then proceed through prayer and meditation to awaken the subjective faculties, and you will become that great orator, or statesman, as the case may be.

You are probably asking the question now, "Why do infant, mathematical prodigies lose the gift as they grow older and become educated?" The child is in tune with the Subliminal Self; the subjective mind is amenable to suggestions, and in ordinary education, children are taught to ignore the Subliminal Self. Instead of being taught to draw out the Wisdom that is within, the latter is usually completely neglected, and the faculty atrophies and disappears. It could be preserved in the child by having the teacher impress the child's mind with the fact that he could always possess the mathematical gift; that he would grow, and expand as he learned the objective rules, figures, numeration, etc. The subjective mind of the child being amenable to suggestion would retain his faculties for "according to his belief," and that of his teacher, would it be done unto him.

Archbishop Whately who was a mathematical prodigy said that as soon as his conscious mind was exercised and educated, this faculty vanished.

Mozart composed music at five years of age. Before he was consciously aware of the laws of harmony, his subliminal or subjective mind knew them; this is true, also, of all men everywhere if we would awaken to the great powers asleep within us.

It was through the subconscious that Shakespeare perceived great Truths hidden from the conscious mind of man. It was due to this fact that Raphael in his meditative moods was en-rapport with the subjective that enabled him to paint madonnas. It was through this same medium Beethoven composed symphonies.

An outstanding violinist told me one time in Vienna, that for hours at a time, he meditated on music and the laws of harmony. "At times," he said, "he was lifted up, and could actually hear the music of the spheres." He added that in these meditative moods, he found himself close to the Universal Pulse Beat and Rhythm of all Creation. He brought forth wonderful music.

Anything any man has done, any man can do. God is within all men, and God is indivisible; therefore, all that is really necessary is for man to awaken to and mentally accept completely these limitless powers within him.

Hamlet must have known this when he said, "There are more things in heaven and earth, Horatio, than are dreamt of in your philosophy."

The Bible in beautiful, poetic, elegant language says, "Eye hath not seen, nor ear heard, neither hath it entered into the heart of man, the things which God hath prepared for them that love him." We are in the Presence of Infinity. We approach It with a sort of mystic awe, realizing the wonder of it all. Imagine and know that never in Eternity could you exhaust the glory and beauty that is within; that is how wonderful you are.

Your subconscious mind is a storehouse of memory, and can be used to furnish you with any data or information you have ever read. Solomon, a Lithuanian Rabbi, had such a remarkable memory that he never forgot whatever he read. He knew the Bible and The Talmuds by heart, and he could quote easily any passage requested. What he did, you can do, this is fundamental and axiomatic.

There is only one Mind. How are you using It? You can succeed in convincing yourself that you can remember everything you read. The Power of retention of whatever you have seen or read is within you. Charge your mind with the belief that it is possible for you to do so, and your mind will respond the same as any one else's.

Edgar Cayce could memorize the contents of a book without ever looking in it. The Subjective Self can see without eyes. Clairvoyance and clair-audience are faculties within all of us. We can develop them and quicken them. This has nothing to do with being born again and again in physical bodies. We do not grow or awaken in sidereal time and space. We must ascend the perpendicular beam within ourselves where dwells the Timeless, Spaceless, Formless, Awareness where all things are, and claim our Divinity here and now.

Cayce's method was to place the volume under his head and sleep on it for awhile. Edgar Cayce had very little ordinary school education. Tuning in on the subconscious mind in sleep or trance state, he was also able to diagnose the ills of patients in any part of the world, even though he knew nothing about materia medica, pharmacology, or the practice of medicine. He simply tapped the Great Unconscious, and

The Meaning of Reincarnation

according to his belief was it done unto him. All the healings that followed were based on belief.

There is only one Healing Presence and Power in the whole world; whatever method, technique, or process used is a means of aligning with the One Healing Presence. The process of all healing is Faith. These words from the Bible state this: "According to your faith, is it done unto you."

Many of you have read about the famous horses that Maeterlinck spoke about. One of the horses spelled out the name of the hotel where he was staying. These horses were trained by a modern trainer called Krall. Krall developed a mathematical prodigy, but it was a stallion. This stallion knew how to extract square and cube roots. He learned to read and spell also. The mathematical problem let us say is 16; there follows six blows of the right foot, and one blow of the left foot. The left foot was for tens, and the right foot for units. The horse was taught to read charts containing all letters of the language. Professors and some of the most learned men in Europe investigated these horses and were amazed. These horses solved the most difficult, mathematical problems with a complete sense of abandonment.

Louis K. Anspacher in *"Challenge of the Unknown"* said that these horses behaved like human, mathematical prodigies. I do not believe that you are now going to say that these horses are incarnations of some former mathematician who lived in time and space. The subjective of the horse is a part of the Great Universal Subjectivity which has the answer to all problems. The unconscious or subjective mind of the horse is amenable to suggestion; the horse's subjective can by training and repetition be conditioned to respond. The subjective of the horse knows all; for there is only One Mind common to all; we are all immersed in It. The belief and faith of the trainer is also communicated to the horse, and a corresponding response comes forth.

The Wisdom of the ages is within every man, awaiting his recognition and claim. The old Hindu idea of Karma, in accordance with which man was punished by successive incarnations here on earth cannot stand the challenge of Jesus: "Be ye perfect as your Father in Heaven is perfect."

Plato and others believe in transmigration and metempsychosis sometimes referred to as reincarnation. Plato also taught that man lost his memory at death. "There is nothing lost in all my Holy Mountain." The subjective retains a memory of everything that has ever transpired.

A drowning man or a man partially asphyxiated sees his whole life instantaneously in every detail; likewise when you pass on to the next dimension the past, present, and future lie stretched before you like a cinema film all in a state of flux.

Nothing is ever lost; a rose that blooms once blooms forever. The modern theory of Time as propounded by Dunne, Einstein, and others was not known in Plato's day or that of Pythagoras.

Time is a state of consciousness. Why postpone your good? Take it now. Whatever you want to be, whatever you want to know, or discover, already is. You could never become something you are not already. God is all, and Creation is finished.

"Be still and know!" *Stillness* is not only keeping quiet; it means there must be no inner dissonance, but rather when man goes within himself, he finds perfect and abiding peace. Knowing that God indwells you, makes you live in a world that is ever peaceful.

Failure to realize God's Holy Presence within causes the average person to live in a series of conditions which grieve him to the end. Man fusses about things which, if he saw them differently, would not cause one moment of unhappiness. In order to awaken to your Inner Powers, and release these God-Qualities within, I suggest that every day of your life you should meditate on Beauty, Love, and Peace. Feel that these Qualities are being resurrected within you. As you meditate daily on this Inner Wisdom and Beauty, feel that you are awakened and illumined like Jesus was. Imagine you are doing the works of Jesus—healing the blind, the halt, and the lame. Sustain this mood; the qualities and powers of God will be resurrected within you. They were always there. You do not create them; you release them. This state of consciousness is not born of woman. The Jesus State of Consciousness is born out of the imagination of man. It is the spiritual rebirth or incarnation of God in your mind and heart. It is your second birth or spiritual awakening.

Meditate from time to time on God and His Qualities. Get immersed in this Holy Presence. By moving inward in meditation, you will feel that your body becomes unreal, and that the earth on which you walk becomes unreal. The external life becomes the dream; the Internal Life awakens;

you move further and further inward. Suddenly you find that by going inward you have found the Universe. The suns, moons, stars, and planets are within. You now discover that planets are thoughts; that suns and moons are thoughts; you discover that your own I AMNESS or Consciousness is the realization which sustains them all. You awaken to the fact temporarily in space are moving the dreams of the Dreamer, and the worlds, suns, moons, and stars are the thoughts of the Thinker. Your eyes are closed; He is meditating, and we are His Meditation. It is God meditating on the mysteries of Himself!

8

The Journey Beyond

Believing in the old concept of reincarnation, think of how many former wives and husbands will be lined up to greet us! Maybe someone might have a million wives waiting for him!

In the twenty-second of Mathew it says, "Therefore in the resurrection whose wife shall she be of the seven? for they all had her."

"Jesus answered and said unto them, 'For in the resurrection, they neither marry, nor are given in marriage, but are as the angels of God in heaven.'"

The Bible is speaking of mental and spiritual laws. The world takes it literally, and thinks because a woman was married to seven brothers here on this plane, they are wondering whose wife shall she be of the seven, for they all had her, or were married to her.

It was the custom in those days that if a man died leaving no issue, his brother would marry the widow in order to perpetuate the name; if he died leaving no issue, the next brother would marry her, and raise up seed, etc.; this has nothing to do with physical marriage. It refers to marriage of the mind.

Whatever you unite with mentally, and accept, or believe, is a mental marriage. You can have false marriages; i.e., you can believe in a false idea, and you will have children by it. The children will be your health, wealth, business, and social relationship. In other words the Bible is always talking about a psychological death; meaning you must die to that which you are, before you can become what you long to be.

I gave advice to a young man one time who lost five positions in five months. He drank excessively, was irresponsible, shiftless, lazy, indolent, crude, lacking in understanding, zeal, and application. He believed in a heaven afar off—a place where you go when you die.

I explained to him he could prove heaven was here now. He followed my advice and took a course in public speaking, and another course at night school where with diligence, personal initiative, and application he learned the rudiments of the commercial world.

He began to pray for guidance and prosperity by claiming these qualities. He began gradually to die to the "old man," and to put on the "new man." He developed enthusiasm, perseverance, stick-to-it-ive-ness, and became foreman of the shop. How happy, spiritual, and joyous he was! He was living in heaven; i.e., he experienced health, harmony, and true expression.

Why postpone heaven? Heaven is here—within you! Peace has not disappeared from the face of the earth; Peace is of God, and God is within you; It is Timeless, Ageless, and Spaceless. Peace is here now in your own mind; tune in on the God of peace, and let His River of Peace flow through you like a summer stream. You do not have to leave this plane to experience peace, joy, happiness, or inspiration. You must, however, die mentally and psychologically; which means you separate yourself from the other false ideas, erroneous opinions, and peculiar ideas about God.

Your ideas control, govern, and rule over you. Enthrone peace, love, and God's guidance. Live with these ideas; marry them by emotionalizing them in your own mind. You can go to heaven now—not when you die. There is no transforming power in death. Fall in love with honesty, integrity, justice, success, peace, and happiness. Move toward these ideals in your mind. Love will take you there. As you unite with these ideas in your mind, there will be a Divine Marriage, and the children that will come forth will be true place, abundance, and security.

The journey for all men is onward, upward, and Godward. Progression is the law of Life. When man sheds the physical body, he enters into the fourth dimension where he has a fourth dimensional focus. There are as Paul says, "Bodies celestial and bodies terrestrial." Death of the physical body is like a journey to a new city, or a new dimension of mind.

I love these words from the Song Celestial:

> *"Never the spirit was born; the Spirit shall cease to be*
> *never;*
> *Never was time it was not; end and beginning are dreams.*
> *Birthless, and deathless, and changeless remaineth the*
> *Spirit forever;*
> *Death hath not touched it at all, dead though the house of*
> *it seems.*
> *Nay, but as one who layeth his worn-out robes away,*
> *And, taking new ones, sayeth, "These will I wear today!"*
> *So putteth by the Spirit*
> *Lightly its garb of flesh,*
> *And passeth to inherit*
> *A residence afresh."*

To say that a man could not pray in the next dimension, and advance spiritually would be to limit The Holy One. Reincarnation—or going to the unmanifest to manifest, or to objectify a greater sense of the Presence—can take place there as well as here. What is true on one plane is true on all planes. We carry over our state of consciousness.

We were met by loving hands here when we came into the third dimensional world; it is reasonable to assume we will meet our loved ones who are in the next dimension when we arrive there after passing from this plane.

We should never really grieve or mourn for loved ones. By radiating the qualities of Love, Peace, and Joy to the loved one who has passed on to the next dimension, we are

The Meaning of Reincarnation

then praying for the loved one in the right manner. We are lifting the other up in our consciousness; this is truly giving the "oil of joy for mourning." We rejoice in their new birthday, knowing the Presence of God is where they are. Where God is, there can be no evil. "God is not the God of the dead, but of the living." Why seek ye the living among the dead?

Realize the loved ones who have passed on are dwelling in a state of beauty and love; then you are lifting them up. They feel your prayers, and thereby they are blessed.

We make them happy by our scientific prayer. Instead of feeling that they are dead and gone, and that their graves are where their bodies are, by an inner mood see them dwelling in a state of indescribable beauty.

Your loved one and all of those you knew on earth, as well as all those people long since gone from the face of the earth, are still living in the next dimension.

For instance, a little child who perhaps died in its mother's womb, or lived for a day, is a grace note in the grand symphony of all creation. She plays through love in the celestial symphony of the spheres. Through love the child is one with its mother, brother, sisters, and with all men—visible and invisible. The child who lived for an hour, or who died in the womb grows, expands, and unfolds in the next dimension. You will again meet the child; however she will not be a child, but she will be fully matured and grown up.

We are all one; the many, apparently separate, human beings are the notes and chords of the eternal symphony of creation.

The loved ones who have passed on still live, and will live forever; for God is Life, and That is their Life. They are functioning fourth dimensionally. Through love you are one with them. Know that they are immersed in God's Holy Omnipresence, and rest assured that Jesus, The Great Conductor, leads them in the Grand Symphony of All Creation.

All things in this relative world of ours are expressions of the Absolute. The One Life is expressed in countless modes. It is all One Reality. The One in the many, and the many in the One. The apparent, separate manifestations are notes in the grand symphony. There is a difference in the notes; they are grouped differently into chords and harmonies; yet, we must remember the symphony is one grace note. Somber notes, and notes used to form part of a magnificent opening chord are not separate; they all are the symphony; the symphony is one and indivisible. The composition is One Reality. Every note shares the beauty, joy and the life of every other note. The Life of the whole is in each note. The part is in the whole, and the whole is in the part. You are the Grand Symphony. You (the Real You—I AM) are the Creator and the Hymn of Creation. The Supreme Reality shares the life of all things.

"Everywhere in heaven is paradise. Even though the grace of the Chief Good does not reign there after only one fashion!" The mystery of the Ultimate Reality is multiplicity in unity. Rejoice in your journey back to God; there is no place else to go. It is the flight of The Alone to the Alone.

IV
Believe In Yourself

(1955)

This short book is the consummate Joseph Murphy. It contains most of the mind-power methods that Murphy brought to worldwide attention in The Power of Your Subconscious Mind *(1963). It also features my favorite of Murphy's passages:*

> *A movie actor told me once that he had very little education, but he had a dream as a boy of being a movie star. Out in the field mowing hay, or driving the cows home, or even when milking them, he said, "I would constantly imagine that I saw my name in big lights in a large theater.*

I kept this up for years until finally I ran away from home; got extra jobs in the motion picture field; and the day came when I saw my name in great big lights, as I did when I was a boy!" Then he added, "I know the power of sustained imagination to bring success."

I am not a cynic in matters of metaphysics. I am a believing historian. And I have had such experiences myself. I ask you to take notice of the counsel about sustained *imagination.* —MH

1

Make Your Dreams Come True

Joseph, in the Bible, means "disciplined or controlled imagination." It is one of the primal faculties of mind, and has the power to project and clothe your ideas, giving them visibility on the screen of space.

Israel loved Joseph. *Israel* is the spiritually awakened man who knows the power of controlled imagination. It is called the "son of his old age." Son means "expression." *Old age* implies wisdom and knowledge of the laws of mind. When you become familiar with the power of imagination, you will call it "the son of your old age." Age is not the flight of years; it is really the dawn of wisdom and Divine knowledge in you. *Imagination* is the mighty instrument used by great scientists, artists, physicists, inventors, architects, and mystics. When the world said, "It is impossible; it can't be done," the man with imagination said, "It *is* done!" Through your imagination, you can also penetrate the depths of reality and reveal the secrets of nature.

A great industrialist told me one time how he started in a small store. He said that he used to dream (Joseph was a dreamer) of a large corporation with branches all over the country. He added that regularly and systematically he pictured in his mind the giant building, offices, factories, and stores, knowing that through the alchemy of the mind, he could weave the fabric out of which his dreams would be clothed.

He prospered, and began to attract to himself—by the universal law of attraction—the ideas, personnel, friends, money, and everything needed for the unfoldment of his ideal. He truly exercised and cultivated his imagination, and lived with these mental patterns in his mind until imagination clothed them in form.

I particularly liked one comment that he made as follows: "It is just as easy to imagine yourself successful as it is to imagine failure, and far more interesting."

Joseph is a dreamer, and a dreamer of dreams. This means he has visions, images, and ideals in his mind, and knows that there is a Creative Power that responds to his mental pictures. The mental images we hold are developed in feeling. It is wisely said that all our senses are modifications of the one-sense-feeling. Thomas Troward, a teacher of mental science, said, "Feeling is the law, and the law is the feeling." Feeling is the fountainhead of power. We must charge our mental pictures with feeling in order to get results.

We are told, "Joseph dreamed a dream, and told it to his brethren, and they hated him." Perhaps as you read this, you have a dream, an ideal, a plan, or purpose that you would like to accomplish. *To hate* is to reject in Bible language. The thoughts, feelings, beliefs, and opinions in your mind are the brethren that challenge you, belittle your dreams, and say to you, "You can't; it is impossible. Forget it!"

Perhaps other thoughts come into your mind that scoff at your plan or ambition. You discover that there is a quarrel in your mind with your own brethren; opposition sets in. The way to handle the opposition in your mind is to detach your attention from sense evidence and the appearance of things, and begin to think clearly and with interest about your goal or objective. When your mind is engaged on your goal or objective, you are using the creative law of mind, and it will come to pass.

"Lo, my sheaf arose, and also stood upright; and, behold, your sheaves stood round about, and made obeisance to my sheaf." Lift your ideal or desire up in consciousness. Exalt it. Commit yourself wholeheartedly to it. Praise it; give your attention, love, and devotion to your ideal; and as you continue to do so, all the fearful thoughts will make obeisance to your exalted state of mind—that is, they will lose their power and disappear from the mind.

Through your faculty to imagine the end result, you have control over any circumstance or condition. If you wish to bring about the realization of any wish, desire, or idea, form a mental picture of fulfillment in your mind; constantly imagine the reality of your desire. In this way, you will actually compel it into being. What you imagine as true already exists in the next dimension of mind, and if you remain faithful to your ideal, it will one day objectify itself. The master architect within you will project on the screen of visibility what you impress on your mind.

Joseph (imagination) wears a coat of many colors. A *coat* in the Bible is a psychological covering. Your psychological garments are the mental attitudes, moods, and feelings you entertain. *The coat of many colors* represents the many facets of the diamond, or your capacity to clothe any idea in form. You can imagine your friend who is poor living in the lap of luxury. You can see his face light up with joy, see his expression change, and a broad smile cross his lips. You can hear him tell you what you want to hear. You can see him exactly as you wish to see him—that is, he is radiant, happy, prosperous, and successful. Your imagination is the coat of many colors; it can clothe and objectify any idea or desire. You can imagine abundance where lack is, peace where discord is, and health where sickness is.

"His brethren said to him, 'Shalt thou indeed reign over us?'" Imagination is the first faculty, and takes precedence over all the other powers or elements of consciousness. You have 12 faculties or brethren, but your imagination, when disciplined, enables you to collapse time and space and rise above all limitations. When you keep your imagination busy with noble, Godlike concepts and ideas, you will find that it is the most effective of all faculties in your ongoing spiritual quest.

The phrase "Joseph is sold into Egypt" means that your concept or desire must be subjectified (Egypt) first before it becomes objectified. Every concept must go "down into Egypt," meaning into the subjective where the birth of ideas takes place.

"Out of Egypt have I called my son": Joseph is the commander of Egypt, which tells you that imagination controls the whole conceptive realm. Whatever prison you may be in, whether it is the prison of fear, sickness, lack, or limitation of any kind, remember that Joseph is the commander in prison and can deliver you. You can imagine your freedom, and continue to do so until it is subjectified; then, after gestation in the darkness, the manifestation comes—your prayer is answered.

Consider for a moment a distinguished, talented architect; he can build a beautiful, modern, 20th-century city in his mind, complete with super highways, swimming pools, aquariums, parks, and so on. He can construct in his mind the most beautiful palace the eye has ever seen. He can see the building in its entirety completely erected before he ever gives his plan to the builders. Where was the building? It was in his imagination.

With *your* imagination, you can actually hear the invisible voice of your mother even though she lives 10,000 miles from here. You can also see her clearly, and as vividly as if she were present; this is the wonderful power you possess. You can develop and cultivate this power and become successful and prosperous.

Haven't you heard the sales manager say, "I have to let John go, because his attitude is wrong"?

The business world knows the importance of "right attitude."

I remember many years ago having printed a small article on reincarnation. These pamphlets were on display on a book counter of a church where I lectured. In the beginning, very few of them were sold because the salesgirl was violently opposed to its contents.

I explained the biblical meaning of reincarnation to her, the origin of the story, and what it was all about. She understood the contents of the drama, and became enthusiastic about the booklets; they were all sold before my lecture series was completed. This was an instance of the importance of the right mental attitude.

Your *mental attitude* means your mental reaction to people, circumstances, conditions, and objects in space. What is your relationship with your co-workers? Are you friendly with people, with animals, and with the universe in general? Do you think that the universe is hostile, and that the world owes you a living? In short, what is your attitude?

The emotional reaction of the above-mentioned girl was one of deep-seated prejudice. That was the *wrong attitude* in selling books; she was biased against the book and the writer.

You can develop the right mental attitude when you realize that nothing external can upset you or hurt you without your mental consent. You are the only thinker in your world; consequently, nothing can move you to anger, grief, or sorrow without your mental consent. The suggestions that come to you from the outside have no power whatsoever, except that you permit them to move you in thought negatively. Realize that you are master of your thought-world. Emotions follow thought; hence, you are supreme in your own orbit.

Do you permit others to influence you? Do you allow the headlines in the newspapers, the gossip, or the criticism of others to upset you or bring about mental depression? If you do, you must admit that you are the cause of your own mood; you created your emotional reaction. Your attitude is wrong.

Do you imagine evil of others? If you do, notice the emotion generated in your deeper self; it is negative and destructive to your health and prosperity. Circumstances can affect you only as you permit them. You can voluntarily and definitely change your attitude toward life and all things. You can become master of your fate and captain of your soul (subconscious mind). Through disciplined, directed, and controlled imagination, you can dominate and master your emotions and mental attitude in general.

If you imagine, for example, that another person is mean, dishonest, and jealous, notice the emotion you evoke within yourself. Now reverse the situation. Begin to imagine the same person as honest, sincere, loving, and kind; notice the reaction it calls forth in you. Are you not, therefore, master of your attitudes?

In reality, the truth of the whole matter is that it is your real concept of God that determines your whole attitude toward life in general. Your dominant idea about God is your idea of life, for God is life. If you have the dominant idea or attitude that God is the Spiritual Power within you responsive to your thought, and that, therefore, since your habitual thinking is constructive and harmonious, this Power is guiding and prospering you in all ways, this dominant attitude will color everything. You will be looking at the world through the positive, affirmative attitude of mind. Your outlook will be positive, and you will have a joyous expectancy of the best.

Many people have a gloomy, despondent outlook on life. They are sour, cynical, and cantankerous; this is due to the dominant mental attitude that directs their reaction to everything.

A young boy of 16 years going to high school said to me, "I am getting very poor grades. My memory is failing. I do not know what's the matter." The only thing wrong was his attitude. He adopted a new mental attitude by realizing how important his studies were in gaining entrance to college in order to become a lawyer. He began to pray scientifically, which is one of the quickest ways to change the mentality.

In scientific prayer, we deal with a principle that responds to thought. This young man realized that there was a Spiritual Power within him, and that It was the only Cause and Power. Furthermore, he began to claim that his memory was perfect, and that Infinite Intelligence constantly revealed to him everything he needed to know at all times, everywhere. He began to radiate love and goodwill to the teachers and fellow students. This young man is now enjoying a greater freedom than he has known for several years. He constantly imagines the teachers and his mother congratulating him on all "A's." It is imagining the desired results that has caused this change of attitude toward his studies.

We have said previously that all our mental attitudes are conditioned by imagination. If you imagine that it is going to be a black day today, that business is going to be very poor, that it is raining, that no customers will come into your store, that they have no money, and so on, you will experience the result of your negative imagery.

One time a man was walking the streets of London, and he imagined that he saw a snake on the street. Fear caused him to become semi-paralyzed. What he saw *looked* like a snake, but he had the same mental and emotional reaction as if it were a snake.

Imagine whatsoever things are lovely, noble, and of good report, and your entire emotional attitude toward life will change. What do you imagine about life? Is it going to be a happy life for you? Or is it one long series of frustrations? "Choose ye whom ye will serve."

You mold, fashion, and shape your outer world of experience according to the mental images you habitually dwell on. Imagine conditions and circumstances in life that dignify, elevate, please, and satisfy. If you imagine that life is cold, cruel, hard, bitter; and that struggle and pain are inevitable, you are making life miserable for yourself.

Imagine yourself on the golf course. You are free, relaxed, and full of enthusiasm and energy. Your joy is in overcoming all the difficulties presented by the golf course. The thrill is in surmounting all the obstacles.

Now let us take this scene: Imagine yourself going into a funeral parlor. Notice the different emotional responses brought forward as you picture yourself in each of the above-mentioned situations. In the funeral chapel, you can rejoice in the person's new birthday. You can imagine the loved one surrounded by his or her friends in the midst of indescribable beauty and love. You can imagine God's river of peace flooding the minds and hearts of all present. You can actually ascend the heavens of your own mind wherever you are; this is the power of your imagination.

"And he dreamed yet another dream, and told it his brethren, and said, 'Behold, I have dreamed a dream more; and behold, the sun and the moon and the eleven stars made obeisance to me.'"

In ancient symbology, the sun and the moon represent the conscious and subconscious mind. The 11 stars represent the 11 powers in addition to imagination. Here again, the inspired writers are telling you that disciplined imagination takes precedence over all other faculties of the mind, and controls the direction of the conscious and subconscious mind. Imagination is first and foremost; it can be scientifically directed.

I was examining one of the Round Towers of Ireland with my father over 50 years ago. He said nothing for one hour, but remained passive and receptive, seeming to be in a pensive mood. I asked him what he was meditating on. This is the essence of his answer: He pointed out that it is only by dwelling on the great, wonderful ideas of the world that we grow and expand. He contemplated the age of the stones in the tower, then his imagination took him back to the quarries where stones were first formed. His imagination unclothed the stones. He saw with the interior eye the structure, the geological formation, and the composition of the stone, and reduced it to the formless state; finally, he imagined the oneness of the stones with all stones and with all life. He realized in his Divine imagery that it was possible to reconstruct the history of the Irish race from looking at the Round Tower!

Through the imaginative faculty, this teacher was able to see the invisible men living in the Tower and to hear their voices. The whole place became alive to him in his imagination. Through this power, he was able to go back in time when there was no Round Tower there. In his mind, he began to weave a drama of the place from which stones originated, who brought them, the purpose of the structure, and the history connected with it. As he said to me, "I am able to almost feel the touch and hear the sound of steps that vanished thousands of years ago."

The subjective mind permeates all things; it is in all things, and is the substance from which they are made. The treasure house of eternity is in the very stones comprising a building. There is nothing inanimate; all is life in its varied manifestations. (The sun and the moon make obeisance to Joseph—imagination.) Truly through your faculty of imagination, you can imagine that the invisible secrets of nature are revealed to you; you will find that you can plumb the very depths of consciousness.

The other night I sat in a park and looked at the setting sun. Suddenly I began to think that the sun is like a house in the city of Los Angeles; there is a greater sun behind our sun, and so on to infinity. It staggers the imagination to ponder and meditate on the myriads of suns and solar galaxies extending into infinity beyond the milky way. This world is only a grain of sand in the infinite seashore. Instead of seeing the parts, let us look at the wholeness, the unity of all things.

We are, as the poet said, "all parts of one stupendous whole, whose body nature is, and God the soul."

It is really out of the imaginative mind of man that all religions are born. Is it not out of the realm of imagination that television, radio, radar, super jets, and all other modern inventions came? Your imagination is the treasure house of infinity, which releases to you all the precious jewels of music, art, poetry, and inventions. You can look at some ancient ruin, an old temple, or pyramid, and reconstruct the records of the dead past. In the ruins of an old church yard, you can also see a modern city resurrected in all its beauty and glory. You may be in a prison of want or lack, or behind stone bars, but in your imagination you can find an undreamed-of measure of freedom.

Remember how Chico, the Parisian sewer cleaner, imagined and lived in a paradisaical state of mind called the seventh heaven even though he never saw the light of day?

Bunyan, in prison, wrote the great masterpiece *Pilgrim's Progress*. Milton, although blind, saw with the interior eye. His imagination made his brain a ball of fire, and he wrote *Paradise Lost*. In this way he brought some of God's paradise to all people everywhere.

Imagination was Milton's spiritual eye, which enabled him to go about God's business whereby he annihilated time, space, and matter, and brought forth the truths of the Invisible Presence and Power.

A genius is a man who is in rapport with his subconscious mind. He is able to tap this universal reservoir and receive answers to his problems; thus, he does not have to work by the sweat of his brow. In the genius type of mind, the imaginative faculty is developed to a very high degree. All great poets and writers are gifted with a highly developed and cultivated imaginative faculty.

I can now see Shakespeare listening to the old stories, fables, and myths of his day. I can also imagine him sitting down listing all these characters in the play in his mind . . . then clothing them one by one with hair, skin, muscle, and bone; animating them; and making them so much alive that we think we are reading about ourselves.

Use your imagination and go about your Father's business. *Your Father's business* is to let your wisdom, skill, knowledge, and ability come forth; and bless others as well as yourself. You are about your Father's business if you are operating a small store, and in your imagination you feel you are operating a larger store giving a greater measure of service to your fellow creatures.

If you are a writer of short stories, you can be about your Father's business. Create a story in your mind that teaches something about the golden rule, then pass that story and all its characters through your spiritualized and highly artistic mentality; your article will be fascinating and intensely interesting to your public.

The truth about man is always wonderful and beautiful. When writing a novel or story we should be sure that we clothe Truth in her garment of loveliness and beauty. You could now look at an acorn, and with your imaginative eye construct a magnificent forest full of rivers, rivulets, and streams. You could people the forest with all kinds of life;

furthermore, you could hang a bow on every cloud. You could look at a desert and cause it to rejoice and blossom as a rose. "Instead of the thorn shall come up the fir tree, and instead of the briar shall come up the myrtle tree." Men gifted with intuition and imagination find water in the desert, and they create cities where formerly other men only saw a desert and a wilderness.

An architect of a city sees the buildings and fountains already in operation before he ever digs a well or builds a house. "I will make the wilderness a pool of water, and the dry land springs of water."

Long hours, hard labor, or burning the midnight oil will not produce a Milton, a Shakespeare, or a Beethoven. People accomplish great things through quiet moments, imagining that the invisible things from the foundation of time are clearly visible.

You can imagine the indescribable beauty of He Who Is being expressed on your canvas, and if you are a real artist in love with beauty, great beauty will come forth effortlessly. Moments of great inspiration will come to you; it will have nothing to do with perspiration or hard mental labor.

In Greenwich Village, I met a poet who wrote beautiful poems; he had them printed on cards, and sold them at Christmastime. Some of these poems were beautiful gems of spiritual love. He said that when he got still, the words would come into his mind accompanied by a lovely scene. Flowers, people, and friends would come clearly into his mind. These images spoke to him. They told him their story. Oftentimes the entire poem, song, or lullaby would appear complete and ready in his mind without the slightest effort. His habit was to imagine that he was writing beautiful poems that would stir the hearts of men.

Shelley said that poetry was an expression of the imagination. When the poet meditates on love and wishes to write on love, the Invisible Intelligence and Wisdom within him stirs his mind; casts the spell of God's beauty over him; and awakens him to God's Eternal Love so that his words become clothed with wisdom, truth, and beauty.

The Great Musician is within. If it is your business to play music or compose music, be sure that you are about your Father's Business. Your Father's Business is first of all to recognize God as the Great Musician; then meditate, feel, pray, and know that the Inner Music sings or plays through you the Song of God's Love, and you will play like you have never played before.

Every invention of Edison's was first conceived in his imagination. The same was true of Tesla, another great inventor and scientist.

I think it was Oliver Wendell Holmes who said that we need three-story men who can idealize, imagine, and predict. I believe it was the capacity to imagine and dream that caused Ford to look forward to putting the world on wheels.

Your capacity to imagine causes you, and enables you, to remove all barriers of time and space. You can reconstruct the past or contemplate the future thought through your inner eye. No wonder it says in Genesis: "Israel loved Joseph [imagination] more than all his brethren." Imagination, when disciplined, spiritualized, controlled, and directed, becomes the most exalted and noblest attribute of man.

I was in a conversation some years ago with a young chemist who stated that his superiors for years had tried to manufacture a certain German dye and failed. He was given the assignment when he went with them. As he commented, he did not know that it could not be done, and synthesized the compound without any difficulty. They were amazed and wanted to know his secret. His answer was that he imagined he had the answer. Pressed further by his superiors, he said that he could clearly see the letters "Answer!" in blazing red color in his mind; then he created a vacuum underneath the letters, knowing that as he imagined the chemical formula underneath the letters, the subconscious would fill it in. The third night he had a dream in which the complete formula and the technique of making the compound was clearly presented.

"Joseph [imagination] is a dreamer, and a dreamer of dreams." "They conspired against him to slay him. And they said one to another, 'Behold, this dreamer cometh.'" Perhaps as you read these Biblical quotations there are thoughts of fear, doubt, and anxiety conspiring in your own mind to slay or kill that desire, ideal, or dream of yours. You look at conditions or circumstances, and fear arises in your mind; yet there is the desire within you which, if realized, would bring you peace and solve your problem.

You must be like Joseph and become a practical dreamer. Decide to make your dreams come true. Withdraw, and take away your attention now from appearances of things and from sense evidence. Even though your senses deny what you pray for, affirm that it is true in your heart. Bring your mind back from its wandering after the false Gods of fear and doubt, to rest in the Omnipotence of the Spiritual Power within you in the silence and quietude of your own mind, dwell on the fact that there is only One Power and One Presence. This Power and Presence is now responding to your thought as guidance, strength, peace, and nourishment for the soul. Give all your mental attention to recognizing the absolute sovereignty of the Spiritual Power, knowing that the God-Power has the answer and is now showing you the way. Trust It, believe in It, and walk the earth in the Light. Your prayer is already answered.

All of us read the story of Columbus and his discovery of America. It was imagination that led him to his discovery. His imagination plus faith in a Divine Power led him on and brought him to victory.

The sailors said to Columbus, "What shall we do when all hope is gone?" His reply was, "You shall say at break of day, 'Sail on, sail on, and on.'" Here is the key to prayer: Be faithful to the end; full of faith every step of the way, and persisting to the end, knowing in your heart that the end is secure because you saw the end.

Copernicus through his vivid imagination revealed how the earth revolved on its axis, causing the old astronomical theories to be discarded.

I think it would be a wonderful idea if all of us from time to time recast our ideas, checked up on our beliefs and opinions, and asked ourselves honestly, "Why do I believe that? Where did that opinion come from?" Perhaps many ideas, theories, beliefs, and opinions that we hold are completely erroneous, and were accepted by us as true without any investigation whatever as to their truth or accuracy. Because our father and grandfather believed in a certain way is no reason why we should.

One woman said to me that a certain idea she had must be true because her grandmother believed it. That is absurd! The race mind believes in many things that aren't true. What came down from generation to generation is not necessarily valid, or the final word and authority.

The above-mentioned woman, who was honest, and well-meaning, had a mind that was very touchy on psychological truths. She took everything in the Bible literally. This mind worked by prejudice and superstition, and opposed everything that was not in accord with her established beliefs, opinions, and preconceived notions.

Our mind must be like a parachute. The latter opens up; if it does not, it isn't any good. Likewise, we must open our eyes and minds to new truths. We must hunger and thirst after new truth and new knowledge, enabling us to soar aloft above our problems on the wings of faith and understanding.

The famous biologists, physicists, astronomers, and mathematicians of our day are men gifted with a vivid, scientific imagination. For instance, Einstein's theory of relativity existed first in his imagination.

Archeologists and paleontologists studying the tombs of ancient Egypt through their imaginative perception reconstruct ancient scenes. The dead past becomes alive and audible once more. Looking at the ancient ruins and the hieroglyphics thereon, the scientist tells us of an age when there was no language. Communication was done by grunts, groans, and signs. The scientist's imagination enables him to clothe this ancient temple with roofs; and surround them with gardens, pools, and fountains. The fossil remains are clothed with eyes, sinews, and muscles, and they again walk and talk. The past becomes the living present, and we find in imagination that there is no time or space. Through your imaginative faculty, you can be a companion of the most inspired writers of all time.

I gave a lecture on the 21st chapter of Revelation sometime ago in the Wilshire Ebell Theater in Los Angeles to our Sunday audience. The previous night while I was meditating on the inner meaning of the following verses, I intuitively and actually felt the presence and the intimate companionship of the mystic seer who wrote the inspired verses.

"And I John saw the holy city, new Jerusalem, coming down from God out of heaven, prepared as a bride adorned for her husband. And I heard a great voice out of heaven saying, Behold, the tabernacle of God is with men, and he will dwell with them, and be their God." (REV. 21:2, 2)

Can't you now walk down the corridor of your own mind, and there see, inwardly perceive, feel, and sense God's river of peace flowing through your mind? You are now in the Holy City—your own mind—inhabited by such lovely people as bliss, joy, faith, harmony, love, and goodwill. Your mind is clothed with God's radiant beauty; and your mood is exalted, noble, and Godlike. You are married mentally and spiritually to God and to all things good. You have on your wedding garment, because you are in tune with the Infinite, and God's Eternal Verities constantly impregnate your mind. In your imagination, you sense and feel that you are the tabernacle of God, and that His Holy Spirit saturates and fills every part of your being. Your imagination now becomes seized with a Divine frenzy. You become God-intoxicated, having received the Divine antibody, the Presence of God in the chamber of your heart.

You can look at a rock, and out of that rock through Divine Imagination you can reveal the Madonna, and portray a vision of beauty and a joy forever. Never permit your imagination to be used negatively; never distort or twist it. You can imagine sickness, accident, and loss and become a mental wreck. To imagine sickness and lack is to destroy your peace of mind, health, and happiness.

On board ship one time, I heard a passenger exclaim when looking at the setting sun, "I am so happy; I hope this lasts forever!"

How often have you seen a glorious sunrise, and perhaps you said, "I hope this lasts forever"? Nothing in this transitory world lasts eternally; however, the Truths of God last forever. Darkness follows night, but morning will come again. Twilight will also come. You do not want things to stand still. You do not want to stand still either, for there are new worlds within and without to conquer. Change eternal is at the root of all life.

You do not want to remain in a rut. Problems are life's way of asking you for an answer. The greatest joy and satisfaction is in overcoming, in conquering. Life would become unbearable and unendurable if we did not experience change. We would be bored by the monotony of things. You meet with night and day, cold and heat, ebb and flow, summer and winter, hope and despair, and success and failure. You find yourself moving through opposites; through your power to imagine what you wish to feel is to reconcile the opposites and bring peace to the mind.

In the midst of sorrow, grief, or the loss of a loved one, your imagination and faith—the two wings of the bird—take you aloft into the very Bosom of God, your Father, where you find peace, solace, and Divine rest for your soul.

In your imagination, you look into the very Face or Truth of God; and God wipes away all tears, and there shall be no more crying. All the mist and fog of the human mind dissolves in the sunshine of God's Love.

"And God shall wipe away all tears from their eyes; and there shall be no more death, neither sorrow, nor crying; neither, shall there be any more pain: for the former things are passed away. Behold I make all things new." (Rev. 4:5.)

When the night is black, you see no way out; that is, when your problem is most acute, let your imagination be your savior.

"I will lift up mine eyes [imagination] unto the hills, from whence cometh my help." (Ps. 121:1.) The hills are of an inner range—the Presence of God in you. When you seek guidance and inspiration, fix your eyes on the stars of God's Truth, such as "Infinite Intelligence leads and guides me," or "Divine Wisdom floods my mind, and I am inspired from on High."

There is a designer, an architect, and a weaver within you; it takes the fabric of your mind, your thoughts, feelings, and beliefs; and molds them into a pattern of life that brings you peace or discord, health or sickness. You can imagine a life that will take you up to the third heaven, where you will see unspeakable and unutterable things of God; or through the distorted, morbid use of your imagination, you can sink to the depths of degradation.

Man is the tabernacle of God, and no matter how low a man has sunk, the Healing Presence is there waiting to minister to him. It is within us waiting for us to call upon It. You can use your imagination in all business transactions in a wonderful way. Always imagine yourself in the other fellow's place; this tells you what to do. Imagine that the other is expressing all that you long to see him express. See him as he ought to be, not as he appears to be. Perhaps he is surly, sarcastic, bitter, or hostile; there may be many frustrated hopes and tragedies lurking in his mind. Imagine whatsoever things are lovely and of good report, and through your imagination you have covered him with the garment of God. God's world of ideals and God's infinite ideas are within him, waiting to be born and released. You can say if you wish, "God waits to be born in him." You can open the door, and kindle the fire of God's Love in that man's heart, and perhaps the spark you lit will burst into a Divine Fire.

The greatest and richest galleries of art in the world are the galleries of the mind devoted to God's Truths and Beauty. Leonardo Da Vinci, through his gift of imagination, meditated on Jesus and the Twelve Disciples, and what they meant. Lost in deep reverie, his imagination secreted the perfect pictures from the Infinite Reservoir within him, and due to his perfect focus, his inner eye glowed with an interior luminosity, so that he was inspired, and out of his Divine Imagery came the masterpiece *The Last Supper*.

You have visited a quiet lake or a mountaintop. Notice how the placid, cool, calm surface reflected the heavenly lights; so does the quiet mind of the spiritual man reflect God's interior Lights and Wisdom.

Picture your ideal in life; live with this ideal. Let the ideal captivate your imagination; let the ideal thrill you! You will move in the direction of the ideal that governs your mind. The ideals of life are like the dew of heaven that move over the arid areas of man's mind, refreshing and invigorating him.

The inspired writer's imagination was fired with Truth when he wrote: "There is a river the streams whereof shall make glad the city of God, the holy place of the tabernacles of the most High." (Ps. 46:4.)

By now you know that imagination is the river enabling *you* to flow back psychologically to God. The streams and rivulets are your ideas and feelings, plus the emanation of love and goodwill that goes forth from you to all men everywhere. Man looks out into the world; and he sees sickness, chaos, and man's inhumanity to man. The man with the disciplined imagination soars above all appearances, discord, and sense evidence, and sees the sublime principle of harmony operating through, in, and behind all things. He knows through his Divine imagery that there is an Everlasting Law of Righteousness behind all things, an Ever-Abiding Peace, a Boundless Love governing the entire Cosmos. These Truths surge through the heart, and are born of the eternal Truth that through the imagination pierces the outer veil, and rests in the Divine meaning of the way it is in God and Heaven.

Imagination was the workshop of God that inspired the writer of the following matchless, spiritual gems—which will go down through the corridor of time and live forever. For tender beauty and for Divine imagery, they are unsurpassed in dealing with the availability and Immanence of God's Presence:

"For he shall give his angels charge over thee, to keep thee in all thy ways." (Ps. 91:11.)

"Whither shall I go from thy spirit? or whither shall I flee from thy presence?"

"If I ascend up into heaven, thou art there. If I make my bed in hell, behold, thou art there."

"If I take the wings of the morning, and dwell in the uttermost parts of the sea; even there shall thy hand lead me, and thy right hand shall hold me."

2

Using the Subconscious Mind in Business

Long before our Bible was published, ancient wisdom said, "As a man imagines and feels, so does he become." This ancient teaching is lost in the night of time; it is lost in antiquity.

The Bible states: "As a man thinketh in his heart, so is he."

Legend relates that many thousands of years ago the Chinese wise men gathered together under the leadership of a great sage to discuss the fact that vast legions of brutal invaders were pillaging and plundering the land. The question to be resolved was: "How shall we preserve the ancient wisdom from the destruction of the invaders?"

There were many suggestions: Some thought that the ancient scrolls and symbols should be buried in the Himalayan mountains. Others suggested that the wisdom be deposited in monasteries in Tibet. Still others pointed out that the sacred temples of India were the ideal places for the preservation of the wisdom of their God.

The chief sage was silent during the entire discussion; in fact, he went to sleep in the midst of their talk and snored loudly, much to their dismay! He awakened in a little while, and said, "Tao [God] gave me the answer, and it is this: 'We will order the great pictorial artists of China—men gifted with Divine imagination [which is the workshop of God]— and tell them what we wish to accomplish. We will initiate them into the mysteries of Truth. They will portray or depict in picture form, the great Truths which shall be preserved for all time, and for countless generations yet unborn. When they are finished with the dramatization of the great Truths, Powers, Qualities, and Attributes of God through a series of picture cards, we will tell the world about a new game that has been originated. Men throughout the world for all time will use them as a game of chance, not knowing that through this simple device, they are preserving the sacred teaching for all generations.'" This was the origin of our own deck of cards.

The ancient Chinese sage, according to the legend, added, "If all the sacred writings were destroyed, they could again be resurrected at any time through the symbolic teachings and inner meanings of the various designs on the playing cards."

Imagination clothes all ideas and gives them form. Through the Divine artistry of imagination, these artists clothed all these ideas with pictorial form. In the act of imagination, that which is hidden in your deeper self is made manifest. Through imagination, what exists in latency or is asleep within you is given form in thought. We contemplate that which hitherto had been unrevealed.

Let us take some simple examples: When you were going to be married, you had vivid, realistic pictures in your mind. With your power of imagination, you saw the minister, rabbi, or priest. You heard him pronounce the words, you saw the flowers and the church, and you heard the music. You imagined the ring on your finger, and you traveled through your imagination on your honeymoon to Niagara Falls or Europe. All this was performed by your imagination.

Likewise, before graduation, you had a beautiful, scenic drama taking place in your mind; you had clothed all your ideas about graduation in form. You imagined the professor or the president of the college giving you your diploma. You saw all the students dressed in gowns. You heard your mother or father or your girl- or boyfriend congratulate you. You felt the embrace and the kiss; it was all real, dramatic, exciting, and wonderful. Images appeared freely in your mind as if from nowhere, but you know and must admit that there was and is an Internal Creator with Power to mold all these forms that you saw in your mind; and endow them with life, motion, and voice. These images said to you, "For you only we live!"

A young man said to me in the army before he was discharged, "I see my mother clearly. I can now imagine her welcome. I see the old home. Father is smoking a pipe. My sister is feeding the dogs. I can see every mark and corner of that home. I can even hear their voices."

Where do all these vivid pictures come from? Keats said that there is an ancestral wisdom in man, and we can, if we wish, drink of that old wine of heaven.

The spirit or God in you is the real basis of imagination. Once in an examination in London, I did not know the answer to an important question. I got still and quiet, and said over and over again slowly, meditating in a relaxed way, "God reveals the answer!" In the meantime, I went on answering the other questions, which were easy.

We know that when you relax the conscious mind, the subjective wisdom rises to the fore. In a short while, the picture of the answer came clearly into my mind. It was there in words like a page of a book, with the entire answer written out as a graph in the mind. A Mightier Wisdom than that of my conscious mind or intellect spoke through me.

I had a very religious school boy about 14 years old come to me. Whenever he had a problem, he said to me that he would imagine Jesus was talking to him, giving him the answer to his problem, and telling him what to do. His mother was very ill; this boy was highly imaginative. He read the story of Jesus healing the woman with the fever. My little friend related to me, "Last night I imagined Jesus saying to me, 'Go thy way; thy mother is made whole!'" He made that drama of the mind so real, vivid, and intense that due to his faith and belief, he convinced himself of the truth of what he heard subjectively.

His mother was completely healed, yet she was considered at that time hopeless and beyond medical help.

Being a student of the laws of mind, you know what happened. He galvanized himself into the feeling of being one with his image, and according to his faith or conviction was it done unto him. There is only One Mind and One Healing Presence. As the boy changed his conviction about his mother and felt her perfect health, the idea of perfect health was resurrected in her mind simultaneously. He did not know anything about spiritual healing or the power of imagination. He operated the law unconsciously, and believed in his own mind that Jesus was actually talking to him; then, according to his belief, was it done unto him.

To believe something is to accept it as true. This is why Paracelsus said in the 16th century, "Whether the object of your belief be true or false, you will get the same results." There is only one spiritual, healing Principle and one Process of healing called *faith*. "According to your faith is it done unto you." There are many processes, methods, and techniques of healing, and all of them get results—not because of the particular technique or method, but because of imagination and faith in the particular process. They are all tapping the One Source of healing, which is God. The Infinite Healing Presence permeates all things and is omnipresent.

The voodoo doctor with his incantations gets results. So does the kahuna of Hawaii with his ministrations, the various branches of New Thought and Christian Science, the Nancy School of Medicine, osteopathy, and so on. All these schools of thought are meeting levels of consciousness and are doing good.

Any method or process that alleviates human misery, pain, and distress is good. Many churches practice the laying on of hands; others make novenas and visit shrines; all are benefitted according to their mental acceptance or belief.

When you are willing to stand alone with God and cease completely giving power to external things; when you no longer give power to the phenomenalistic world, which means to make a world of effect a cause; and when all your allegiance is given to the Spiritual Power within you, realizing it as the only Presence and the only Cause, you will not need any props of any kind. The Living Intelligence that made your body will respond immediately to your faith and understanding; and you will have an instantaneous, spiritual healing. If you are not at that level of consciousness where you can grow a tooth through prayer, the obvious thing to do is to go see a dentist. Pray for him and for a perfect, Divine, oral adjustment. As long as you believe in external causes, you will seek external remedies.

To illustrate further the power of imagination, I will tell you about a close relative of mine who had tuberculosis. His lungs were badly diseased, so his son decided to heal his father. He came home to Perth, Western Australia, where his father lived, and said to him that he had met a monk who sold him a piece of the true cross, and that he gave him the equivalent of $500 for it. (This young man had picked up a splinter of wood off the sidewalk, went to a jeweler's, and had it set in a ring so that it looked real.) He told his father that many were healed just by touching the ring or the cross. He inflamed and fired his father's imagination to the point that the old gentleman snatched the ring from him, placed it over his chest, prayed silently, and went to sleep. In the morning, he was healed; all the clinic's tests were negative.

You know, of course, that it was not the splinter of wood from the sidewalk that healed him. It was his imagination aroused to an intense degree, plus the confident expectancy of a perfect healing. Imagination was joined to faith or subjective feeling, and the union of the two brought about the healing. The father never learned the trick that had been played upon him; if he had, he probably would have had a relapse. He remained completely cured, and passed away 15 years later at the age of 89.

I know a businessman here in Los Angeles who has reached the top in his field. He told me that for 30 years, the most important decisions he ever made were based on his imaginary conversations with Paul. I asked him to elaborate, and he remarked that few people in the business world realized the wonderful guidance and counsel they could receive by dramatizing in their imagination that they were receiving counsel from the writers or great seers of the Bible.

I will quote this successful executive as accurately as I can: "Many times my decisions might have prospered the company or plunged it into bankruptcy. I vacillated, wavered, and got high blood pressure and heart disease. One day the idea came to me: Why not ask Jesus or Paul? I loved the Epistles of Paul, so when an important decision was to be made, I would imagine Paul was saying to me: 'Your decision is perfect; it will bless your organization. Bless you, my son! Keep on God's path.' After imagining I saw Paul and heard him, a wave of peace and inner tranquility would seize me; I was at peace about all decisions."

This was this businessman's way of receiving Divine Guidance by using his imagination to convince himself that right action was his. There is only one Principle of Intelligence in this world; all that is really necessary is to say and believe, "God is guiding me now, and there is only right action in my life."

The mind, as Troward tells you, works like a syllogism. If your premise is correct, the conclusion or result will correspond. The subjective reasons deductively only, and its sequence or conclusion is always in harmony with the premise. Establish the right premise in your mind; you will be subjectively compelled to right action. Inner movement of the mind is action. The external movements and action is the automatic response of the body to the internal motion of the mind. Hearing a friend or associate congratulate you on your wonderful decision will induce the movement of right action in your life.

The man who used St. Paul to impregnate his mind with the belief of right action was using the One Eternal Principle of Intelligence. His technique of arriving at that place in his mind does not really matter.

Goethe used his imagination wisely when confronted with difficulties and predicaments. His biographers point out that he was accustomed to filling many hours quietly holding imaginary conversations. It is well known that his custom was to imagine one of his friends before him in a chair answering in the right way. In other words, if he were concerned about any problems, he imagined that his friend was giving him the right or appropriate answer, accompanied with the usual gestures and tonal qualities of the voice, making the entire imaginary scene as real and vivid as possible.

I was very well acquainted with a stockbroker in New York City who used to attend my classes at Steinway Hall there. His method of solving financial difficulties was very simple. He would have mental, imaginary conversations with a multimillionaire banker friend of his who used to congratulate him on his wise and sound judgment, and compliment him on his purchase of the right stocks. He used to dramatize this imaginary conversation until he had psychologically fixed it as a form of belief in his mind.

Mr. Nicols, Ouspensky's student, used to say, "Watch your inner talking, and let it agree with your aim."

This broker's inner talking or speech certainly agreed with his aim to make sound investments for himself and his clients. He told me that his main purpose in his business life was to make money for others, and to see them prosper financially by his wise counsel. It is quite obvious that he was using the laws of mind constructively.

Prayer is a habit. This broker regularly and at frequent intervals during the day returned to the mental image in his mind; he made it a deep, subjective pattern. That which is embodied subjectively is objectively expressed. It is the *sustained* mental picture that is developed in the dark house of the mind. Run your mental movie often. Get into the habit of flashing it on the screen of your mind frequently. After a while it will become a definite, habitual pattern. The inner movie that you have seen with your mind's eye shall be made manifest openly: "He calleth things that be not as though they were, and the unseen becomes seen."

Many people solve their dilemmas and problems by the play of their imagination, knowing that whatever they imagine and feel as true, will and must come to pass.

Sometime ago, a certain young woman was involved in a complicated lawsuit that had persisted for five years. There was one postponement after another, with no solution in sight. At my suggestion, she began to dramatize as vividly as possible her lawyer having an animated discussion with her regarding the outcome. She would ask him questions, and he would answer her appropriately; then she condensed the whole thing down to a simple phrase, as suggested years ago by the French School of Mental Therapeutics. She had him repeat it over and over again to her. The phrase she said was: "There has been a perfect, harmonious solution. The whole case is settled outside court."

She kept looking at the mental picture whenever she had a spare moment. While in a restaurant for a cup of coffee, she ran the mental movie with gestures, voice, and sound equipment. She could imagine easily the sound of his voice, smile, and mannerisms. She ran the movie so often that it became a subjective pattern—a regular train track. It was written in her mind, or as the Bible says, it was "written in her heart and inscribed in her inward parts." Her conclusion was: "It is God in action," meaning all around harmony and peace.

(*Harmony* is of God, and what you want in a legal case is a harmonious solution.)

In the science of imagination, you must first of all begin to discipline your imagination and not let it run riot. *Science* insists upon purity. If you wish a chemically pure product, you must remove all traces of other substances as well as extraneous material. You must, in other words, separate out and cast away all the dross.

In the science of imagination, you eliminate all the mental impurities, such as fear, worry, destructive inner talking, self-condemnation, and the mental union with other miscellaneous negatives. You must focus all your attention on your ideal, and refuse to be swerved from your purpose or aim in life. As you get mentally absorbed in the reality of your ideal, by loving and remaining faithful to it, you will see your desire take form in your world. In the book of Joshua it says, "Choose ye this day whom ye shall serve." Let your choice be, "I am going to imagine whatsoever things are lovely and of good report."

I know and have talked to many people who diabolically invert the use of their God-given faculty. The mother, for example, imagines that something bad has happened to her son, John, because he is late coming home. She imagines an accident, a hospital, Johnny in the operating room, and so on.

A businessman whose affairs are prospering, yet dwells on negativity, is another example of the destructive use of imagination. He comes home from the office, runs a motion picture in his mind of failure, sees the shelves empty, imagines himself going into bankruptcy, an empty bank balance, and the business closed down . . . yet all the time he is actually prospering. There is no truth whatsoever in that negative mental picture of his; it is a lie made out of whole cloth. In other words, the thing he fears does not exist save in his morbid imagination; the failure will never come to pass, except he keeps up that morbid picture charged with the emotion of fear. If he constantly indulges in this mental picture, he will, of course, bring failure to pass. He had the choice of failure or success, but he chose failure.

There are chronic worriers; they never seem to imagine anything good or lovely. They seem to know that something bad or destructive is always going to happen. They cannot tell you one reason why something good should and could happen; however, they are ready with all the reasons why something dire and evil should occur.

Why is this? The reason is simple: These people are habitually negative; that is, most of their thinking is of a negative, chaotic, destructive, morbid nature. As they continue to make a habit of these negative patterns of thought, they condition their subconscious mind negatively. Their imagination is governed by their dominant moods and feelings; this is why they imagine evil, even about their loved ones.

For example, if their son happens to be in the army, they imagine that he is going to catch cold, become an alcoholic, or become loose morally; or if he is in combat, they imagine he will be shot, and all manner of destructive images enter their minds. This is due to the hypnotic spell of habit, and their prayers are rendered null and void.

Make a choice now! Begin to think constructively and harmoniously. *To think* is to speak. Your thought is your word. Let your words be as a honeycomb, sweet to the ear, and pleasant to the bones. Let your words be "like apples of gold in pictures of silver." The future is the present grown up; it is your invisible word or thought made visible. Are your words sweet to the ear? What is your inner speech like at this moment? No one can hear you; it is your own silent thought. Perhaps you are saying to yourself, "I can't; it is impossible." "I'm too old now." "What chance have I?" "Mary can, but I can't. I have no money. I can't afford this or that. I've tried; it's no use." You can see your words are not as a honeycomb; they are not sweet to your ear; they do not lift you up or inspire you.

Ouspensky was always stressing the importance of inner speech, inner conversation, or inner talking. It is really the way you feel inside, for the inside mirrors the outside. Is your inner speech pleasant to the bones? Does it exalt you, thrill you, and make you happy?

Bones are symbolic of support and symmetry. Let your inner talking sustain and strengthen you.

"But the word is very nigh unto thee, in thy mouth, and in thy heart, that thou mayest do it. See, I have set before thee this day life and good, and death and evil."

Decree now, and say it meaningfully: "From this moment forward, I will admit to my mind for mental consumption only those ideas and thoughts that heal, bless, inspire, and strengthen me." Let your words from now on be as "apples of gold in pictures of silver." An apple is a delicious fruit.

Gold means "power." *Pictures of silver* in the Bible means "your desires." The picture in your mind is the way you want things to be. It is the *picture* of your fulfilled desire. It could be a new position or health. Let your words, your inner silent thought, and feeling coincide and agree with the *picture of silver* or your desire. Desire and feeling joined together in a mental marriage will become the answered prayer.

Be sure you follow the imagination of the Bible, and let your words be sweet to the ear. What are you giving *your* ear to now? What are you listening to? What are you giving attention to? Whatever you give attention to will grow, magnify, and multiply in your experience.

"Faith cometh by hearing," Paul says. Listen to the great truths of God. Listen to the voice of God. What language does He speak in? It is not Gaelic, French, or Italian; but the universal language or mood of love, peace, joy, harmony, faith, confidence, and goodwill. Give your ear to these qualities and potencies of God. Mentally eat of these qualities; and as you continue to do so, you will be conditioned to those positive, enduring qualities, and the Law of Love will govern you.

You have heard this oft-repeated quotation: "Man is made in the image and likeness of God." This means that your mind is God's mind, as there is only One Mind. Your Spirit is God's Spirit, and you create in exactly the same way, and through the same law as God creates. Your individual world; that is, experiences, conditions, circumstances, environment, as well as your physical health, financial states, and social life, and so on, is made out of your own mental images and after your own likeness.

Like attracts like. Your world is a mirror reflecting back to you your inner world of thought, feeling, beliefs, and inner conversation. If you begin to imagine evil powers working against you, or that there is a jinx following you, or that other forces and people are working against you, there will be a response of your deeper mind to correspond with these negative pictures and fears in your mind; therefore, you will begin to say that everything is against you, or that the stars are opposed to you; or you will blame karma, your past lives, or some demon.

Truly the only sin is ignorance. Pain is not a punishment; it is the consequence of the misuse of your inner power. Come back to the one Truth, and realize that there is only One Spiritual Power, and It functions through the thoughts and images of your mind. The problems, vexations, and strife are due to the fact that man has actually wandered away after false Gods of fear and error. He must return to the center—the God-Presence within. Affirm now the sovereignty and authority of this Spiritual Power within you—the Principle of all life. Claim Divine guidance, strength, nourishment, and peace, and this Power will respond accordingly, I will now proceed to point out how you may definitely and positively convey an idea or mental image to your subconscious mind. The conscious mind of man is personal and selective. It chooses, selects, weighs, analyzes, dissects, and investigates. It is capable of inductive and deductive reasoning. The subjective or subconscious mind is subject to the conscious mind. It might be called a servant of the conscious mind. The subconscious obeys the order of the conscious mind. Your conscious thought has power. The power you are acquainted with is thought. In the back of your thought is Mind, Spirit, or God. Focused, directed thoughts reach the subjective levels; they must be of a certain degree of intensity. Intensity is acquired by concentration.

To *concentrate* is to come back to the center and contemplate the Infinite Power within you that lies stretched in smiling repose. To concentrate properly, you still the wheels of your mind and enter into a quiet, relaxed mental state. When you concentrate, you gather your thoughts together; and you focus all your attention on your ideal, aim, or objective. You are now at a focal or central point, where you are giving all your attention and devotion to your mental image. The procedure of focused attention is somewhat similar to that of a magnifying glass, and the focus it makes of the rays of the sun. You can see the difference in the effect of scattered vibrations of the sun's heat, and the vibrations that emanate from a central point. You can direct the rays of the magnifying glass so that it will burn up a particular object upon which it is directed. Focused, steadied attention of your mental images gains a similar intensity; and a deep, lasting impression is made on the sensitive plate of the subconscious mind.

You may have to repeat this drama of the mind many times before an impression is made, but the secret of impregnating the deeper mind is continuous or sustained imagination. When fear or worry comes to you during the day, you can always immediately gaze upon that lovely picture in your mind, realizing and knowing that you have operated a definite psychological law that is now working for you in the dark house of your mind. As you do so, you are truly watering the seed and fertilizing it, thereby accelerating its growth.

The conscious mind of man is the motor; the subconscious is the engine. You must start the motor, and the engine will do the work. The conscious mind is the dynamo that awakens the power of the subconscious.

The first step in conveying your clarified desire, idea, or image to the deeper mind is to relax, immobilize the attention, and get still and quiet. This quiet, relaxed, peaceful attitude of mind prevents extraneous matter and false ideas from interfering with your mental absorption of your ideal; furthermore, in the quiet, passive, receptive attitude of mind, effort is reduced to a minimum.

In the second step, you begin to imagine the reality of that which you desire. For example, you may wish to sell a home. In private consultation with real-estate brokers, I have told them of the way I sold my own home; they have applied it with remarkable results. I placed a sign in the garden in front of my home that read: "For sale by owner." The second day after placing the sign, I said to myself as I was going to sleep, "Supposing you sold the house, what would you do?"

I answered my own question, and I said, "I would take that sign down and throw it in the garage." In my imagination, I took hold of the sign, pulled it up from the ground, placed it on my shoulders, went to the garage, and threw it on the floor, saying jokingly to the sign, "I don't need you anymore!" I felt the inner satisfaction of it all, realizing that it was finished. The next day a man gave me a deposit of $1,000 and said, "Take your sign down; we will go into escrow now."

Immediately I pulled the sign up and took it into the garage. The outer action conformed to the inner. There is nothing new about this. "As within, so without," meaning according to the image impressed on the subconscious mind, so is it on the objective screen of your life.

This procedure or technique is older than our Bible. The outside mirrors the inside. External action follows internal action.

I was engaged by a very large organization to do some spiritual work for them. Through fraudulent means, others were trying to lay claim to their vast mining and other interests. They were harassing the company by legal trickery, and trying to get something for nothing. I told the lawyer to dramatize vividly in his imagination several times daily the president of the company that he represented congratulating him on the perfect, harmonious solution. As he sustained the mental picture through continuous mental application, the subjective wisdom gave him some new ideas—as he said, "Right out of the blue!" He followed these up, and the case was closed soon afterward.

If a person has a mortgage due at the bank and he does not have the money to cover it, and if he will faithfully apply this principle, the subconscious mind will provide him with the money. Never mind how, when, where, or through what source. The subjective mind has ways you know not of; its ways are past finding out. It is one of the instruments or tools that God gave man, so he could provide himself with all things necessary for his welfare. The man who hasn't the money to meet the mortgage can imagine himself depositing a check or currency required in the bank; that is, giving it to the cashier. The important point is to become intensely interested in the mental picture or imaginary act, making it real and natural. The more earnestly he engages his mind on the imaginary drama, the more effectually will the imaginary act be deposited in the bank of the subconscious mind. You can take a trip to the teller's window in your imagination, and make it so real and true that it will actually take place physically.

There is a young lady who comes to our Sunday-morning lectures regularly. She had to change buses three times; it took her one-and-a-half hours each Sunday to get there. In the sermon, I told how a young man prayed for a car and received one. She went home and experimented as follows: Here is her letter, in part, published with her permission:

"Dear Dr. Murphy:
This is how I received a cadillac [sic]; I wanted one to come to the lectures on Sunday and Tuesdays. In my imagination I went through the identical process I would go through if I were actually driving a car. I went to the show room, and the salesman took me for a ride in one. I also drove it several blocks. I claimed the Cadillac car as my own over and over again. I kept the mental picture of getting into the car, driving it, feeling the upholstery, etc., consistently for over two weeks. Last Sunday I drove to your meeting in a cadillac. My uncle in Inglewood passed away; left me his cadillac and his entire estate."

If you are thinking, *Well, I do not know of any way to get the money to pay off the mortgage*, don't worry about it. To worry means to strangle. Realize that there is a Power inherent within you that can provide you with everything you need when you call upon It. You can decree now with feeling and conviction: "My house is free from all debt, and wealth flows to me in avalanches of abundance." Do not question the manner in which the answer to your prayers will come. You will do the obvious things necessary, knowing that the subconscious intelligence is directing all your steps, for it knows everything necessary for the fulfillment of your dreams. You can also imagine a letter from them mortgage company informing you that you are paid up; rejoice in the image, and live with that imaginary letter in your mind until it becomes a conviction.

Become convinced now that there is a power within you that is capable of bringing what you imagine and feel as true into manifestation. Sitting idly by, daydreaming, and imagining the things you would like to possess, will not attract them to you. You must know and believe that you are operating a law of mind; become convinced of your God-given power to use your mind constructively to bring into manifestation the thing you desire.

Know what you want. The subconscious mind will carry out the idea, because you have a definite, clear-cut concept of what you wish to possess. Imagine clearly the fulfillment of your desire; then you are giving the subconscious something definite to act upon. The subconscious mind is the film upon which the picture is impressed. The subconscious develops the picture; and sends it back to you in a material, objectified form.

The camera is *you* consciously imagining the realization of your desire through focused attention. As you do so in a relaxed, happy mood, the picture is cast on the sensitive film of the subconscious mind. You also need a time exposure; it may be two or three minutes or longer depending on your temperament, feeling, and understanding. The important thing to remember is that it is not so much the time as the quality of your consciousness, degree of feeling, or faith. Generally speaking, the more focused and absorbed your attention is, and the longer the time, the more perfect will be the answer to your prayer. *Believe* that you have received, and ye shall receive. "Whatsoever ye shall ask in prayer, believing, ye shall receive." *To believe* is to accept something as true, or to live in the state of being it; as you sustain this mood, you shall experience the joy of the answered prayer!

3

How to Imagine Success

God is always successful in His undertakings. Man is equipped to succeed because God is within him. All the attributes, qualities, and potencies of God are within.

You were born to win, to conquer, and to overcome! The Intelligence, Wisdom, and Power of God are within you, waiting to be released, and enabling you to rise above all difficulties.

There are many men who quietly use the abstract term *success*, over and over many times a day until they reach a conviction that success *is* theirs. Remember that the *idea of success* contains all the essential elements of success. As a man repeats the word *success* to himself with faith and conviction, his subconscious mind will accept it as true of himself, and he will be under subjective compulsion to succeed.

We are compelled to express our subjective beliefs, impressions, and convictions. The ideal way to succeed is to know what you want to achieve. If you do not know your right place, or what you would like to do, you can ask for guidance on the question. The deeper mind will respond; as a result, you will find a push or tendency in a certain field of activity.

The deeper mind is responsive to your thought. The subconscious—sometimes called "subjective or deeper mind"—sets in operation its unconscious intelligence that attracts to the individual the conditions necessary for his success. Man should make it a special point to do the thing he loves to do. When you are happy in your endeavor, you are a success.

Accept the fact that you have an inner Creative Power. Let this be a positive conviction. This Infinite Power is responsive and reactive to your thought. To know, understand, and apply this principle causes doubt, fear, and worry to gradually disappear.

If a man dwells on the thought, for example, of failure, the thought of failure attracts failure. The subconscious takes the thought of failure as his request, and proceeds to make it manifest in his experience, because he indulges in the mental practice of conceiving failure. The subconscious mind is impersonal and non-selective.

A business friend of mine, a tailor by trade, has a favorite saying: "All I ever do is add. I never subtract." He means that *success* is a plus sign. *Add* to your growth, wealth, power, knowledge, faith, and wisdom.

Life is addition! Death is subtraction. You add to your life by imagining whatsoever things are true, lovely, noble, and Godlike. Imagine and feel yourself successful, and you must become successful. You are never a slave to circumstances, environment, or conditions. You are a master of conditions. You can become a victim of conditions by mentally acquiescing to things as they are. As you change your mind, you change conditions.

A movie actor told me once that he had very little education, but he had a dream as a boy of being a movie star. Out in the field mowing hay, or driving the cows home, or even when milking them, he said, "I would constantly imagine that I saw my name in big lights in a large theater. I kept this up for years until finally I ran away from home; got extra jobs in the motion picture field; and the day came when I saw my name in great big lights, as I did when I was a boy!" Then he added, "I know the power of *sustained* imagination to bring success."

What does *success* imply to you? You want undoubtedly to be successful in your relationship with others. You wish to be outstanding in your chosen work or profession. You wish to possess a beautiful home, and all the money you need to live comfortably and happily. You want to be successful in your prayers, and in your contact with the Universal Power within you.

Imagine yourself doing the thing you long to do, and possessing the things you long to possess. Become imaginative; mentally participate in the reality of the successful state; enter into that state of consciousness frequently;

make a habit of it; then you will find you will be guided to do everything necessary for the realization of your dream. Go to sleep feeling successful every night and perfectly satisfied. You will succeed eventually in implanting the idea of success in your subconscious mind.

I know a drugstore clerk who was a licensed pharmacist receiving $40 a week plus his commission on sales. "After 25 years," he told me, "I will get a pension and retire."

I said to him, "Why don't you own your own store? Get out of this place. Raise your sights! Have a dream for your children. Maybe your son wants to be a doctor or your daughter desires to be a musician."

His answer was that he had no money! He began to awaken to the fact that whatever he could conceive as true, he could give it conception.

The first step toward your goal is the *birth of the idea* in the mind, and the second step is the *manifestation of the idea*. He began to imagine that he was in his own store. He participated in the act mentally. He arranged the bottles, dispensed prescriptions, and imagined several clerks in the store waiting on customers. He visualized a big bank balance. Mentally he worked in that imaginary store. Like a good actor, he lived the role. (Act as though I am, and I will be.) This drugstore clerk put himself wholeheartedly into the act . . . living, moving, and acting in the assumption that his store was his.

The sequel was interesting. He was discharged from his position, went with a large chain store, became manager, and then district manager. He made enough money in four years to make a down payment on a drugstore of his own. He called it his "dream pharmacy." "It was," he said, "exactly the store he saw in his imagination." He became successful in his chosen field, and was happy doing what he loved to do.

The individual who habitually maintains a mental attitude of faith and expectancy of the best is bound to succeed and advance in life. The individual who is depressed, dejected, morbid, and despondent attracts failure all along the line. Fear is truly a lack of faith in Divine supply. It is faith misplaced. Fear is faith in the wrong thing. Fear is a belief in lack, or that man's good is being withheld from him.

"Son, thou are ever with me, and all that I hath is thine." All things you need are in the invisible. It could be said that all things needed are in the abstract. You must desire to be greater than you are, in order to advance in life. Desire comes first, followed by a recognition of the Power within you enabling you to manifest what you want. The subconscious mind is the medium through which all that you desire can be brought into objectivity. You are the one giving orders in the form of habitual thinking, feeling, opinions, and beliefs. The subconscious mind obeys the orders given by the conscious mind. If your conscious mind is opposed to all negative thoughts, they can make no impression upon your subconscious mind. You become immunized.

If, for example, you say, "I wish I were healthy, then I could be much more successful in my work;" begin *now* to realize that your body is your mind expressed. The subconscious mind is the builder of the body, and controls all its vital functions. Your conscious mind has the power to change any idea or group of thoughts held in the subconscious mind. You can impress the idea of health on your subconscious mind when you know that it can be done. A conviction and sincere belief is necessary. Affirmative statements establish a definite impression on the subconscious mind.

A wonderful way to impress the subconscious is through disciplined or scientific imagination. By illustration, if your knee is swollen and you are lame, imagine that you're doing the things you would do if you were in perfect health. You might say that I would go downtown on a bus, visit friends, ride horseback, go swimming, or hiking. First, in your imagination you go on these psychological journeys, making them as real and natural as possible. *Continue* to go on these psychological journeys! You know that self-motivation is yours. All movement is first of the mind or consciousness of man before any external movement can take place.

By example, the chair does not move of itself. You must impart motion to it. The same is true of your body. As you continue to do all the things you would do were you healed, this inner movement will cause the subconscious to build the body in accordance with the image back of it.

The following is a wonderful prayer for perfect health. A minister I knew in South Africa applied this prayer and healed himself. Several times a day he would affirm slowly and quietly, first making certain that he was completely relaxed mentally and physically: "The perfection of God is now being expressed through me. The idea of health is now filling my subconscious mind. The image that God has of me is a perfect image, and my subconscious mind re-creates my body in perfect accordance with the perfect image held in the mind of God." This is a simple, easy way of conveying the idea of perfect health to your subconscious mind.

You can develop confidence by knowing and realizing that nothing can prevent you from achieving success. Develop a certainty in your mind that this Inner Power can be called upon to overcome all obstacles. There must be an assurance and determination on your part that you can achieve and accomplish what you set out to do. This positive, affirmative attitude constitutes confidence.

You have heard the Biblical expression "According to your faith is it done unto you." Faith in God is the realization that there is only One Spiritual Power that is Omnipresent, Omniscient, Omnipotent, All Love, All Light, All Beauty, All Life, and An Ever-Present Help in time of trouble. Know that His Power responds to your thought.

V
Stay Young Forever

(1958)

Joseph Murphy knew something about staying young. He did not publish his first book until he was 47. (I had a similar trajectory in my writing career.) He did not write his landmark The Power of Your Subconscious Mind *until he was 65. The title* Stay Young Forever *may sound unserious, especially since its author left us in 1981. But he hits upon two vital points. The first point is validated by contemporary placebo studies. If you maintain an active, engaging, and involved mindset, and if you are immersed in stimulating and novel surroundings, especially ones that evoke your youth, you demonstrate measurable resilience in markers like blood pressure, flexibility, muscle mass, weight, mood, and even eyesight. Murphy's second point—a centerpiece of his philosophy—is that since all of us emerge from Universal Mind, the ancient Greeks called it* Nous, *it stands to reason that we all eternally endure.*

—MH

Stay Young Forever

A few months ago I called on an old friend of mine in London, England, who was very ill. He said to me, "We are born, grow up, become old and good-for-nothing, and that's the end." This mental attitude of futility and worthlessness was the chief reason for his sickness. He was frustrated, weak, and almost lifeless. He felt his advancing years (over 80) gave him no hope. His cry was that he was useless and that no one wanted him. He was looking forward to senescence and after that—nothing.

Unfortunately many people have the same attitude as this man. They are afraid of what they term old age, the end, and extinction which really means that they are afraid of Life; yet Life is endless. Wisdom teaches that age is not the flight of years, but age is the dawn of wisdom. Spirit in man was never born and can never die. Spirit is God, and God hath no beginning nor end. Man's body is really the garment God wears when He takes the form of man. In order to manifest Itself, Spirit needs a form. Man's body is the instrument through which the Spirit functions on this plane. The Spirit and the body are not separate; man's body is Spirit or Life reduced to the point of visibility. Matter and Spirit are not different—they are the same. Spirit is the highest degree of matter, and matter is the lowest degree of Spirit. Man will always have a body. When he leaves this plane, he will put on a fourth-dimensional body, and so on to infinity; for there is no end to the glory which is man's.

Life is progression; the journey is ever onward, upward, and Godward. All formed things in the universe are gradually returning to the formless and the formless life is forever taking form. Anything that hath a beginning hath an end. Our body has a beginning; it will again return to the formless primordial substance, and we will put on a new body for every end is a beginning.

Old age is not a tragic occurrence. What we call the aging process is change. It is to be welcomed joyfully and gladly as each phase of human life is a step onward on the path which has no end. Man has powers which transcend his body; he has senses which transcend his five senses. Scientists today are setting forth positive, undisputable evidence that man can leave his present body and travel thousands of miles and see, hear, touch, and speak to people even though his physical body is on a couch thousands of miles away. Man's life is spiritual and eternal; he never grows old for Spirit or Life cannot grow old. Life is self-renewing, eternal, and indestructible. God is Life, and Life is the reality of all men. The evidence of the immortality of man is overwhelming. The scientist cannot see with his eyes an electron; yet he accepts it as a scientific fact because it is the only reasonable conclusion which coincides with other observed phenomena. We can't see God or Life; however we know we are alive. Life is, and we are here to express It in all Its beauty and glory.

The Bible says, *This is life eternal, that they might know Thee the only true God*. JOHN 17:3. The man who thinks or believes that the earthly cycle of birth, adolescence, youth, maturity, and old age is all there is to life, is indeed to be pitied; such a man has no anchor, no hope, no vision, and to him life has no meaning. This type of belief brings frustration, stagnation, cynicism, and a sense of hopelessness resulting in neurosis and mental aberrations of all kinds. If you can't play a fast game of tennis or swim as fast as your son, or if your body has slowed down, or you walk with a slow step, remember Spirit is always clothing Itself anew. What men call death is but a journey to a new city in another mansion of our Father's house.

I say to men and women in my lectures that they should accept what we call old age gracefully. Age has its own glory and beauty which belongs to it. Love, beauty, peace, joy, happiness, wisdom, good will, and understanding—these qualities never grow old and never die. Emerson said, "We do not count a man's years until he has nothing else to count." Your character, the quality of your mind, your faith, and convictions are not subject to decay.

I met a surgeon in England, age 84, who operates every morning, visits patients in the afternoons, and writes in the evening. He is young at 84, full of life, zeal, enthusiasm, love, and good will. He has not surrendered to advancing years; he knows that he is immortal. He said to me, "If I should pass on tomorrow, I would be operating on people in the next dimension, not with a surgeon's scalpel, but with mental and spiritual surgery."

John Wesley was very active in expounding his convictions about God and His laws when he was close to ninety. Our own President Herbert Hoover is very active and performing monumental work on behalf of the government at the age of eighty-three. He is healthy, happy, vigorous, and full of life and enthusiasm. I have listened to him speak over the radio; his mind is clear and decisive. I believe his mental acumen and sagacity are much greater now than when he was forty. He finds life interesting and fascinating. I read recently where he spends all the time available in writing the life of former President Woodrow Wilson. Mr. Hoover is a very religious man and is full of faith in God, life, and the universe. He was subjected to a barrage of criticism and condemnation in the years of the depression, but he weathered the storm and did not grow old in hatred, resentment, ill will, and bitterness. On the contrary he went into the silence of his soul and communing with the Indwelling God he found the peace which is the power at the heart of God.

The greatest of all shock absorbers and preventatives of decrepitude and mental and physical disorders is peace at the Divine Center within you. Tune in and feel it now. All the barbs, criticism, anger, and hate aimed at you will be absorbed, neutralized, and lost in the great ocean of God's love and peace within you; this is the secret of remaining young forever.

My father learned the French language at sixty-five; became an authority on it at seventy; he also made a study of Gaelic when he was over sixty, and became a famous teacher of the language. He actively assisted my sister in a school of higher education and continued to do so until he passed away at ninety-nine. His mind was as clear at ninety-nine as it was when he was fifty; moreover, his handwriting and his reasoning powers had improved through the years. Cato learned Greek at eighty, and Mme. Schumann-Heink reached the pinnacle of her musical success when she was a grandmother. There is an old saying which has an underlying truth and that is that a man is as old as he feels. You are as old and as young as your thought. Reason it out for yourself. Ask yourself a simple question such as this: "When was my mind born? When will it die? Hath mind and spirit a beginning? How could there be an end to that which has no beginning or end?"

Life was never born and it will never die. Water wets it not, fire burns it not, wind blows it not away. You know these things to be true. How could you say, "I'm old, I am useless, I am unwanted, etc." Never in Eternity could you exhaust the glories and beauties that are within you, for Infinity is within you. There is no end to man, since there is no end to God. To maintain this concept will keep you forever young, vital, keen, alert, alive, and full of the Light that never grows dim. Your gray hairs are a great asset to you; they symbolize wisdom, understanding, forbearance, and strength of character. Many clergymen receive all manner of wonderful offers when they are over sixty; people believe that they know something by that time. One man said to me recently, "The only reason I come to see you is because you have gray hairs; I believe you have been through the mill, and that you are talking from experience." Ministers find it very easy to get a good position at forty-five, sixty, and over. A retired priest recently informed me that he has been receiving fabulous offers from many sources; he is seventy. Truth, Love, and Wisdom have no age. It is possible for a boy of twelve years of age who studies the laws of mind and the way of the Spirit to have a greater knowledge of God than his grandfather who refuses to open his mind to the Truths of God.

Don't ever quit a job and say, "I am retired, I am old, I am finished." That is stagnation, death, and you are finished. Some men are old at thirty and others are young at eighty. The mind is the master-weaver, the architect, the designer, and the sculptor. George Bernard Shaw was quite active at ninety, and the architectural quality of his mind had not relaxed from active duty. I meet men and women who tell me that some employers almost slam the door in their faces when they say that they are over forty. This attitude on the part of these employers is to be considered cold, callous, evil, and completely void of compassion or understanding. The total emphasis seems to be on youth; i.e., you must be under thirty-five. The reasoning behind this is certainly very shallow. If the employer would stop and think, he would realize that the man or woman was not selling his age or gray hair, rather he was willing to give of his talents, his experience, his wisdom gathered through years of experience in the market place of life. By means of practice and application the man's age should be a distinct asset to the organization. His gray hair, if he had any, should stand for greater wisdom, skill, and understanding. A man or woman with emotional and spiritual maturity is a tremendous blessing to any organization. A man should not be asked to resign when he is sixty-five; that is the time of life when he could be most useful in handling personnel problems, making plans for the future, shaping decisions, and in the realm of creative ideas based on his experience and insight into the nature of the business.

A motion picture writer in Hollywood told me that he had to write scripts which would cater to the twelve year old mind. This is a tragic state of affairs which indicate that the great masses of people have not become emotionally and spiritually mature. It means that all the accent is placed on youth, and youth stands for inexperience, lack of discernment, and hasty judgment. I am now thinking of a man of sixty years of age who is trying frantically to keep young. He swims with young men every Sunday, goes on long hikes, plays tennis, and boasts of his prowess and physical powers saying, "Look, I can keep up with the best of them, etc." He has forgotten the great truth: *As a man thinketh in his heart, so is he*. Diets, exercise, and games of all kinds will not keep this man young. It is necessary for him to see that he grows old or young through his processes of thinking. The Spirit is conditioned by thought; if his thoughts are on the beautiful, the noble, and the good, he will be young regardless of his chronological years.

Job said, "The thing which I greatly feared is come upon me." There are many people who fear old age and are uncertain about the future expecting mental and physical deterioration as the years advance. What they think and feel come to pass. We grow old when we lose interest in life, when we cease to dream, to hunger after new truths and worlds to conquer. When the mind is open to new ideas, new interests, and when we raise the curtain and let in the sunshine and inspiration of new truths of God and His universe, we will always be young and vital. If you are ninety or ninety-nine, realize you have much to give. You can help stabilize, guide, and direct the younger generation; you can give of your knowledge, your experience, and your wisdom; you can always look ahead for you are gazing into Infinity. You will find that you can never cease to unveil the glories and the wonders of the Infinite One. Veil after veil is lifted, and Its Face becomes more august and wonderful. Try to learn something new every moment of the day and you will find your mind will always be young.

I was introduced to a man in Bombay who said he was one hundred ten years old; he had the most beautiful face I have ever seen. He seemed transfigured by the radiance of an inner light. There was a rare beauty in his eyes indicating he had grown old with gladness.

I receive many letters from men and women who say, "I was turned down because I am over forty." This is a stupid indifference to the sincere desire of these workers to express their talents and abilities. It would seem that we have created a new cult called the "Thirty-five Cult." One man told me that he could not be hired because he was thirty-six and the company would have to pay a few dollars more for insurance premiums. How narrow-minded, short-sighted, and revolting is such an attitude. The reverse should be true. There should be a respect for the man's experience and capacities. The newspapers are taking cognizance of the fact that the voting population of the elderly in California elections is increasing by leaps and bounds; this means their voice will be heard in the legislature of the State and also in the halls of Congress. I believe there should be a federal law enacted prohibiting employers from discriminating against men and women just because of age. A man of sixty-five may be younger mentally, psychologically, and physically than many men at thirty. It is stupid and ridiculous beyond words to tell a man he can't be hired because he is over forty. It is like saying to him that he is ready for the scrap heap or the junk pile. What is a man of forty or over to do—bury his talents and hide his light under a bushel? Men who are deprived and prevented from working because of age must be sustained by government treasuries at county, state, and federal levels; the very organizations who refused to hire them and benefit from their wisdom and experience will be taxed to support them. They are biting off their nose to spite their face; it is a form of financial suicide.

Man is here to enjoy the fruit of his labor and is here to be a producer and not be a prisoner of a society which compels him to idleness. Man's body slows down gradually as he advances through the years, but the mind can be much more active, alert, alive, and quickened by the Holy Spirit. Man's mind does not have to grow old. Job said, *Oh that I were as in months past, as in the days when God preserved me; When his candle shined upon my head, and when by his light I walked through darkness; As I was in the days of my youth, when the secret of God was upon my tabernacle.* JOB 29:2–3–4.

The secret which Job speaks of is Joy. All of us can capture our youth by stirring up the gift of God within us. Every time we recognize the Spirit within as Lord Omnipotent, and reject the power of false beliefs of the world we are stirring up the gift of God within us. In Him there is fullness of Joy. *The joy of the Lord is my strength.*

Feel the Miraculous, Healing, Self-Renewing, Ever-Living God moving through your mind and body. Know that you are inspired, lifted up, rejuvenated, and strengthened; then you will feel a deep response and become rejuvenated, revitalized, and recharged spiritually. You can bubble over with enthusiasm and joy as in the days of your youth for the simple reason that you can always recapture the joyous state mentally and emotionally. The candle which shines upon your head is Divine Intelligence which reveals to you everything you need to know and enables you to affirm the presence of your good regardless of appearances. You walk by His Light, because you know the dawn appears and all the shadows flee away.

Instead of saying, "I am old," say, "I am wise in the ways of God." You are never a failure for you know, "He never faileth." You can always travel in your mind and conquer new fields. Don't let the race mind, corporations, newspapers, statistics hold a picture before you of old age, declining years, decrepitude, senility, and uselessness. Reject it for it is a lie. You can rise above the race-mind and refuse to be hypnotized by such propaganda. Affirm Life—not death. Realize you live forever, and Spirit is your reality. Get a vision of yourself as happy, radiant, successful, serene, and full of the Light of God. If you are retired, get interested in the Bible, its inner meaning. Get a new vocation, do something you always loved to do. Go to the University and take up subjects you always wanted to study. Travel, explore, investigate, and pray as follows: *As the hart panteth after the water brooks, so panteth my soul after thee, O God.* PSALM 42:1.

Be sure that your mind never retires. It must be like a parachute which is no good except it opens up. Be open and receptive to new ideas. I have seen men of sixty-five and seventy retire; they seem to rot away and in a few months pass on; they felt life was at an end. This retirement was a new venture, a new challenge, a new path, the beginning of the fulfillment of a long dream. It is inexpressibly depressing to hear a man say, "What shall I do, I'm retired?" He is saying in effect, "I am mentally and physically dead. My mind is bankrupt of ideas." All this is a false picture. The real truth is you can accomplish more at ninety than you did at sixty because each day you are growing in wisdom and understanding of God and His universe through your new studies and interest.

His flesh shall be fresher than a child's: he shall return to the days of his youth. JOB 33:25. Realize you will never have an old mind, except you think you have. Learn to give all allegiance and devotion to the Indwelling God which is supreme, the only cause and power. To give power to the race mind, to senescence, sickness, to people, conditions, and events divides your allegiance and instills conflict and fear. You might be eighty years chronologically speaking, but if you are cranky, irritable, irascible, petulant, and cantankerous, you are really old regardless of the number of years you have accumulated whether thirty or ninety. Old age means the contemplation of the truth of God from the highest standpoint. This brings you to the well of God where you drink of the waters of life which keep you forever refreshed and God-intoxicated.

Look forward to a greater degree of spiritual awareness and realize that you are on an endless journey, a series of infinite steps in the ceaseless, tireless, endless ocean of God's Love; then with the Psalmist you will say, *They shall still bring forth fruit in old age; they shall be fat and flourishing.* PSALMS 92:14. *The fruit of the Spirit is love, joy, peace, patience, gentleness, goodness, faith, meekness, temperance: against such there is no law.* GAL. 5:22–23.

You are a son of the Infinite which knows no end and you are a child of Eternity.

VI
Nuclear Religion

(1961)

Murphy was eager to marry his metaphysis to new findings in science, technology, and psychology. He titled this pamphlet Nuclear Religion *to make the point that all the technologies we know of are nothing but tools of the individual mind and stem from Universal Mind. Murphy would certainly say the same today of the binary coding and digital connectedness that has remade our world, for good and ill. All forces of life are expressions of the One Mind and are subject to the ethics and insights of individual minds. Our use of technology reflects back to us the scale of our own development.* —MH

1

Nuclear Religion

People speak of the electronic age, the atomic age, and of inconceivable nuclear power. Wherever you go, you hear people speaking of the marvelous discoveries in the scientific field; some of our modern scientists speak of interplanetary travel in the not-too-distant future.

In reference to the powers within man, this is very interesting and significant; but the greatest discovery of all time is that Omnipotence is within you. Every man has within him Infinite Intelligence, Boundless Wisdom, and the Power that moves the world.

Some time ago I read about a woman who lifted a truck which had pinned down her husband. The neighbors marveled and wondered how she did this because subsequently four men could not lift the same truck. How is it that this frail woman was able to do what four men were unable to do? Seeing the urgent need, she automatically called upon the Power within her and—never doubting—she received all the strength she needed for the occasion. This same Power in all of us is capable of extraordinary and superhuman effort, and in times of emergency and great need, we call it forth. It is the faith that moves mountains.

Mrs. Olive Gaze, wife of the late philosopher, Dr. Harry Gaze, brought to my attention the story of a boy called Michael Little, fifteen years old, who single-handedly lifted a gatepost weighing over three hundred pounds which had fallen on a little girl. Later two strong men could not budge the gate.

Begin now to think, feel, and know that Omnipotence is within you. Contemplate your Transcendental Power. The Bible says that God indwells man, and with this God-Power all things are possible. This is the greatest find of all time, far more important than any discovery ever made by man. No matter what the problem is, no matter what the difficulty, *you* can momentarily call forth the Transcendental God-Power which can do all things. The atomic energy and thermonuclear power are perfectly harmless, for the forces and powers of nature are not evil, they are neutral.

Nuclear or atomic energy have no particular purpose of their own. Man gives purpose to them. The same wind which will blow a boat upon the rocks will also carry it safely to the harbor. Fire will burn man or warm him, depending on how he uses it. Water will quench your thirst, but you also can use it to drown a child. Electricity can be used to light the house, vacuum the floor, fry an egg, drive a train, and for countless other purposes to bless and alleviate the burdens of mankind, but man also can use the same electrical energy to electrocute someone, or he can make electrical mines for destroying his fellowmen. Good and evil are the movements of man's mind relative to the LifePrinciple which forever seeks to express Itself through each one of us as harmony, health, peace, and true expression.

The word *evil* comes from live. When you invert it, you have the word *evil* which means you are living life backwards. The word *devil* means de-evil or of evil. A simple way for the man who walks the street to look at good and evil is to say to himself, "How am I using this Life-Principle? Am I letting this Power flow through me constructively or destructively?" Think good, and good follows. Think evil, and evil follows. The nuclear religion deals with the One Universal Power within all men which should be used constructively, harmoniously, peacefully, lovingly, and for the purposes of blessing all humanity.

The word *religion* means to tie back to God; it means your personal and intimate relationship with the Divine Life-Principle within you which is frequently called God.

The Bible says, *God is Life*. You are alive with the Life of God. There is only one Life-Principle and that Life is coursing through your veins now. If you will pray in this simple way which I am suggesting here, I feel sure that you will transform your life. For about fifteen minutes every morning and night sit down quietly, relax, let go, and softly, lovingly, and reverently affirm as follows: "God flows through me as harmony, health, peace, joy, wholeness, beauty, true place, love, and abundance. I rejoice and give thanks that I am a free-flowing channel for the Divine Forces." When fear or worry-thoughts come into your mind, affirm boldly, "God's love, peace, and power are flowing through me." Do not fight negative thoughts.

When your room is dark, you do not say to yourself that you will shovel out the darkness. On the contrary, you turn on the light. Learn to chant the beauty of the good. Do it a thousand times a day if necessary. To *pray* is to think. Your thought is your prayer. What are you thinking now? The basis of the universal, nuclear religion is given in the Book of Proverbs, *As a man thinketh in his heart, so is he*. Actually, this Bible truth is the basis of all religions when they are stripped of all external wrappings and trappings.

For instance, the *heart* is an old Chaldean word meaning your subconscious mind; it is called the subconscious or subjective mind, because it is subject to the habitual thinking of your conscious, reasoning, analytical mind. The meaning of the quotation is obvious; it means that the way you really think and feel about life, yourself, your neighbor, and the world, you express and manifest in all phases of your life.

Thoughts are things. Your thoughts are creative. Emerson says, "Man is what he thinks all day long." Thought and feeling create your destiny. This is why you mold, fashion, and shape your own future. This is what religion is all about, regardless of all labels. The thought, idea, or mental picture, which you feel is true, is impressed on your subconscious mind, and whatever is impressed is expressed.

For example, you can entertain the thought that this atomic power shall be used to propel ships over the sea, drive trains, automobiles, airplanes, heat and light homes, direct ships under water, and perform countless other services—all for the express purpose of making life more wonderful. You can, likewise, invert the use of this power and direct that atomic energy for the purposes of destruction. Again it is a result of the movement of your own mind; it is not the fault of the atomic or thermonuclear energy. The power is in man and not in the nuclear energy.

All the wonderful inventions in the world are thoughts of men expressed. The Bible says, *Death and life are in the power of the tongue.* Are you using your power of speech to decree health, harmony, and happiness? To *think* is to speak. Your words are thoughts expressed. You have or can have control over your thoughts, and therefore, your speech.

Another beautiful Bible quotation is, *Choose ye this day whom ye shall serve.* Choose life, love, truth, beauty, security, and wealth. You are here on this planet to reproduce the qualities, attributes, potencies, and aspects of God. You are here to discover the joy of living and to make this world a better place to live in for your children and their children's children; you are here to better humanity and promote peace. As a result, they could say of you that the world was blessed because you walked this way.

God or this Infinite Intelligence who created all things is Infinite. There cannot be two Infinites, since one would cancel out the other, and there would be chaos and discord everywhere. Infinity cannot be divided or multiplied. God is Omnipotent, the Creator of all things visible and invisible. *Omnipotence* means the All-Powerful One without anything to oppose or challenge It. If there were any power to challenge, neutralize, or thwart omnipotence, God would not be supreme.

The words *devil, satan, etc.*, mean misunderstanding, misapplication, and misinterpretation of the Laws of Life. The ancient Hebrews said the devil means God upside down, meaning man's twisted, distorted concept of God. Your good and evil experiences depend on how you use this Life-Principle within you, which is forever whole, pure, and perfect in Its ultimate nature. There is evil in the world because men think destructive, vicious thoughts; moreover, they cheat, rob, defraud, lie, murder, etc. Man's inhumanity to man makes countless thousands mourn, but this does not mean that there is an evil power contending with good. It is man's misuse of his mind to maim, injure, and destroy. There is no law compelling man to hate, resent, and entertain vengeful and hostile thoughts. These mental poisons generate emotions which get snarled up in the subconscious mind and being negative must have a negative outlet resulting in ulcers, high blood pressure, gastritis, arthritis, and various other psychosomatic disorders.

All scientific thinkers today do not look upon the Bible in the traditional way. The Bible is a textbook of psychology dealing with spiritual laws. It tells us how we get into trouble and then relates how to get out of trouble. The Bible says that as a man soweth, so also shall he reap. This infers that all our external experiences, conditions, and events are the result of our internal thinking.

If man gets his thought right, his actions inevitably will be right, in the same way that a certain chemical reaction will follow a certain combination of the necessary ingredients. If you want to change conditions, you must change your thoughts and see things as they ought to be. If a man does not know the powers of his mind, minimizes intangibles, and fails to see the power of ideas charged with enthusiasm, he is out of touch with the causative world within him.

Remember that the Life-Principle is within you. This Life-Principle is called by many names such as God, Reality, Infinite Intelligence, Nature, Allah, Brahma, Infinite Mind, Universal Mind, I AM, Aum, Wisdom, The Ancient of Days, The All-Seeing Eye, Our Father, The Only One, The Infinite Healing Presence, The Christ Within—all these and many more are equivalents for God in all languages of the world. *God is Spirit*, as Jesus says. You cannot see Spirit with your eye, but you know that you can feel the Spirit of Truth, Goodness, and Beauty moving in your heart. You cannot see Love, but you know that love wells up in your heart when you look at your own child. There is the love of a mother for her child, of the boy for his dog, of the father for his son; in fact, he may sacrifice much in order to get a healing for his son. Then there is the love of country where some men give their lives for ideals.

Love gives itself. You cannot buy it. Love is kindness, justice, mercy, and peace. You love another when you love to see the other become and express all that he longs to become. You love when you sincerely wish for the other health, happiness, peace, and all the blessings of heaven. Love frees, Love gives, Love is the Spirit of God moving in the hearts of men. Love unites; hate divides. Hatred is Love in reverse. Hatred, envy, jealousy, and revenge are called the devils which bedevil us in the Bible. Jesus cast these obnoxious, vicious patterns of thought out of the minds of men by contemplating God's Love and God's Peace as the Truth of Being, and they were healed. Love dissolves everything unlike itself in the mind and body of man.

You love your wife when you see the peace of God in her and call that Presence forth. When you radiate this love sincerely, God's Love will shine forth in all Its pristine glory. If you love your husband in the true sense of the term, you will quietly know, feel, and believe that the Presence of God is functioning in him, through him, and all around him. You will picture him in your mind as he ought to be—radiant, happy, successful, and peaceful. When you love your husband, you do not attach yourself mentally to his shortcomings, derelictions, abnormalities, or idiosyncracies. Neither do you dwell on negative symptoms, but you go straight to the God-Presence which indwells him, affirming, feeling, and rejoicing that God is flowing forth through him as harmony, joy, peace, success, vitality, and beauty. Remember, your husband will be to you what you believe him to be. You are always living with your real belief and convictions as you go through life with your wife or husband.

If a man loves a woman, he will not do anything unloving. For example, he will not come home drunk, neither will he criticize or condemn her. He will not be sadistic with his tongue, neither will he flirt and show disrespect for his wife in public or any other place. Love does not do these things. Love cannot do anything unloving. Love is kind; it vaunteth not itself; it is not puffed up. Love envieth not. Love always forgives. Love always blesses. Love heals all conditions. Love, freedom, and respect are one, and whenever one is missing, love is not present. Love is not possessive. Love does not coerce. If a man loves his wife, he does not try to make her a second edition of himself by causing her to think the way he does, nor does he try to submerge her personality in any way. A man who loves his wife will be delighted to see her fully expressed and divinely happy. He wants to make her happy, therefore, his thoughts, speech, and actions will reveal his love for his wife. Many women are frightfully frustrated in the home; they have wonderful talents which are going to waste, causing confusion with its usual accompaniments, such as neurosis, insomnia, and other illnesses. Many women are not fully expressed in their home or in the kitchen; so the husbands should encourage them in their full expression at all times. If husbands and wives began to see the God in each other and nourish the qualities which endeared them one to the other, the marriage would grow more blessed though the years, and the atmosphere of the home would be one of peace, harmony, and joy.

Children grow up in the image and likeness of the mental and emotional climate or atmosphere of the home. Parents' love for their children causes them to practice the Presence of God in their thoughts, feelings, and actions all day long. When you enter such a home, you know God or Love dwells there, and God is Love. This is the Nuclear Religion and the practice of it is nothing more than the practice of the Presence of God; it is powerful beyond imagination. Let us not overlook it because of its utter simplicity.

The first step in the practice of the Nuclear Religion is to realize that God or the Life-Principle is the only Presence and the only Power. God is that Invisible Spirit and Mind in you. The peace, the love, and the joy that you feel at times welling within is the Presence of God in you.

When you solve a difficult problem, it is the Infinite Intelligence which created all things and knows all things which gives you the answer. There is as much God in you as there is love, peace, joy, wisdom, understanding, and goodwill. God is the highest and best in every man. As we have already said, "God is Boundless Love, Infinite Intelligence, Absolute Harmony, Supreme Wisdom, Boundless Joy, Infinite Life, and God is All Powerful."

The whole world is God or the Life-Principle in infinite differentiation. Everything in the universe is alive. God is the life of the fish, the bird, the dog, the horse, and of all trees and vegetation. All minerals and the stones in the field also are alive.

There are different degrees of awareness. Infinite Intelligence is God. There is more Intelligence operating in a dog, for instance, than there is in the goldfish in the bowl. The Life-Principle reaches Its highest degree of intelligence in man who has the power to reason and consciously tune in on the Infinite Power, thereby enabling him to rise higher and higher in the scale of living. The more Intelligence operating in man the more freedom, happiness, and peace of mind he possesses. He rises above restrictions, limitations, and environmental circumscriptions, because his thoughts and imagery are creative, enabling him to change conditions and solve all problems which face him.

The following is a wonderful prayer to realize. It is the essence of the Nuclear Religion and is contemplated by scientific thinkers all over the world. These men relax quietly ten or fifteen minutes every day and meditate on the fact that God is the only Presence and the only Power. They let their thoughts dwell on this profound Truth, looking at it from all angles. They begin by thinking that every person they meet is an expression of God. In fact, everything they see is God made manifest, for there is only God who is in all, over all, and all in all. They realize the whole world and all things therein contained represent God dramatizing Himself for the joy of expressing Himself. They continue to do this regularly, systematically, and lovingly. As a result, they find their whole world changing; they experience better health, outer conditions improve, and they are possessed of a new vitality and energy.

I would strongly suggest that you think all day long from the standpoint of the One God about every person and every situation you meet. Pray at work by realizing God is your partner, and God is in action through all your associates. Pray while driving your car, realizing the vehicle is God's idea moving from point to point freely, joyously, and lovingly. Pray when you go into a store by realizing God directs your purchases, that God is prospering the clerk who waits on you, and that the store is being governed and directed by God's Wisdom.

A young lady told me that she lost her purse a few Sundays ago. She became still and said, "Infinite Intelligence knows where my purse is and leads me to it, and I follow the lead when it comes." The idea popped into her mind to go to the telephone booth in a large drug store which was one of the many places she had visited during the day. This lady's subconscious mind knew where the purse was and responded to her request. The Bible says, *Taste the Lord for he is good*. She tasted the Lord (the subconscious mind) in the sense that she experienced the way it works by responding to her request, and she recognized the lead when it came.

Let prayer be the orderly, right way of doing everything. God cannot do anything unloving because God is Absolute Love. God cannot send pain because God is Absolute Peace. God cannot send sickness or disease, for God is Wholeness, Beauty, and Infinite Life; likewise the Presence never grows old or decays. God cannot deceive you, trick you, or test you because God is Absolute Truth. God cannot cause discord, confusion, and chaos in your life, as God is Absolute Harmony. We bring misery, suffering, and tragedy into our lives by our own wrong thinking and misuse of the laws of our mind. The Bible says, *God is Love, and Love is Life*. The tendency of Life is to express Itself as harmony, beauty, love, and joy.

To be religious is to experience the joy of living. There are as many religions as there are individuals in the world. Your personal religion is really your real concept and conviction about this Presence and Power within you regardless of your religious affiliation. You are always bound by your belief. *To believe* is to accept something as true. If you believe Santa Barbara is in New York State, your letters will go astray; or if you believe three and three are seven, you will be in trouble in the financial world as long as you believe the lie.

Religion means a real knowledge of God and an inner experience of God in your heart. If I gave you a lecture on common table salt, describing its chemical composition, its atomic weight, uses, etc., you might say that it was a very interesting lecture, but if you had not tasted the salt, you would not know its savor.

You will find that all the great religions of the world have one fundamental unity; also, they have a great number of things in common. Actually all of them borrowed from each other. All religions can be summed up in this Truth: *Know ye not that ye are the temple of God and that the Spirit of God dwelleth in you*. This means that God indwells you.

The truths of the Bible cannot be taught on the level of terminology. You have to discover the meanings of the allegories, parables, myths, and cryptograms. The Bible is replete with figurative, idiomatic, oriental expressions. The Hebrew mystics who wrote the Bible have always stated that there is a hidden meaning behind the words. As the Spirit of God is hidden within you, so is there a hidden meaning to every part of the Bible. You are much more than your body;

likewise the Bible is much more than a body of words. *Except by parable, spake he not unto them.* Man must learn the meaning of the parable and realize that there is a deep, inner meaning to every parable and allegory.

The letter of the Law killeth, and the Spirit giveth Life. You must find the meaning behind the words. People with little faith or understanding are always arguing doctrinal points. There are people who spend a great part of their lives proving that the many incidents in the Bible are not historical; you can get many books along this line. The important point to consider is that all the stories in the Bible are psychologically and spiritually true even though historically unprovable.

The Bible speaks in a language of symbolism. A *shepherd* in the Bible means a man who is spiritually enlightened. The star which he sees is a realization of the Divine Presence within him which will guide, direct, and protect him from all harm. If you are to be a good shepherd, you will trust God in all your ways; then you will find the still waters (the quiet mind) within yourself. You are not religious or devout if you nurse grievances, grudges, and perpetuate animosities. Neither can man say he is religious if he has not found it in his heart to forget, forgive, and release others. There is no consolation in a religious affiliation apart from the commandment of *Love ye one another.*

The first step in the religious life is to cleanse the mind of all grievances. What is the use of talking about religious beliefs if you are bitter, cynical, and the heart is corroded with psychic traumas of guilt, grudges, and bitter memories? The self-pitying and the hateful can never know the blessings of God. It is no use to pray for release from misery, pain, and suffering until you cleanse the heart first. The teachings of all religions of the world are beautifully summarized in a few verses from the Bible, *There is no fear in Love, but perfect Love casteth out fear, because fear hath torment. He that feareth is not made perfect in Love. If a man say, I love God, and hateth his brother, he is a liar: for he that loveth not his brother whom he hath seen, how can he love God whom he hath not seen? And this commandment have we from him, That he who loveth God loves his brother also.*

Since the dawn of time in countless modes, man venerated a deity. He humbled himself and exalted the Divine Being. He felt the impulse of God within him. The various creeds are opposed or differ in form, ritual, and interpretation of symbols. All of them agree on the existence of God and the virtues such as purity, goodness, love, beauty, and faith. Let these qualities rule. Whenever men gather to worship a Transcendent Ideal, they should not be criticized or attacked. The important thing is to develop what is within them, to better themselves, and to come closer to God. The rest is secondary.

People differ on which road to take to God. You will find God through a heart full of love and goodwill. Guides come and people follow. Some go one way, others choose a different path. All are convinced and sincere that their path or trail is the best one. *Whatever road I take leads to Thee.* When we meet at the top, there is no use fighting and saying my road is the only one, or that my road is absolutely best and there is no other; that would be absurd. We will all awaken to God's Glory and Love some day, and we will all meet at the Summit.

Divine inspiration, molded by external conditions, varying according to climates, adapted to soil, and to the period's traditions, brought about the world's great religions, the source of which was Divine. Intolerance and bigotry are proofs of incomprehension and denote a lack of love. Many intelligent men and women feel abandoned. Their hearts are full of disturbing and unanswered questions. There is only One Truth, One God, but there are many and varied mentalities. What is obvious to some may seem obscure and unacceptable to others.

Religion must not fight science. We must not entrench ourselves behind absolute dogmas and intransigent interpretations. Do not stagnate. Man would go far if it were revealed to him that there is no conflict between science and religion. I look upon science and religion as two arcs of a circle which unite and form a whole. The laws underlying physics, chemistry, and mathematics are not different from the operation of the laws of our mind.

There must be a scientific approach to prayer, and it is as follows: *Go thy way and as thou hast believed, so be it done unto thee*. To believe something is to accept it as true. Whatever you mentally accept and feel to be true will come to pass. The Law of Life is the law of belief. What should you believe in? Creeds? Dogmas of churches? Grandfather's religious concepts? Opinions of men? No! It is none of these. It is belief in the workings of your subconscious mind, in the creative laws of life, in the goodness and guidance of God, in the love of God, and the tendency of Life to express Itself through us as joy, love, beauty, harmony—in other words, the life more abundant. It is what you really believe deep down in your heart that matters, not what you say with your lips or give intellectual assent to. As you really think and feel in your heart, so are you—this is your real religion, regardless of your labels.

2

Nuclear Religion
In Human Relations

Do people bore you, or do you find them interesting? For example, do you say, "He bores me to tears," and so forth? Such a complaint is a subconscious indication of apathy and listlessness within ourselves. All men and women are interesting because we are all God's children. Every individual is in essence an epitome of the whole human race. The Divine Intelligence operates in each person and is responsive to us when we recognize It in others. Each person is unique. You are an individualized expression of God, and no one in all the world is like you because you are you.

Let us use a chemical analogy. The chemicals, such as calcium, phosphorous, sulphur, etc., are not in exactly the same proportions in each person. No two individuals are chemically alike. All of us know that certain chemicals have an affinity for one another; others are more or less inert when they are mixed together. This would be true whether they are in a chemical laboratory or in the human body. To continue with the chemical analogy, I might say that all our relations with people, hostile, friendly, or indifferent, are determined by the relations of the chemicals of which we and they are composed.

Let us suppose for a moment that a qualified chemist goes into a laboratory containing all kinds of chemicals; he knows very well the atomic and molecular structure of each chemical. He knows that in the raw or natural state some of these chemicals will combine according to their qualities, i.e., they will react on each other naturally. Take notice of what the chemical scientist does: He utilizes his knowledge of the science and art of chemistry to make complex chemical compounds which bless humanity in countless ways. The chemist with his understanding blends together harmoniously various chemicals and brings forth plastic goods, rubber goods, and synthetic drugs. He enters into the field of radio, television, aeronautics, and telephonic communications, bringing about magnificent contributions to the human race which would be absolutely impossible in ordinary circumstances—such as trusting Nature alone to do so.

Let us begin to see the truth of the chemical analogy to our problems in human relations. Suppose that you say to me, "My neighbors are dull, insipid, boring, and impossible." This means that you are a chemist in your own laboratory and doing nothing at all with your chemicals. You could mix, rearrange, combine your chemicals in such a way that you would get a wonderful, warm, cordial, and friendly response from what seems to you to be impossible neighbors. If you say, "I find one interesting and the other boring," you are like a laboratory full of chemicals with no chemist present who could manufacture marvelous and useful combinations with these chemicals in your neighbor's laboratory.

You are here to study the mysteries of life, to understand humanity, to love your neighbors, to get along with others, to take a deep interest in humanity, in God, in nature, and appreciate the fact that every man is an epitome of the entire human race. You are here to take charge of your thoughts, feelings, responses, and reactions to life. Likewise, we have charge over all the chemicals and elements in our body. If we are good spiritual chemists, we will combine with the chemical elements in other people and establish harmonious human relations.

Place the spiritual chemist in charge of your mental and physical laboratory. Do not be a laboratory without a chemist or spiritual director. You are the master of your thoughts. You are the only thinker in your universe; therefore you know that you alone are responsible for the way you think. The other fellow is not responsible for the way you think about him. Wake up the spiritual chemist within you. Identify with the God in the other, and let the chemistry of love, peace, and goodwill flow from you and touch the God in the other. Your moods, like chemical elements, have their affinities. God's Love emanating from you will combine chemically with God's Love in the other. A deep, vital understanding takes place; you find the former so-called enemy is a co-worker on the way.

A spiritual chemist does not depend on people or surroundings to stimulate or interest him. If he did, he would be a laboratory without a scientist present. He is not at the mercy of people, hoping that they are nice, interesting, and loving; he makes desirable and useful chemical combinations with all people. If a man continues to act according to his natural conditioning or natural affinities, his likes and dislikes, his prejudices and fears, he could be called a mineral or vegetable man living and dying a mere passive and mechanical machine-type individual, reacting in a stereotyped way to all the events of the day. Let every encounter with others be a chemical experiment in prayer. Say to yourself whenever you meet another person, "God is in that person; he possesses all the qualities, attributes, and potencies of God. I am a spiritual chemist; I know that all the chemicals in the ocean and in the earth are within this man. I can combine the chemicals in myself with this man harmoniously and make a wonderful compound which will bless us both and all humanity. The God in me salutes the God in him. I direct the chemical and spiritual waves which flow forth from me. I know as a scientist that the lamp of love burning in my heart kindles a chemical fire in the other, bringing about a Divine fusion, causing me to realize the profound truth, *I sought God, and I found Him, and He delivered me from all my fears.*"

You are a human being; you should be vitally interested in the Life-Principle animating all people. Know that the other is looking for someone who will overlook his frailties, shortcomings, and derelictions, and like Paul of Tarsus declare, *Christ in you, the hope of glory.* COLOSSIANS 1:27.

This is how to chemically and spiritually unite with another person by affirming silently as follows: "Divine Love is flowing harmoniously and peacefully through him, and there is harmony, peace, and understanding between us. God reveals to me what I should say, and Divine Wisdom reigns supreme."

This attitude of mind brings about a rearrangement of the atomic and molecular structure of your thought which blends harmoniously with the other, resulting in a joyous union between you. The Bible says, *Stir up the gift of God within you*. Release the power, the joy, and the love of God lodged within you. Cease saying, "He bores me," which is an unconscious confession of guilt within yourself, indicating you are all wrapped up in yourself and looking for someone to lift you out of your despondency or "self-centeredness." Every time you meet another, stir up the spiritual chemist within and say to yourself, "I behold the presence of God in the other, and I know that at this moment there is a rearrangement of the chemical elements in both of us whereby we blend harmoniously, peacefully, and lovingly." Thoughts are things, and whatever we think about another we are thinking about ourselves.

Some years ago Dr. Charles Littlefield, a scientist, discovered the truth of the Biblical statement, *As a man thinketh in his heart, so is he*. While concentrating on a saline solution by peering through a microscope, he discovered that his focused thought took form. One day he concentrated his attention on a frail elderly lady; he stood gazing intently at her for some time. When he turned back to look at the saline solution, he was surprised to find a miniature form of this woman. Day after day he concentrated on certain mental pictures, and he was amazed to see his mental imagery take form in the shapes developed by the crystals in the saline solution under the microscope.

Man is what he thinks all day long. Our thoughts are the tools and instruments which fashion, mold, and shape our destiny. Your thoughts can be photographed. They have form, shape, and structure in your brain now, and are gradually being condensed into muscle, skin, and cells, as well as experiences, events, and conditions.

There is a revolution going on today in the field of chemistry and physics. The chemistry which the writer studied in college is outmoded, antiquated, and completely irrelevant to modern discoveries. For example, the postulate of immutable elements is gone; this dogma disappeared with the discovery of radioactivity. Scientists today point out that we are living in a dynamic, changing, evolving universe.

In our periodicals, magazines, and newspapers of today, man is reading about the discoveries of modern science. The late Robert Andrews Millikin, who was head of the California Institute of Technology at Pasadena for many years, said that the two fundamental principles, conservation of mass and conservation of energy, are now gone as distinct and separable verities.

Einstein and other scientists have also pointed out the interconvertibility of energy into mass and mass into energy. In other words, our modern scientists are saying that energy and mass are one and the same thing, operating at different levels of vibration. I read an article some years ago in which someone asked Einstein what matter was, and he replied, "Energy reduced to the point of visibility." The conceptions of the conservation of energy and the conservation of mass are considered no longer sacrosanct.

Your body is plastic, porous, and pliable. It consists of waves of light vibrating at different rates of vibration. Modern science teaches that the only difference between one substance and another is the number and rate of motion of the electrons revolving around a nucleus, proving the dictum of Pythagoras that the world was ruled by number and motion. There were scientists in the nineteenth century who were under the impression that all the great discoveries in physics had already been made. Some said that all we had to do was to make more exact quantitative measurements upon the old phenomena.

You cannot measure love with a slide rule, neither can you measure peace, happiness, wisdom, or understanding. We are dealing with the intangible, the invisible, the imponderable. You cannot see the power that moves your finger to write; surely you do not think the finger moves itself! The body moves as it is moved upon. The body acts as it is acted upon. Your body is characterized by inertia, and your thoughts, emotions, and imagery are played upon it for good or ill. You can play a melody of God on the tissues of your body or a song of hatred or ill will.

You will find that the dogma of many religious groups asserts or affirms some things to be true which completely contradict modern scientific findings. There are people living in this country today who believe that the world was made in six days and that God somehow got tired and rested on the seventh day. Geologists, paleontologists, archaeologists, anthropologists, physicists, astronomers, and other scientists realize that the cosmos took form according to a definite cosmic design and took countless millions of years to assume the form it now has. All these changes took place in Divine order and sequence according to an archetypal design of the Infinite Intelligence which is the only creative power.

Judge Troward who perceived the creative process, intuitively stated as follows: "The physical history of our planet shows us first an incandescent nebula dispersed over vast infinitudes of space; later this condenses into a central sun surrounded by a family of glowing planets hardly yet consolidated from the plastic primordial matter; then succeed untold milleniums of slow geological formation; an earth peopled by the lowest forms of life whether vegetable or animal; from which crude beginnings a majestic, unceasing, unhurried, forward movement brings things stage by stage to the conditions in which we know them now."

You could look at the six days of creation as six great stages in the evolution of the cosmos. The story in Genesis also portrays the six steps in prayer followed by the seventh day or Sabbath of God in which you reach the point of conviction or inner certitude that your prayer is answered. There is also a spiritual or esoteric meaning to all parts of the Bible, and except we have the inner meaning, we actually have no Bible. In psychological parlance, the six days represent the length of time it takes you to impress or convey your idea or concept on the subconscious mind. As soon as you succeed in impregnating the subconscious by imagining the reality of your desire and feeling the thrill of fulfillment, you impress the subconscious mind. Then, impregnation has taken place, the work of the six days is finished, followed by a period of rest called the Sabbath or seventh day, which is the interval of time between the impregnation and the manifestation.

The modern physicist, astronomer, or scientist cannot afford to have a closed mind. New discoveries and revelations are compelling scientists to discard the old mechanistic and materialistic concepts of the nineteenth century, and dynamically reveal that we are living in an ever-changing, fluidic universe of dancing forces, and that the universe is a mental phenomenon.

The new, nuclear physics, with great courage and faith, has without hesitation discarded the gross atomistic concepts of yesterday. These scientists have demonstrated their own miracles, such as nuclear transubstantiation, time-space fusion, television, radio, inter-atomic energy, etc. Science is beginning to kneel and pray before the altar of being.

In materia-medica circles it is customary to discard the textbooks of yesterday's pathologies and nostrums. Likewise, you must discard old superstitions, and false beliefs about an avenging God, hell, purgatory, devil, evil forces, and realize that all these are simply states of mind, created by man himself, due to his ignorance and lack of understanding. Arrive at the hour of decision in your own mind where *none but the best wine* of spiritual wisdom shall be put forth for the guests who hunger for a more wholesome fare. Become an open-minded seeker after Truth.

When a man says that God is punishing him or that God will judge him on the last day, he must ask himself such questions as follows: Where did such an idea come from? Who said it? Why was it said? Is there any sense or meaning to it? Have I been brainwashed since my youth? Am I a hypnotized victim of ignorance, superstition, and fear? Where did such ideas originate? Primitive men, not knowing where God was, originated and postulated a God outside themselves; furthermore, in their primitive state of mind they attributed to God all the passions, such as jealousy, hate, envy, anger, etc., which they found within themselves.

Primitive and prehistoric man realized that he was subjected to forces over which he seemed to have no control. The sun gave him heat, but it also scorched the earth. The fire burned him, the thunder terrified him, the water flooded his lands, and his cattle were drowned. His idea of external powers was the primitive and fundamental type of every idea of God. He conceived for these elements or forces of nature love or aversion, and fear and hope gave rise to the first idea of religion. Primitive man, in his infantile reasoning with himself, perceived that when another man, stronger than he, was about to injure him, he was able to bribe him or offer him certain gifts and in other ways abase himself, thereby mollifying the other's attitude. From this crude reasoning he proceeded to supplicate the intelligences of the winds, the stars, the waters, hoping that they would hear him and answer his prayers. He proceeded to make offerings and sacrifices to the gods of the wind and the rain.

The first men conceived the universe to be filled with innumerable gods. Their ideas of God were divided according to the sensations of pleasure or pain, and derived solely from the forces of nature. They divided the gods and genii into beneficent and malignant powers—hence, the universality of these two characters in all the systems of religion.

God is the Life-Principle animating all things. This Life-Principle seeks to express Itself through all men as harmony, health, peace, joy, wholeness, beauty, and perfection. Align yourself with this Creative Life Force and flow along with this God-Presence by realizing you are a channel for the Divine. If you swim against the current or against the waves of the sea, you get shaken up quite a bit. Swim with the tide, go along with the currents of life, love, truth, and beauty. If you get angry, resentful, or jealous, you are going contrary to Life; you are inverting the stream of Life.

You are here to express Life fully and to be healthy, happy, and in your true place, doing what you love to do. If you apply a mental tourniquet and say, "I'm too old," "I can't do that," "It is too late now," "I'm stymied," "I'm blocked," etc., you are damming up the free flow of the Spirit. In other words you are being frustrated in that you are bottling up the creative forces within you and not realizing your objectives. You can let the creative forces flow through you as art, music, painting, research work, or mathematics, according to your natural endowments. When you mentally block your good by entertaining the belief in obstacles, delays, and difficulties, your emotions get snarled up in the subconscious mind, and being of a negative nature, these destructive moods come forth as sickness, disease, mental disturbances, and various other forms of psychoneurosis.

Never entertain fixed beliefs about religion. Look at your religion as your personal relationship to God, your fellowman, and the universe. You must not assert as true about God and the Universe that which modern science knows to be completely false, such as the six-day creation of the earth, the end of the world at a certain time, etc. The God of Science is the principle of Infinite Intelligence operating in all men, animals, and in the entire cosmos. God is the Spirit of Divine Order and of orderly development.

Voltaire wrote, "If God did not exist, it would be necessary to invent him." To deny the existence of a Creative Intelligence is a complete contradiction of the evolutionary findings of all modern science. Your religious concepts should change. Your grandfather rode on a donkey or a horse, today you ride in a modern jet. People communicated with each other in this country at one time by pony express. Today you may phone or wire your family, or perhaps see them on television even though they may be thousands of miles away. What about your religious concepts? Are they of the horse and buggy type, or have you advanced with the electronic and jet age?

Truth has been discovered in the past, it is being discovered now, and will continue to be discovered. Religion is undergoing a revolution. There are probably about fifteen million people in America reading and studying about mental and spiritual laws free from the superficialities, wrappings, and trappings of creed, dogma, and tradition. As you begin to read what modern science is discovering in this space age in the field of astrophysics, mathematics, time, chemistry, extra sensory perception, scientific prayer therapy, etc., you develop a deep sense of humility and receptivity. Modern science is walking humbly with God, and our greatest scientists are true mystics.

Micah said, twenty-five hundred years ago, *What doth the Lord require of thee but to do justice, to love mercy, and to walk humbly with thy God?* Einstein once said that the most beautiful and most profound emotion we can experience is the sensation of the mystical. It is the source of all true science. Einstein recognized the Illimitable Superior Spirit which revealed Himself in all phases of the incomprehensible universe. I look upon Einstein as one of the world's greatest mystics. A mystic is a man who intuitively perceives the great truths of God without any conscious process of reasoning. Einstein had the ability to inwardly sense the invisible things of the Spirit, and through feeling, present them to the intellect. That which the intuition reveals, the intellect may later analyze. It is this feeling, back toward spiritual prototypes, that marks the work of the true mystic in any age.

There is an atomic science of the Spirit also with its own wavelengths and electronics. Let us enter into the high oscillations of the Spirit by focusing our attention on God, the only Presence and the only Power, and then we will discover the great truths of the Bible: *If thine eye be single, thy whole body is full of light. With mine eyes stayed on Thee, there is no evil on my pathway.*

3

The Wonders of the Subconscious and the Science of Prayer

Our mind is a garden. In this garden which is called the Garden of Eden, or the Garden of God, we plant seeds. Regardless of what we sow with our conscious mind, our subconscious will bring it to pass. Therefore, let us sow the thoughts of peace, happiness, guidance, and goodwill. Let us meditate on these qualities and accept them in our conscious reasoning mind. Whatever we accept in our conscious reasoning mind our subconscious, which is like the soil, will accept without question and bring it to pass.

Man's subconscious assumption and convictions of himself dictate and control all his conscious actions. This is why man is belief expressed. Believe nothing, therefore, which does not contribute to your health, happiness, and peace of mind. Your subconscious mind will objectify faithfully the habitual thinking of your conscious mind. Whatever you believe is true in your conscious mind, your subconscious will accept without question; be very careful that you accept only that which is true, noble, and Godlike.

Whatever you impress on your subconscious mind is expressed on the screen of space as conditions, experience, and events. As ye sow in your subconscious mind, so shall ye reap in your body and environment.

One time Caruso was struck with stage fright. He said his throat was paralyzed due to spasms caused by intense fear which constricted the muscles of his throat. Perspiration poured copiously down his face. He was ashamed because in a few minutes he had to go out on the stage, yet he was shaking with fear and trepidation. He said, "They will laugh at me. I can't sing." Then he shouted in the presence of those behind the stage, "The little me wants to strangle the Big Me within." He said to the little me, "Get out of here, the Big Me wants to sing through me." By the Big Me he meant God, the Limitless Power within him, and he began to shout, "Get out, get out, the Big Me is going to sing!" This released the Almighty Power within him. When the cue came he walked out on the stage and sang gloriously, majestically, enthralling the audience.

In your subconscious mind, as William James wrote, is the Power that moves the world. It is the Almighty Power of God. Your subconscious is one with Infinite Intelligence and Boundless Wisdom. It is fed by hidden springs and is called the Law of Life. Whatever you impress upon the subconscious, the latter will move heaven and earth to bring it to pass. It knows no obstacles. We must impress it with the right ideas and constructive thoughts. Your subconscious mind is impersonal and nonselective. It is called the wife. The Bible says, *The husband shall be head of the wife*. Many people take these statements literally with all kinds of absurd consequences. The Bible is a psychological textbook dealing with the principles and modes of living. It deals with moods, tones, and vibrations; it talks about the male and female principle within each of us.

The conscious mind is the husband. It is head of the wife because the subconscious is amenable to suggestion and controlled by suggestion. Whatever your conscious mind decrees, your subconscious will honor and execute accordingly. You can believe a lie, and your subconscious will express whatever is impressed upon it, good, bad or indifferent, and will bring it to pass.

The reason there is so much chaos and misery in the world is because people do not understand the interaction of the male and female principle within themselves. When these two principles work in accord, in concord, in peace, and synchronously together, we have health, happiness, peace, and joy. There is no sickness or discord when the conscious and subconscious work together harmoniously and peacefully. What is true subjectively is true objectively also. For example, a woman loves to follow a man who leads. *Man*, in the Bible, is a person who plans, chooses, directs, imagines, decides, and gets things done.

What are we planting with our conscious mind? The conscious mind is the reasoning mind; it analyzes, weighs, dissects, investigates, scrutinizes, and chooses. *Choose ye this day whom ye will serve*. What are we choosing? If we are resentful or hateful, we are sowing these seeds, and we may have growths in our bodies to conform to our destructive mental attitude. The growths may appear in different parts of the body.

The tomb of Hermes was opened with a sort of mystic awe because people believed that the greatest secret of the ages was contained therein. The secret was, *As within, so without. As above, so below*. In other words—whatever is impressed in the subconscious is expressed. These were truths proclaimed by Moses, Isaiah, Jesus, Buddha, Zoroaster, Laotze, and all the illumined seers of the ages. The spiritually minded man who is alert and alive knows that the greatest secret in the world is the discovery of the Presence of God in man.

The great secret of the ancient mystery temple schools was that the I AM in you is God. That was the great secret. When you say, I AM, you are announcing Pure Being, Life, Undifferentiated Awareness, and the Presence of God in you. This is the great secret. The so-called secret of Hermes' tomb, *As within, so without*, is no secret; it has always been known. In other words, whatever you feel as true subjectively is expressed as conditions, experiences, and events. We can never deviate from the truth, that as a man thinks and feels, so is he. Your thought and feeling control your destiny. The intake and outgo must be equal. Motion and emotion must balance. As in heaven (your own consciousness), so in earth (in your body and environment). This is the Law of Life.

You will find throughout all nature the law of action and reaction, of rest and motion. These two must balance; then there will be balance and equilibrium. Realize that within us is the very life of the Divine. We are here to let it flow through us rhythmically and harmoniously.

Pray frequently as follows: "God flows through me as harmony, health, peace, beauty, and right action. God speaks, thinks, and acts through me now, and I am expressing the Life Divine."

Everyone can do something far more wonderful than he or she is doing. Every boy wants to be a hero. He must be taught to express and direct his talents and express his desires in the right way along Godlike channels. Something within the boy tells him he is born to be victorious and triumphant. God whispers to him through urges and intimations, "Go forth and conquer." The Higher Self knows he can do it. The desires, ideas, plans, and purposes that you have are the qualities of the God-Presence in you saying that you can be, you can do, and you can have; otherwise, you would not have the desire.

Your subconscious is impersonal and nonselective; it is all-wise and knows the answers to all questions. It does not argue with you controversially. It does not say, "You must not impress me with that."

The husband impregnates his wife, and she brings forth a child. If they hate each other, the child may be born blind, deaf, or deformed. The creative act should be based on Divine Love where each one sees the God in the other. As a result the child comes forth corresponding to that creative mood; it is a lovely child spiritually, mentally, and physically. You know in your heart that this is true.

Psychologically speaking, the husband is the idea, and feeling is the mother. These two must agree, producing a child of the mind which is answered prayer. There is an intelligence in the atom—there must be—when two atoms of hydrogen combine with one of oxygen and create a molecule of water.

There is life, intelligence, and power in all nature which operates instinctively, automatically, mechanically, and mathematically. How will you get your subconscious to work for you? First of all, realize the great secret that the intake and the outgo must be equal. The impression and the expression must be equal. All frustration is due to unfulfilled desires. For example, when you say, "I can't do this," "I am too old now," "I can't meet this obligation," "I was born on the wrong side of the tracks," "I don't know the right politician," you are putting up resistance, and frustration sets in. You are blocking your own good.

When we set up obstacles and delays in our minds, we are saying in effect that we do not believe that the Infinite Intelligence which gave us these desires can fulfill them. We are denying the Presence and the Power of God which is within our own subconscious mind. We are setting up opposition, friction, delays, impediments, and difficulties. This generates congestion, followed by sickness, frustration, and neurotic tendencies.

Affirm boldly: "The God Presence which gave me this desire leads, guides, and reveals to me the perfect plan." This causes the intake and the outgo to become equal; the motion and the emotion, the impression and the expression are one; as within, so without. What you felt within is expressed in the without, and there is balance, equilibrium, and equanimity.

If you think negatively, destructively, and viciously, these thoughts generate emotions which must be expressed, and being negative find an outlet—perhaps as ulcers, heart trouble, tensions, and anxieties. All this is due to the fact that we have placed delays, obstacles, and impediments in our own minds.

Cease blocking the Divine Energy which always seeks to flow harmoniously through us. We must become channels for the Divine. We are here to release the Love, the Light, the Truth, and the Beauty of God. This is the Will of God for every single being in the world. You are here to express wave upon wave of joy, peace, and happiness; all these are the qualities of God seeking expression through you. The Bible says, *Out of the heart are the issues of Life. The heart is a Chaldean word meaning the subconscious. Keep thy heart with all diligence, for out of it are the issues of life. As a man thinketh in his heart, so is he.*

Whatever you consciously think and feel as true, your subconscious will bring it to pass. If you say, "Whenever I eat mushrooms, I get acute indigestion," the subconscious mind will take that suggestion as a request. When the time comes for you to eat mushrooms, the subconscious says, "The boss doesn't like mushrooms." For example, if you say, "If I take coffee at night before going to bed, I cannot sleep," the subconscious reacts as if to say, "The boss doesn't want to sleep tonight." If you say, "There is no way out, I am lost, there is no way out of this dilemma, I am stymied and blocked," you will be blocked. You will be frustrated; you will get no answer or response from your subconscious.

If you want the subconscious mind to work for you, give it the right request and attain its cooperation. It is always working for you; it is controlling your heartbeat this minute and also your breathing. It heals a cut on your finger, and its tendency is lifeward, forever seeking to take care of you and preserve you. The subconscious has a mind of its own, but it accepts your patterns of thought and mental imagery. If you are the captain on the bridge and give the wrong orders to the men below, they will follow your instructions; the ship may go on the rocks.

Say to your subconscious, "I know there is an answer. I accept it now and give thanks." This affirmative attitude should produce a response from your Deeper Mind which knows only the answer. Your subconscious can read the contents of a closed safe; it knows the motives of another person. Suppose you are called upon to sign a document and you are wondering whether you should do so or not. Affirm as follows: "Infinite Intelligence guides, directs, and tells me what to do." You will get a response, perhaps a persistent feeling which tells you not to sign it. You asked and received an answer. It did not speak in a voice, but you felt an urge or predominant feeling. Listen to this silent inner knowing which follows true prayer.

What is your idea or feeling about yourself now? Every part of your being expresses that idea; your vitality, body, financial status, friends, and social status represent a perfect reflection of the idea you have of yourself.

When you pray for guidance, the answer is in your subconscious mind; it knows the answer to everything. However, if you say, "I don't think there is any way out. I am all mixed up and confused. Why don't I get an answer?" you are neutralizing your prayer, and like the soldier marking time, you do not get anywhere.

We injure ourselves by the ideas which we entertain. How often have you wounded yourself by getting angry, fearful, jealous, or vengeful? These are the poisons that enter your subconscious. You were not born with these negative attitudes. Many people say that they are victims of the past and blame the subconscious. Feed your subconscious mind lifegiving thoughts, and you extirpate and expunge all the negative patterns lodged therein. Tune in on the Infinite Life, Love, and Power of God and become a channel for His Love now; then all the past is wiped out and remembered no more.

Let us dwell on a simple truth about your subconscious—it is a one way mind. If you say, "How will I get the subconscious to work for me?" The answer is: watch your conscious mind and make sure the thoughts you habitually think are based on whatsoever things are true, lovely, just, and of good report. Your mission is to take care of your conscious mind, and the subconscious will take care of itself.

The subconscious never ceases to function. Feed it with true premises. The intimations and urges of the subconscious are always lifeward. For example, if you took some bad food, it would cause you to regurgitate. If you took some poison, the subconscious would neutralize it if you completely trusted its wonder-working power. However, if you persist in giving it negative patterns, it has to follow your orders. By filling your mind with the Truths of God, you crowd out of your mind everything unlike God. The lower is subject to the higher. Begin now to take care of your conscious mind, knowing in your heart and soul that your subconscious mind is always expressing, reproducing, and manifesting, according to your habitual thinking. The subconscious mind is the preserver of your body; it watches over you while you sleep and digests your food.

If you want to heal yourself tonight, sit down quietly and relax your body. Affirm slowly, peacefully, and lovingly: "My toes are relaxed, my feet are relaxed, my ankles are relaxed, my shoulders are relaxed, my neck is relaxed, my head is relaxed, my face is relaxed, my abdominal muscles are relaxed, my whole being is completely relaxed, and I feel wonderful."

In this relaxed state pray as follows: "The Miraculous Healing Power is saturating every cell of my being. My whole body is now being transformed into the pattern on the Mount. The Infinite Healing Presence which created me is now making me whole and perfect, and I rejoice that this is so."

Do this quietly several times, feeling the truth of what you affirm. You know what you are doing and why you are doing it. Your thoughts of wholeness, beauty, and perfection sink down into the subconscious which releases the Healing Presence, making you whole, pure, relaxed, and perfect. Your subconscious has the perfect pattern of your lungs, heart, eyes, and all the organs of your body. There is one prerequisite before using the subconscious to heal—you must not have any anger, ill will, or hatred toward anyone. You cannot expect the Healing Presence to flow through a contaminated consciousness. Water does not flow through a pipe filled with debris and rust. You must forgive everyone.

If someone has hurt you, pray as follows: "I wish for him (or her) harmony, health, peace, joy, and all the blessings of heaven. I do this sincerely. He is free and I am free. I know when I have forgiven the other because when I meet him in my mind a wave of peace goes forth to him, and I sincerely rejoice in hearing good news about him."

The subconscious will respond, but it expects you to come to a decision, to a true judgment in your conscious mind. Come to a conclusion, be definite and specific in your mind. When you say meaningfully, "Divine Order is mine, Divine right action is mine, a happy ending is mine," the subconscious will respond accordingly. Wish for everyone what you wish for yourself. Be sincere and honest about it. As you bless others, you are blessing yourself.

Affirm boldly: "Success is mine, wealth is mine, Divine right action is mine, Divine guidance is mine, I mean this, I am sincere." Do not equivocate or vacillate, and you will discover wonders happening in your life. If you say, "I don't know the way out," you will get no response whatever, and more confusion will be yours. If there is inharmony in the office, pray as follows: "The harmony and the love of God reign supreme in the minds and hearts of all. I decree this, and it comes to pass in Divine Order." You will get results from your subconscious mind because you came to a definite decision.

Do you trust this Deeper Mind? Do you say, "It is the Great Executive, it knows the answer"? If you do, you will get results; the Divine solution will follow through the Wisdom and Intelligence of the Almighty.

Another great secret of the subconscious is that the subconscious deals with ends, not with means. It knows how to bring your request to pass. If you are planning how you are going to get an answer: "Whence?" "When?" "Where?" you are defeating the purpose. You are blocking the action of your subconscious. It says in effect, "You don't trust me. You do not believe me. You don't think that I am the Great Executive. You do not know that I have the know-how of accomplishment." That is what it seems to say to you.

Go to the end in prayer. See and feel the happy ending, the joyous solution, the way out, and the subconscious will release its majesty and wisdom in your behalf. Do not try to browbeat, intimidate, or coerce the subconscious. If you are using effort and force, you are presupposing an opposing power. This indicates a conflict in the mind. There is only One Power. If there were two powers, one would cancel out the other, resulting in strife and contention everywhere.

You sign blank checks when you make such statements as: "There is not enough to go around," or "There is a shortage," "Maybe I can't pay the mortgage," etc. If you are full of fear about the future, you are also writing a blank check and attracting negative conditions to yourself. The subconscious mind takes your fear and belief as your requests, proceeding in its own way to bring obstacles, delays, lack, and limitation into your life. To him that hath the feeling of wealth, more wealth shall be added; to him that hath the feeling of lack, more lack shall be added.

The subconscious mind also gives you compound interest. Every morning as you awaken, deposit thoughts of prosperity, success, wealth, and peace; dwell upon these concepts; busy your mind with them as often as possible. These positive thoughts will find their way as deposits in your subconscious mind and bring forth abundance and prosperity.

I can hear you saying, "Oh, I did that and nothing happened." You did not get the results because you indulged in fear thoughts perhaps ten minutes later and neutralized the good you had affirmed. When you place a seed in the ground, you do not dig it up. Suppose, for example, you are going to say, "I shall not be able to make that payment." Before you get further than, "I shall—" stop the sentence, and dwell on a positive, constructive statement such as, "By day and by night I am being prospered in all my ways."

To prosper means to advance along all lines in wisdom, understanding, and material possessions. Money represents wealth; it is a symbol of exchange. It represents freedom, opulence, luxury, and refinement. I do not know of anyone who says that he has too much; in all probability he is looking for more.

If you are experiencing a financial block, the obstruction is in your own mind. You can now destroy that mental block. Get on mental good terms with everyone.

As you go to sleep tonight, practice the many techniques which we occasionally refer to. Repeat the word, "Wealth," quietly, easily, and feelingly. Do this over and over again as a lullaby. Lull yourself to sleep with the word, "Wealth." You should be amazed at the results. Wealth should flow to you in avalanches of abundance; this is another example of the miracles of the subconscious mind.

VII
Why Did This Happen to Me?

(1962)

This short work lays out Murphy's most radical thesis, and it has some commonality with Christian Science. He writes that even someone possessed by loving thoughts can fall ill or experience other forms of suffering if the individual believes in the reality of his condition. *Murphy's point is that the ultimate law of mind and the ultimate reality of life are goodness, health, and growth. That is the true nature of things. I think he would agree with the statement that while evil* occurs, *it does not actually* exist.   —MH

Remember ye not the former things,
neither consider the things of old.
ISAIAH 43:18.

. . . But this one thing I do,
forgetting those things which are behind,
and reaching forth unto those things which are before,
I press toward the mark for the prize . . .
PHIL. 3:13–14.

Why Did This Happen To Me?

Whatsoever a man soweth, so also shall he reap. This means that if we plant thoughts of peace, harmony, health, and prosperity, we shall reap accordingly; and that if we sow thoughts of sickness, lack, strife, and contention, we shall reap these things. We must remember that our subconscious mind is like the soil; it will grow whatever type of seed we plant in the garden of our mind. We sow thoughts, Biblically speaking, when we believe them wholeheartedly, and it is what we really believe deep down in our hearts that we demonstrate.

I had a friend who was bedridden with disease and on visiting her at a hospital in London, England, she said to me. "Why did this happen to me? What did I do to deserve this? Why is God angry at me? Why is God punishing me?" Her friends pointed out to me how kindhearted and deeply spiritual she was, and that she was a pillar of the church, etc.

It is true that she was an excellent person in many ways, but she believed in the reality of her sickness and that the condition was incurable. She believed that her heart was governed by laws of its own, independent of her thinking. This was her belief, so naturally, she demonstrated accordingly. She changed her belief and began to realize that her body was spiritual and that when she changed her mind, she changed her body. She began to cease giving power to the sickness in her thought and prayed as follows: "The Infinite Healing Presence is flowing through me as harmony, health, peace, wholeness, and perfection. God's Healing Love indwells every cell." She repeated this prayer frequently, and following her change of belief she had a wonderful healing. This woman lived in fear of a heart attack for several years, not knowing that what we fear most comes to pass.

The law of life is the law of belief. Trouble of any kind is nature's alarm signal that we are thinking wrongly in that direction, and nothing but a change of thought can set us free. Man is belief expressed (Quimby), and we demonstrate what we really believe. There is a law of cause and effect operating at all times, and nothing happens to man without his mental consent and participation. You do not have to think of an accident to have it befall you.

Dr. Paul Tournier, famous French psychiatrist, writes about a man who cut his hand with a saw and blamed the so-called accident on the fact that the wood which he was cutting was very wet. Dr. Tournier knew that there was a mental and emotional cause behind the severe cut on the man's hand. He discovered that the man was very irritated toward his employer, and furthermore he had considerable rancor and hostility toward a former employer who had discharged him. Dr. Tournier explained to the man that when he is irritated and upset emotionally, his efforts become uncoordinated and jerky, and thus the accident had happened.

In the thirteenth chapter of Luke we read the following: *There were present at that season some that told him of the Galilaeans, whose blood Pilate had mingled with their sacrifices. And Jesus answering said unto them, Suppose ye that these Galilaeans were sinners above all the Galilaeans, because they suffered such things? I tell you, Nay: but, except ye repent, ye shall all likewise perish. Or those eighteen, upon whom the tower in Siloam fell, and slew them, think ye that they were sinners above all men that dwelt in Jerusalem? I tell you, Nay: but, except ye repent, ye shall all likewise perish.*

Jesus denies categorically that the victims of such calamities are worse sinners than other men, and added *Except ye repent, ye shall likewise perish.* Misfortune, accidents, and tragedies of various kinds are signs of mental and emotional disorders that have broken out into manifestation. To repent means to think in a new way, to turn back to God and align our thoughts and mental imagery with the Infinite Life, Love, Truth, and Beauty of God, and then we become channels for the Divine.

Still your mind several times a day and affirm slowly, quietly, and lovingly, "God flows through me as harmony, health, peace, joy, wholeness, and perfection. God walks and talks in me. God's spell is always around me, and wherever I go God's Wisdom governs me in all my ways, and Divine right action prevails. All my ways are ways of pleasantness, and all my paths are peace."

As you dwell on these eternal verities, you will establish patterns of Divine Order in your subconscious mind, and whatever you impress is expressed; therefore, you will find yourself watched over at all times by an Overshadowing Presence, your Heavenly Father, who responds to you when you call upon Him.

All of us are in the race mind, the great psychic sea of life. The race mind believes in sickness, accident, death, misfortune, and tragedies of all kinds, and if we do not repent, i.e., if we do not do our own thinking, the race mind will do our thinking for us. Gradually the thoughts of the race mind impinging on our consciousness, may reach a point of saturation and precipitate an accident, sudden illness, or calamity. The majority of people do not think, they think they think. You are thinking when you differentiate between that which is false and that which is true. To think is to choose. You have the capacity to say yes and no. Say yes to the Truth and reject everything unlike God or the Truth. If the mental instrument could not choose, you would not be an individual. You have the ability to accept and reject. *Think on whatsoever things are lovely, whatsoever things are just, whatsoever things are honest, whatsoever things are pure . . . think on these things.*

You are thinking when you know that there is an Infinite Intelligence which responds to your thoughts and that no matter what the problem is, as you think about a Divine solution and the happy ending, you will find a subjective wisdom within you responding to you and revealing to you the perfect plan and showing you the way you should go.

Some months ago a woman visited me, stating that she had an organic lesion for several years which failed to heal. She had taken all kinds of therapy including X-ray. She had prayed and sought prayer therapy from others without results. She told me, "God has it in for me. I'm a sinner, this is why I am being punished." She also told me that she went to a man who hypnotized her, read her past, and had the effrontery and the audacity to tell her that she was a victim of karma, that she had wounded people in a former life, punishing them unjustly, and that now she was suffering and reaping her just deserts. Poignantly she asked, "Do you think this is why I can't be healed?"

All this is so much folderol and a monstrous absurdity. The above explanation compounded the misery and pain of the woman and offered no cure or solace. I explained to her an age-old Truth that there is but one Power called God. It is the Creative Intelligence in all of us which created us. This Power becomes to us what we believe It to be. If a person thinks that God is punishing him and that he must suffer, *according to his thought and belief is it done unto him. As a man thinketh in his heart so is he.* This means that man's thoughts and feelings create his destiny. Man is what he thinks all day long, and if a man fails to think constructively, wisely, and judiciously, then someone else or the race mind will do his thinking for him, and perhaps make a complete mess of his life.

If you believe that God is Infinite Goodness, Boundless Love, Absolute Harmony, and Boundless Wisdom, the

God-Presence will respond accordingly to you by the law of reciprocal relationship, and you will find yourself blessed in countless ways. The forces of life are not evil; it depends how we use them. Atomic energy is not evil, it is good or bad depending on the way we use it. Man can use electricity to kill another or to vacuum the floor. You can use water to quench a child's thirst or drown it. The wind which blows the ship on the rocks can also carry it to safety. The uses to which all things or objects in the world are put are determined by the thoughts of man. It is the mind of man which determines the use of the forces and objects in the world. Good and evil are movements in the mind of man relative to the One Power which is whole, pure, and perfect. The Creative Force is in man. There is no power in the manifest universe except we give power to externals. This woman was seeking justification and alibis for her suffering. She was looking outside herself instead of realizing the cause is always in her subconscious mind.

I asked her to tell me about her relationship with men. She confessed that she had an illicit love affair five years previously and that she felt guilty and full of remorse. This unresolved remorse was the psychic wound behind her organic lesion. She realized that God was not punishing her, but she was punishing herself by her own thoughts. The lesion was solidified thought which she could unthink. Life or God does not punish. If you burn your finger, Life proceeds to reduce the edema, gives you new skin, and restores it to wholeness. If you eat some tainted food, Life causes you to regurgitate and seek to restore you to perfect health. The ancients said that the doctor dresses the wound, and God heals it.

The lesion and the morbid symptoms that no medical treatment or prayer therapy could heal, or had been able to cure, disappeared in a week. There is no worse suffering than a guilty conscience and certainly none more destructive. This woman had been punishing herself for five years by her destructive thinking, and when she ceased to condemn herself and began to claim that the Infinite Healing Presence was saturating her whole being and that God indwells every cell of her body, the lesion disappeared. If you had been misusing the principle of electricity or chemistry for fifty years and you suddenly used it correctly, surely you would not say that the principle of electricity had a grudge against you because you had misused it. Likewise, no matter how long you may have used your mind in a negative and destructive manner, the minute you begin to use it the right way, right results follow. *Remember not the former things, neither consider the things of old.* ISAIAH 43:18.

A man who came to see me some months ago was gradually losing his vision. He was attributing it to lack of vitamins, heredity factors, and pointed out that his grandfather went blind at eighty years of age. He belonged to a strange cult, and the cult leader, after reading his horoscope, said the planets were in a malefic configuration and that this was the cause of his failing vision. It is well known in psychosomatic circles today that psychic factors play a definite role in all disease. Nearsightedness can be brought on by workings of the mind. Treating the mental and emotional factors of the individual rather than the eye may reveal the basic emotional factor, the reason why the subconscious mind is selecting an ailment which tends to shut out everything except the immediate surroundings.

Dr. Francis Dunbar states that certain emotional reactions can cause the involuntary muscles to twist the eyeball out of shape. In talking to this man, he revealed that he hated the sight of his mother-in-law who was living in his home. He was full of suppressed rage, and his emotional system which could not stand the strain any longer selected the eyes as the scapegoat. The explanation was the cure in this case. He was surprised to learn that negative emotions, if persisted in, snarl up in the subconscious mind and being negative must have a negative outlet. The negative commands to his subconscious mind, "I hate the sight of her," "I don't want to see her anymore," were accepted by the deeper mind as a request which brought it to pass.

He made arrangements for his mother-in-law to live elsewhere and prayed for her by releasing her to God and wishing for her all the blessings of Heaven. His vision began to improve almost immediately, and in two weeks his eyesight was restored to normal. He knew he had forgiven his mother-in-law because he could meet her in his mind, and there was no longer any sting. He was trying to justify his failing vision by explaining it in terms of outside causes rather than his own mind.

A deficiency of Vitamin A can cause ophthalmia which is an inflammation of the conjunctiva or of the eyeball; nevertheless, this could be due to ignorance, indifference, or negligence on the part of the individual. The cause in this case would be stupidity or carelessness, and the latter is a state of mind or simply a lack of knowledge. Vitamin A is omnipresent and we should have the intelligence to use it.

You cannot dodge or circumvent the law of mind. It is done unto you as you believe, and a belief is a thought in the mind. No external power or evil entity is trying to lure or harm you. People are constantly attributing their ailments to the atmosphere, the weather, to malpractice, evil entities, germs, viruses, and diet. Man pollutes the air with his strange notions and false doctrines. If a man believes that by being near an electric fan he will catch cold or get a stiff neck, that belief when accepted by him becomes his master and ruler and causes him to experience a cold. This is why the Bible says, *According to your faith is it done unto you*. The fan has no power to give anyone a stiff neck; it is harmless. Your faith can be used two ways. You can have faith in an invisible virus to give you the flu, or you can have faith in the Invisible Spirit within you to flow through you as harmony, health, and peace.

Realize God cannot be sick and the Spirit in you is God; what is true of God is true of you. Believe this and you will never be sick for *according to your faith* (in health and happiness) *is it done unto you*. Emerson said, "He (man) thinks his fate alien because the copula is hidden. But the soul contains the event that shall befall it; for the event is only the actualization of its thoughts, and what we pray to ourselves for is always granted. The event is the print of your form. It fits you like your skin." *Fate* by R. W. Emerson.

The Devil in the Bible means ignorance or misunderstanding. Spell live backward and you have evil. Your evil is an inversion of the Life-Principle which is God. God moves as a unity and seeks to express Himself through you as beauty, love, joy, peace, and Divine Order. The false idea in your mind is called the adversary, devil, Satan, etc. The devils which bedevil man are enmity, strife, hatred, revenge, hostility, self-condemnation, and other negative emotions. If man fails to believe in the goodness of God and in a God of Love, the extent to which he believes this can well be his so-called devil which is the source of his pains, aches, and misfortunes.

A woman wrote me stating that her daughter was watching a group of men fighting on the streets of New York and that a bullet hit her daughter necessitating the amputation of two fingers—and what was the cause of it? Was it God's will? Was it punishment for her sins that this accident occurred? The answer is in the negative to all these questions of the mother. God does not judge or punish; good and evil are the movements of man's own mind. It is very primitive thinking to believe that God is punishing us or that a devil is tempting us. Our state of consciousness is always made manifest. Men, women, and children are constantly testifying to our state of consciousness. Our state of consciousness is always cause.

We do not know the contents of this girl's mind. If she were hateful, resentful, or full of hostility and self-condemnation, she could have attracted such a condition to herself. We must remember that the majority of people do not discipline, control, or direct their thinking and mental imagery along God-like channels; therefore, their failure to think constructively and harmoniously from the standpoint of the Infinite One means that they leave their minds open to the irrational mass mind which is full of fears, hates, jealousies, and all kinds of negative happenings.

Man's failure to think the right way is as bad as thinking negatively and destructively. As a boy, I remember a farmer in Ireland who waited behind a fence every day for over a week in order to shoot the landlord when he passed by. One day he was going behind the usual fence and he stumbled, the rifle went off, and he was shot fatally. I did not understand the reason at that time, and like others, I believed it to be an accident. There are no accidents; there is a mind, a mood, a feeling behind that car, train, bicycle, and also behind the gun. This man had murder in his heart for a long time, and his subconscious responded accordingly.

No manifestation cometh unto me, save I the Father draw it. The father is your state of consciousness, your own creative power, and no experience comes to you except there is an affinity in your own mind. Two unlike things repel each other. If you walk and talk with God and believe that God is guiding you and that the Law of Harmony is always governing you, then you cannot be on a train that is wrecked because discord and harmony do not dwell together. The mother added in her letter as a postscript, "My daughter cannot get her fingers back through prayer." I don't know why people are so decisive and categorical in their statements that a man cannot grow a leg or finger if missing.

Let me quote from *He Heals To-Day* by Elsie Salmon: "Mildred was three years old when brought to me. She was born without a left hand. The arm ended in a point no bigger than the size of an index finger well above the wrist. Within a month the point at the end of the deformed arm had doubled in size and was quite plump, whereupon the father, now seeing this remarkable development, said, 'Anything can happen.' The following month there was a formation which looked like a thumb and which, at the time, we thought was a thumb. About three months following we found that this was not a thumb at all but that the growth was the whole hand at the end of the arm and this was unfolding like a flower before our eyes."

She concludes by saying that those who were skeptical are now accepting it as an established fact. Perhaps we should take a lesson from the rhinoceros. When you take off his horns and cut out the roots, he grows new horns. Cut the legs off a crab, and he grows new legs. If a man believed he could grow a new finger, leg, or any organ, he could experience his belief.

Let us cease blaming others, let us look within for the cause of all. Believe in God, in the goodness of God, in the love of God, and in God's guidance, and you will find that all your ways will be those of pleasantness, and all your paths will be paths of peace. You are belief expressed.

Afterword

Takeaway Points

My hope this that this collection will grant you new insights every time you return to it. Do not be afraid to change your ideas—refining old ideas, arriving at new ones, and discarding what proves unhelpful or unverifiable. Too often we approach spiritual teachings with an "all or nothing" attitude, feeling that we must be in total agreement with what we read or otherwise move on to another set of ideas. Allow Murphy's insights, gathered over a lifetime, to sit with you for a time. Below are some points that I hope will help you on your journey. —MH

1. Nearly every religious, psychological, and classical philosophy agrees: *What you think dramatically affects your quality of life.* That statement may mean different things to different people, but it is the closest we possess to a universal ethic.

2. We all possess a quality of mind that goes beyond the cognitive and analytic—a storehouse of emotive thoughts, mental pictures, and deep-seated memories. Call it the psyche, the subconscious, or the creative mind, this storehouse harbors deeply insightful and causative power, if properly harnessed. This suggestive power can solve problems and shape circumstances in ways that we do not always suspect.

3. You can tap the positive agencies of your mind by setting aside time just before going to sleep at night to reflect on a cherished aim, or the solution to a problem. This is a supple period in which to impress suggestions on your psyche or subconscious.

4. Form vivid, believable, emotionally charged mental pictures—*and stick with them*. Consistency is key in training your subconscious. You may be surprised by an uncanny symmetry between long-ago mental pictures and your current circumstance.

5. Never force a mental image. Forced effort invites failure. Be relaxed, calm, and confident when impressing the subconscious. If you find this difficult, take a break and return to it when you're in a calm and confident mood. There is nothing wrong with stepping away from your efforts and returning when your emotions are on your side.

Afterword

6. Once you have acted to impress your creative mind with an image or outcome, do not dwell on the ways and means of your accomplishment—these will reach your conscious mind in the form of hunches, "happy accidents," fortuitous relationships, and breakthrough ideas.

7. Your solutions, however remarkable, are likely to reach you through *established means*. This is one of subtlest and most important points of practical spirituality. A desired thing is likely to arrive through channels and mechanics that are already established: something will not appear from out of the blue but may come in a manner that first seems ordinary or conventional. Hence you are apt to overlook it. A solution, condition, or object may reach you in ways that differ from your expectations. Be watchful and flexible.

8. Specialize in a field of work that you love, and strive to know more about it than anyone else. Passion, concentration of energies, and mental focus act powerfully upon your psyche. A deeply felt, well defined, and unconflicted aim is the surest way to harness the energies of your mind.

9. Do not get dejected or stuck if some of the methods and ideas that you encounter in your spiritual search seem paradoxical. Not everything will reveal itself

along neat and stratified lines. Learning to live with paradox is one of the hallmarks of maturity.

If you want to make one definite and gainful investment in your future, cultivate a positive, meditative, and confident state of mind. Your sense of self-respect and capability will impress itself on your psyche and bring you unexpected opportunities, relationships, and ideas. You are as your mind is.

Joseph Murphy Timeline

This timeline is intended as a resource for writers, seekers, and students of Joseph Murphy and of the American metaphysical tradition in general. It is also intended as a corrective to some of the misinformation that has circulated about Murphy, such as his studying with Swami Vivekananda (1863–1902), English judge and mystic Thomas Troward (1847–1916)—both of whom lived and worked at disparate times and distances from Murphy—or dubious details about his childhood home and educational background. This timeline represents the most complete information that I could locate through immigration records, Murphy's few interviews, and cross-referenced sources. —MH

1898

Joseph Denis Murphy is born on May 20, the fourth of five children (three girls and two boys) to a devout Catholic family on the Southern Coast of Ireland in Ballydehob, County Cork. Murphy's father was headmaster of a local boys high school.

Circa 1914–1915

After being educated locally, Murphy studies chemistry in Dublin. Bowing to his parents' wishes he enrolls briefly in a Jesuit seminary. Dissatisfied with his studies, and unbelieving of the doctrine of no salvation outside the church, Murphy leaves seminary.

Circa 1916–1918

Murphy works as a pharmacist for England's Royal Army Medical Corps during World War I.

1918–1921

Murphy works as a in pharmacist in Dublin. He earns a monthly salary of about $10.

1922

Dissatisfied with traditional religion and finding limited opportunities to practice as a chemist, Murphy just shy of age 24 arrives in New York City on April 17, 1922. He is accompanied by his wife, Madolyn, who is eight years his senior (wedding date unknown). He arrives with $23. Applies for citizenship in August.

1923–1938

Murphy works as a pharmacist in New York City including at a pharmacy counter at the Algonquin Hotel. He deepens his study into metaphysics and years later recounts having studied with the figure of Abdullah, a black man of Jewish descent whom Murphy's contemporary and fellow New Yorker, Neville Goddard (1905-1972), wrote that he studied with. Murphy reports that Abdullah tells Murphy that he

Joseph Murphy Timeline

actually had three brothers, not two. Upon checking with his mother, Murphy discovers that he had a third brother who died at birth and was never spoken of.

Circa 1931
Murphy begins attending the Church of the Healing Christ in New York City, presided over by Emmet Fox.

Circa 1938
Murphy is ordained as a Divine Science minster. He continues to work as a druggist and chemist.

1941
Murphy begins broadcasting metaphysical sermons over the radio.

1942
Murphy enlists as a pharmacist in the New York State National Guard, a post he holds until 1948.

1943
Murphy studies Tarot in New York City and comes to believe in symbolic correspondences between the Tarot cards and Scripture.

1945
Murphy writes his first book, *This Is It: The Art Of Metaphysical Demonstration*.

1946
Murphy is ordained as a Religious Science Minister in Los Angeles. He soon takes over the pulpit of the Institute

for Religious Science in Rochester, New York. He publishes the short works *Wheels of Truth*, *The Perfect Answer*, and *Fear Not*.

1948
Murphy publishes *St. John Speaks*, *Love is Freedom*, and *The Twelve Powers Mystically Explained*.

1949
Murphy is re-ordained into Divine Science and becomes minister of the Los Angeles Divine Science Church, a post he will hold for the next 28 years. Services become so popular that they are held at the Wilshire Ebell Theater.

1952
Publishes *Riches Are Your Right*.

1953
Publishes *The Miracles of Your Mind*, *The Fragrance of God*, and *How to Use the Power of Prayer*.

1954
Publishes *The Magic of Faith* and *The Meaning of Reincarnation*, one of his most controversial books.

1955
Publishes *Believe in Yourself* and *How to Attract Money*, one of his most enduringly popular works.

1956
Murphy writes *Traveling With God* in which he recounts his international speaking tours, comparing New Thought with

various global traditions. He also publishes *Peace Within Yourself* (*St. John Speaks* revised) and *Prayer Is the Answer*.

1957
Publishes *How to Use Your Healing Power*.

1958
Publishes the short works *Quiet Moments with God*, *Pray Your Way Through It*, *The Healing Power of Love*, *Stay Young Forever*, *Mental Poisons and Their Antidotes*, and *How to Pray With a Deck of Cards*.

1959
Publishes *Living Without Strain*.

1960
Publishes *Techniques in Prayer Therapy*.

1961
Publishes *You Can Change Your Whole Life* and *Nuclear Religion*.

1962
Publishes *Why Did This Happen to Me?*

1963
Publishes *The Power of Your Subconscious Mind*, which becomes a worldwide bestseller and a landmark of New Thought philosophy. The book's publication makes Murphy into one of the most widely known metaphysical writers in the world.

1964
Publishes *The Miracle of Mind Dynamics*.

Joseph Murphy Timeline

1965

Publishes *The Amazing Laws of Cosmic Mind Power*.

1966

Publishes *Your Infinite Power to Be Rich*.

1968

Publishes *The Cosmic Power Within You*.

1969

Publishes *Infinite Power for Richer Living*.

1970

Publishes *Secrets of the I Ching*.

1971

Publishes *Psychic Perception: The Magic of Extrasensory Perception*.

1972

Publishes *Miracle Power for Infinite Riches*

1973

Publishes *Telepsychics: The Magic Power of Perfect Living* (1973)

1974

Publishes *The Cosmic Energizer: Miracle Power of the Universe* (1974)

1976

Murphy's first wife Madolyn dies. He remarries his secretary, Jean L. Murphy (nee Wright), also a Divine

Science minister. He writes *Great Bible Truths for Human Problems*.

1977
Publishes *Within You Is the Power*

1979
Publishes *Songs of God*

1980
Publishes *How to Use the Laws of Mind*

1981
Murphy dies on December 16 in Laguna Hills, CA, where he and his wife Jean are living at the Leisure World retirement community, now known as Laguna Woods Village.

1982
These Truths Can Change Your Life is published posthumously.

1987
Canadian writer Bernard Cantin publishes the French language work *Joseph Murphy se raconte à Bernard Cantin* [*Joseph Murphy Speaks to Bernard Cantin*] with Quebec's Éditions Un Monde Différent. The book is based on an extended series of interviews Cantin conducted with Murphy before his death and provides a rare window into Murphy's career. It does not appear in English. *The Collected Essays of Joseph Murphy* is published posthumously.

About the Authors

A native of Ireland who resettled in America, JOSEPH MURPHY, Ph.D., D.D. (1898–1981) was a prolific and widely admired New Thought minister and writer, best known for his metaphysical classic, *The Power of Your Subconscious Mind*, an international bestseller since it first appeared on the self-help scene in 1963. A popular speaker, Murphy lectured on both American coasts and in Europe, Asia, and South Africa. His many books and pamphlets on the autosuggestive and metaphysical faculties of the human mind have entered multiple editions. Murphy is considered one of the pioneering voices of affirmative-thinking philosophy.

MITCH HOROWITZ is a PEN Award-winning historian and the author of books including *Occult America*, *One Simple Idea*, and *The Miracle Club*. His G&D Media titles include *The Miracle Habits*, *Secrets of Self-Mastery*, *The Power of the Master Mind*, and *The Miracle of a Definite Chief Aim*. Follow him on Twitter @MitchHorowitz and on Instagram @MitchHorowitz23.

www.ingramcontent.com/pod-product-compliance
Lightning Source LLC
Chambersburg PA
CBHW052011070526
44584CB00016B/1710